THE ORA

Reclaiming Liberalism

THE
ORANGE
BOOK

RECLAIMING LIBERALISM

Edited by Paul Marshall and David Laws

P

PROFILE BOOKS

First published in Great Britain in 2004 by
Profile Books Ltd
58A Hatton Garden
London ECIN 8LX
www.profilebooks.co.uk

A CIP catalogue record for this book is available from the British
Library.

ISBN 1 86197 797 2

Typeset in Minion by MacGuru Ltd
info@macguru.org.uk

Printed and bound in Great Britain by Hobbs the Printers

Contents

About the contributors

Vince Cable MP

Dr Cable has worked as adviser to the World Commission on Environment and Development, Head of the Economics Programme at Chatham House, and Chief Economist at Shell International. He was elected as Member of Parliament for Twickenham in 1997. Dr Cable served as Liberal Democrat Trade and Industry Spokesman from 1999 and was appointed Shadow Chancellor of the Exchequer in 2003. He is the author of various books and pamphlets including *Protectionism and Industrial Decline* (1983) and *Globalisation and Global Governance* (1999).

Nick Clegg

Nick Clegg worked as a political consultant before being elected to the European Parliament as Liberal Democrat MEP for the East Midlands in 1999. Nick was the Trade and Industry Spokesman for the Liberal Democrat Group in the European Parliament. He was a member of the Trade, Industry, Research and Energy Committee and has taken a leading role in political debates concerning international trade policy and the World Trade Organisation. Nick Clegg's publications include *Doing Less To Do More: A New Focus for the EU* (2000), *Trading for the Future: Reforming the WTO* (2001), and *Reforming the European Parliament* (2003).

Edward Davey MP

Edward Davey worked as Senior Economics Adviser for the

Liberal Democrats before moving into management consultancy and becoming Director of Omega Partners. Edward was elected Member of Parliament for Kingston & Surbiton in 1997. He was appointed Shadow Chief Secretary to the Treasury in 2000 and served on the Treasury Select Committee between 1999 and 2001. Edward was made Shadow Secretary for the Office of the Deputy Prime Minister in 2001. He is the author of *Making MPs Work for Our Money: Reforming Parliament's Role in Budget Scrutiny* (2000).

Christopher Huhne MEP

Chris Huhne, MEP for South East England, is the European Liberal Democrat and Reformist Group's economics spokesman and sits on Parliament's Economic and Monetary Affairs Committee. Chris chaired the Liberal Democrat Public Services Policy Commission, the expert group on Britain's adoption of the euro, and the Policy Commission on Globalisation. Chris is an award-winning former economic journalist, was for some time a City economist, and has written four books, including two on European monetary union.

Rt Hon. Charles Kennedy MP

Charles Kennedy MP was elected to Parliament in 1983 at the age of 23 to become the youngest MP in the House of Commons. In 1999, he was elected as the Leader of the Liberal Democrats. Charles Kennedy is the author of *The Future of Politics* (2000).

Susan Kramer

Susan Kramer is a leading businesswoman with wide experience of finance and transport. In 1988, she became a Vice-President of Citibank, based in Chicago, and in 1993 she started working in Eastern Europe and set up her company, Kramer & Associates, which dealt in financing infrastructure projects in Hungary, Poland, Romania and Austria. She stood as Liberal Democrat candidate for London Mayor in 2000, and is a member of the Board of Transport for London and Vice-Chair of its Rail Advisory Committee. Susan Kramer is currently Director of Infrastructure Capital Partners Ltd, and Liberal Democrat PPC for Richmond.

David Laws MP

David Laws was a Vice-President at J. P. Morgan and Co. and then a Managing Director at Barclays de Zoete Wedd before becoming Director of Policy for the Liberal Democrats, 1997–99. David was elected Member of Parliament for Yeovil in 2001 and was a member of the Treasury Select Committee, 2001–03. He joined the Liberal Democrat Shadow Cabinet as Shadow Chief Secretary to the Treasury in 2003.

Paul Marshall

Paul Marshall is co-founder of Marshall Wace Asset Management, one of Europe's leading hedge fund institutions. In 1985, Paul was Research Assistant to the Rt Hon. Charles Kennedy MP and in 1987 SDP/Liberal Alliance candidate for Fulham. Formerly a Director of Mercury Asset Management Plc and Chairman of the City Liberal Democrats, Paul is Chairman of the Liberal Democrat Business Forum.

Mark Oaten MP

Mark Oaten was Managing Director of Westminster Public Relations before standing as Member of Parliament for Winchester in 1997. Mark's two-vote victory in the May 1997 election was challenged but he won the subsequent by-election with a majority of 21,556. After the 2001 election, Mark Oaten was elected Chairman of the Parliamentary Party of the Liberal Democrats. In October

2003, he took over from Simon Hughes as Liberal Democrat Shadow Home Secretary.

Steve Webb MP and Jo Holland

Steve Webb is Member of Parliament for Northavon and the Liberal Democrat Shadow Work and Pensions Secretary. After graduating in 1986, he worked for nine years for the independent Institute for Fiscal Studies, specialising in the workings of the personal tax and benefit system. At the same time, he served as a specialist adviser to the House of Commons Social Security Select Committee. In 1995, Steve was appointed Professor of Social Policy at Bath University and was elected to Parliament in 1997. Jo Holland is the Senior Researcher for Steve Webb MP.

Sub-editors: Gordon Mead, Julia Pitman and Matthew Sheldon.

Figures and tables

Foreword

Liberalism boasts a proud tradition of radical and pioneering thought, and I am delighted that this collection of essays sits so well within that tradition.

While some competing political creeds look tired and outdated, the extent to which the principles of Liberalism have stood the test of time is striking. Liberalism is as compelling at the beginning of the 21st century as it was two hundred years ago.

The contributors to this book have drawn on these Liberal traditions to produce a challenging set of policy ideas, which are hard-headed in their economic liberalism but equally committed to the vision of a fairer society and greater opportunity for all that is at the heart of the modern Liberal Democrat Party.

Not all of the ideas in *The Orange Book: Reclaiming Liberalism* are existing party policy, but all are compatible with our Liberal heritage. It is right that we should be a party of lively debate, for debate of this type is the mark of a confident and growing party that expects to be at the heart of government.

Charles Kennedy

Introduction

Paul Marshall

Liberalism is arguably one of the most successful creeds in political history. Its founding fathers, Jeremy Bentham, James Mill, Adam Smith and John Stuart Mill, would have been proud of their heritage. Within seven years of the publication of James Mill's 'Essay on Government' (1825), Britain had begun the process of extending the franchise, which was ultimately to culminate in universal suffrage. Likewise, the Corn Laws were repealed within a decade of the formation of the Manchester League, and economic liberalism and free trade became the defining principles behind Britain's economic management throughout the nineteenth century. The twentieth-century experiment with state socialism and the mixed economy now looks like just an expensive interlude, and even the modern Labour Party has accepted most of the tenets of economic liberalism.

Political and economic liberalism have also been hugely successful exports. Political liberalism has been at the root of the worldwide spread of democracy, and was also the inspiration behind the post-war international settlements, now sadly under so much pressure. Economic liberalism has been the guiding light for the world's most successful economy and was the victor in the Cold War.

John Stuart Mill, the founding father of personal liberalism, was described by Herbert Asquith as the 'Purveyor-general of thought for the early Victorians', and his *On Liberty* has been an inspiration for those who have struggled for freedom and civil liberties across the world ever since.

Later, the philosophy of social liberalism, developed by late-nineteenth-century thinkers such as L. T. Hobhouse and J. A. Hobson, provided the inspiration for many of the important social reforms introduced by the Asquith government, arguably one of the greatest reforming governments this country has produced. The lineage of social liberalism can be traced all the way through to modern formulations of the enabling state and to the primacy given to education both by modern Liberal Democrats and US Democrats.

However, the Liberal Party has been much less successful than the Liberal creed. Whether because it was the victim of its own success, or because of its failure to adapt to the class-based divisions of the industrial age, the Liberal Party found itself confined for most of the twentieth century to, at best, influence, not power. Many of its ideals were absorbed into the conventional wisdom of a liberal, democratic Britain, and some were co-opted by the other parties. But some of them were also trampled on by the state socialism that disfigured British politics in the twentieth century, and others are still being eroded by the privileges that are for ever creeping into the structures of power.

As we enter a new century, and a post-industrial age where society is more at ease with itself, less hidebound by class, sex or race, there is a good argument that Liberalism, and the Liberal Democrat Party, will be more attuned to the aspirations of an educated and self-confident citizenship than either of the outworn creeds of socialism or conservatism. (The founding principles of Liberalism arguably have a stronger resonance today than at any time in the twentieth century.)

This is the perspective of *The Orange Book: Reclaiming Liberalism*. The contributors have sought to examine how the principles of Liberalism can be applied to a range of problems facing Britain at the beginning of the 21st century. In part, this has been about reapplying the founding principles of Liberalism; in part, it has been about re-examining those Liberal principles in light of the changed circumstances of modern society.

The range of issues covered is not, and cannot be, exhaustive, but should be of sufficient scope to illustrate the continuing force of Liberal logic. Equally, the views expressed are those of the individual authors and are not necessarily party policy. However, taken together, they do represent a hard-headed, coherent whole which illuminates the practical relevance of Liberalism, classical and 'New', to contemporary problems.

Three chapters of the book are broadly concerned with issues of political liberalism, applying in turn a local, European and global perspective. Although early Liberalism achieved its foremost aim of extending the franchise, there are many other battles still to be fought, both in relation to extending the principles of political liberalism into our international arrangements (and notably the EU), and also in relation to restoring the principles of accountability, pluralism and democracy to domestic politics.

Edward Davey sets out in his chapter just how far the 'century of centralism' eroded the traditions and fabric of local democracy.

> During the twentieth century, Britain became one of the most
> centralised democracies in the western world, as both socialist
> thinkers and conservative forces saw central state power as
> the best way to impose their order. On the left, the Fabians
> in particular saw national government as the only way to
> promote equality and redistribution, with the state grappling
> with the capitalist forces they opposed. On the right, central

power was seen as necessary to tame nationally organised labour and other opponents such as 'loony left' councils that challenged national public spending controls.

However, as we move into the 21st century, the changing nature of society and of political debate requires the British state to take a more pluralistic, democratic and accountable (i.e. liberal) shape, says Davey: 'As the main battlefield has moved away from the economic and industrial sphere towards public services and quality of life, the all-powerful Westminster-Whitehall model is under strain.'

Davey seeks to show how stronger local government and new regional assemblies 'can be mechanisms for checking state power and for promoting quality and choice in public services for the individual'. Decentralisation should enable much greater freedom to experiment (cheaply), to innovate, 'to embrace the choice agenda, so crucial to the reform of public services'.

Nick Clegg applies the same principles of political liberalism to Britain's engagement in the EU. When it comes to Europe, the principles of political liberalism have to be squared with the Liberal Democrats' strong tradition of internationalism and their constructive approach to European cooperation. This leads to a much more complex and subtle discussion of Europe than the common caricature of the Liberal Democrat position. Clegg shows how a Liberal approach to the exercise of power in the EU, 'which insists on checks and balances, on diffused centres of power and on the greatest degree of parliamentary accountability', leads to strong criticism of the unaccountable way in which decision-making power is currently exercised by national governments in the Council of Ministers and to a 'natural scepticism towards the European Commission'. The quest for greater accountability would imply a more substantive role for the European Parliament, but the problem here is the absence of a fully formed and engaged community of voters, or *demos*. 'In the absence of a European *demos*, it must be accepted that the primary source of meaningful political legitimacy in the EU remains the nation state, at least for the foreseeable future.' This conclusion leads Clegg to be very cautious about the allocation of additional powers to the EU – 'the allocation of authority at EU level must only ever be countenanced if there is an overwhelming and compelling reason to do so.'

A rigorous application of the principles of subsidiarity and proportionality to the scope of the EU's existing powers leads to some equally hard-headed conclusions. Clegg shows how many of the EU's existing powers (notably the CAP – a 'wasteful and economically perverse support system') are a result of political accident rather than logic, while other powers that should be exercised at the European level are wrongly restricted to national governments. His prescription is clear. Liberal Democrats should push for the repatriation of certain existing EU powers – much of agricultural, regional and social policy, for instance – whilst arguing for the elevation of certain new powers where the value of collective European action is compelling – in areas of foreign, asylum and immigration policy – to the EU.

Chris Huhne applies almost identical principles to Nick Clegg in his review of the present systems of global governance:

> For any institutional change, there should perhaps be three
> guiding principles. The first is that the institution should
> be able to deal with the cross-border problem it is designed
> to tackle. The second is that the institution should be as
> democratically accountable as possible, and at the very least
> should be open and transparent. The third is the old Liberal
> principle that decisions should be taken as closely as possible

to the people affected by them (now dignified with the ungainly description of subsidiarity).

Huhne finds the existing framework of global governance – whether it be in the political, security, economic or environmental fields – creaking under the pace of change, and reform hindered by the conservatism or suspicion of domestic opinion: 'Problems may be global, but politics is local.'

In an age where disorder in failing states – in Cambodia, Rwanda, Bosnia-Herzegovina, Kosovo, Sierra Leone, Colombia and Afghanistan – 'has been the most significant cause of abject human misery in our times', Huhne advocates reform of the UN in a Gladstonian direction. Designed to deal with the kind of intra-state conflicts that had occurred between the wars, the UN has been ill-equipped to deal with problems of civil conflict, humani-tarian outrage and failing states which are its diet today. It needs to change its approach to domestic sovereignty, which currently forbids intervention in the internal affairs of its members. 'UN members must have the collective capacity to challenge the sover-eignty of other members for gross and persistent abuse of human rights, the denial of the right to peaceful coexistence of nations and communities, or wilful and widespread environmental damage.'

For this to work, of course, the UN needs to enhance its own legitimacy – 'the UN does not look behind the principle of state representation, regardless of whether those states broadly repre-sent their peoples (the democracies) or merely an unaccountable regime (China).' Huhne advocates a constitutional convention to draft a new charter more in keeping with the security and political challenges the world now faces.

In the security field, Huhne advocates measures to counter the trend towards US unilateralism by introducing a greater balance of responsibilities for policing the world's trouble spots.

'The European Union can do much to strengthen the multilateral system by creating its own rapid reaction force, and being prepared to commit that force to UN tasks. The USA bears too high a share of the burden of global security ... Europe cannot expect to have the influence it would like when its own contribution to global order is so feeble.'

In the economic sphere, Huhne turns his attention to the problems of debt and poverty relief and, apart from further extensions to free trade, advocates a number of changes to the existing practices of the IMF that would be more supportive to the fabric of countries in economic difficulty. He also argues for a strengthening of global cooperation in the environmental field through the creation of an international governmental organisation for the environment.

In Chapter 5, 'Liberal economics and social justice', Vince Cable uses the benchmark of economic liberalism to conduct a wide-ranging audit of Britain's economic arrangements and concludes that there is much work to be done. He argues that it is Britain's responsibility to be the flag-bearer of economic liberalism within the EU, highlighting the injustice of the Common Agricultural Policy ('an economic, environmental and moral disaster') and the need to make a stand against the growing threat of 'regulatory protectionism'.

At home, Cable launches a strong attack on the 'new mercantilism' of the industrial welfare state, proposing that many of the industrial support functions of the DTI, like the DTI itself, could be dismantled. He also argues that economic liberals should take on a new challenge, of downsizing of the 'regulatory state'. Although the growth of regulation was initially part of a liberalising move away from the 'command and control' structures of the mixed economy, Cable is concerned that regulation is going too far, undermining the ability of companies to adapt and change rapidly enough in an enterprise economy. Amongst his proposals are 'sunset clauses' for all regulators and regulatory bodies; the use of markets instead of regulation where possible (e.g. recycling levies on first users of cars and bottles, congestion charging); a new system of 'regulatory impact assessment'; and higher standards of accountability (including parliamentary scrutiny) for regulators. Cable also applies Liberal principles to the debate about the delivery of public services. 'One of the defining characteristics of economic liberalism is a belief that a system with many individual consumers and competing providers will provide a more satisfactory outcome than one based on monopoly, either of the private sector or the state.' Cable advocates 'as much individual choice as possible, albeit within the constraints of a universal service'. While he stops short of advocating a voucher system in mainstream health or education provision, due to the problems of capacity shortages and the resultant social injustice, Cable is more favourably disposed to exploring the potential of voucher systems in further and vocational education.

Vince Cable's most resounding message, especially in the context of current political debate, is the need for a plurality of providers:

> The vision should be one in which a mixture of public sector,
> private and mutually owned enterprises compete to provide
> mainstream services. The private sector already provides
> nursery, special needs and vocational education for LEAs
> or government. Voluntary organisations like churches are
> already substantial providers of schooling. Provided the state
> performs its central function of ensuring that there is a regime
> for standard-setting and testing, and providing resources to
> pay for a quality service, there is no overriding reason why the
> state itself should provide the service.

With regard to the boundaries between the public and private sector, Cable argues for a new fiscal rule setting the share of public spending to GDP (using present levels as an appropriate base). Such a constraint would have the merit of forcing policy-makers to define priorities and to focus on how to get greater value from the same level of financial input into public services. Similar constraints should apply to the tax system, and Cable proposes two guiding principles – the state should not take more than 40% of GNP in tax (the present level is 37%) and marginal rates of direct tax should not exceed 50%.

He also proposes reforms to the tax system in the name of social justice, highlighting the creeping regressivity of the British tax system (the highest 20% of income earners pay a smaller proportion of their income in tax [35%] than the lowest 20% [40%]). These tax reforms should be accompanied by other measures to simplify the tax system, including the scrapping of many tax reliefs and the abolition of a separate capital gains tax.

Chiming with the vision set out by Cable, Susan Kramer and David Laws examine the constructive role that the principles of economic liberalism can play in achieving Liberal Democrat goals in the fields of environmental and health policy.

The central argument of Susan Kramer's chapter is that we can achieve our environmental goals more effectively, and with greater public acceptance, by harnessing market forces than through the traditional methods of regulation and taxation. The critical step is to attach proper economic value to environmental 'goods'.

> Traditionally, full economic value has not been attached to the
> environment, and many of what are now being recategorised
> as environmental and ecosystem 'goods' have been regarded as
> free. Carbon storage, water purification, habitat, pollination
> (by insects) etc. would all cost billions if not provided by

9

nature, yet are critical to sustaining life and the quality of life. The use of markets and trading mechanisms therefore offers a major benefit in the search to enhance environmental sustainability by starting to establish widely accepted values for environmental goods.

Kramer reviews the recent experiments with 'user charging' and 'depletion/pollution trading schemes' and concludes that these market-based approaches should become a central feature of Liberal Democrat thinking.

David Laws comes to a similar conclusion when examining the potential of economic liberalism to deliver answers to the problems of the UK health service. Starting with a 'Liberal' vision, which includes access for all regardless of ability to pay, fairness, choice and competition, he examines four alternative models for the delivery of UK health services. These include 'a better funded status quo', the current government programme of 'investment and reform', and the Conservative alternative of choice for those who can afford it. His conclusion is that none of these alternatives delivers on a truly social liberal vision and that the Liberal Democrats should push for far-reaching reform based on a 'national health insurance scheme'. Every UK citizen would be a member of the scheme, choosing either the NHS or an alternative insurance provider. Insurers would have to accept any applicant, regardless of health risk characteristics, and every insurer would levy the same maximum annual charge for membership of the scheme. The state would pay the annual charge for each citizen for the full range of clinical services through a hypothecated tax on income; and each individual would be free to choose between health providers.

Laws' vision for healthcare reform has strong parallels with the proposal set out in Chapter 10 for pension reform. Both use the strategy of a universal compulsory levy, based on the contributory principle, to ensure not only that reform is properly funded, but more importantly that people can see where their money goes, are encouraged to take more responsibility for how it is spent, and are able to choose between different providers of the service they have paid for.

David Laws is thus able to use economic liberal principles to deliver social liberal goals. Indeed, the chapters reviewed so far all draw on what might be called 'classic Liberalism', demonstrating just how much the traditions of economic and political liberalism are relevant to contemporary problems. Other issues tackled in the book, such as family policy, pensions and penal reform, are more challenging and the solutions proposed draw on later strands of the Liberal tradition, notably the thinking of T. H. Green, Hobhouse, Hobson and, more latterly, Sir William Beveridge.

Hobhouse, whose writings have a particular resonance today, developed a reformulation of Liberalism emphasising the positive role the state can play in equipping its citizens to participate fully in society. One of Hobhouse's most important insights was that Liberalism needed to graduate from its origins as a movement of protest towards a more constructive role in equipping citizens to enjoy their freedom:

> The modern state ... starts from the basis of an authoritarian order, and the protest against that order, a protest religious, political, economic, social, and ethical, is the historic beginning of Liberalism. Thus Liberalism appears at first as a criticism, sometimes even as a destructive and revolutionary criticism. Its negative aspect is for centuries foremost. Its business seems to be not so much to build up as to pull down, to remove obstacles, which block human progress, rather than to point the positive goal of endeavour or fashion the fabric of civilisation. It finds humanity oppressed, and would set it free.

> It finds a people groaning under arbitrary rule, a nation in bondage to a conquering race, industrial enterprise obstructed by social privileges or crippled by taxation, and it offers relief. … [But] is Liberalism at bottom a constructive or only a destructive principle?

Modern Liberalism needs to balance the 'negative' and 'positive' elements of freedom to which Hobhouse refers, without losing sight of the primacy of liberty and without falling into a philosophical no-man's land. On the one hand, it must not lose the élan of protest, the determination to champion individual rights and democracy wherever they are threatened. On the other, it must ceaselessly strive to equip and encourage each individual to realise his full potential and play his full part in society.

Perhaps the best embodiment of this balance is the 'principle of citizenship', a principle which Hobhouse referred to as the characteristic of 'the higher civilisation'. Citizenship is an overused term, but for Liberals it has the immense appeal of combining the 'negative' and 'positive' connotations of freedom – the negative connotation of rights (freedom from …) which stem from your status as a citizen, and the positive connotation of responsibility (to family, children, the community, environment …) and participation (in the workplace, schools, housing associations, neighbourhood watches and in local and national government).

The notion of responsibility has arguably been neglected in a Liberal tradition so closely associated with the struggle for individual rights. But the two go together. A society of responsibilities without rights is reminiscent of the post-feudal order against which the early Liberals were reacting. A society of rights without responsibilities leads eventually to the kind of civic disaggregation which is depicted all too sombrely in Chapter 9. The balance has to be found in a mutual reciprocity between individual and society, which Hobhouse refers to in his definition of the civic bond: 'it consists essentially in a certain reciprocity of obligation as between the individual members of the state, and also as between the state and its members.'

This is the spirit that animates the chapters on penal reform, family policy and pensions. The central and most radical proposal in Mark Oaten's chapter on reform of the justice system is the introduction of a regime of compulsory targeted education. Oaten shows how the existing policy of 'locking them up and throwing away the key' contributes to a situation where 71% of all 18- to 21-year-olds in prison go on to reoffend. This creates a vicious circle of reoffending which, apart from being highly expensive, restricts the liberty of other citizens and inhibits people's quality of life. Education is the key to successful rehabilitation and Oaten proposes an 'enforced' regime of basic numeracy and literacy lessons for every prisoner who does not possess these skills, together with vocational training and a continuing programme of educational and occupational development after release. Oaten's vision is strongly Liberal. Even J. S. Mill, the greatest proponent of negative freedom, saw the merits of compulsory education: 'Is it not almost a self-evident axiom that the state should require and compel the education up to a certain standard of every human being who is born its citizen?'[1]

Mill is also an inspiration to Steve Webb as he explores the complex and sensitive issue of family policy. As he states in his introduction, 'By instinct, Liberals are suspicious of the power of the state ... and ... in few areas is this wariness of state interference more acute than in our approach to what might loosely be described as "family policy".' Yet, in a society increasingly paying the consequences of family breakdown, 'Standing idly by whilst pressures on families are causing real problems for children and parents alike is not a liberal response. It is an irresponsible response.'

Steve Webb's response is to use a constructive definition of freedom in a way that clearly evokes the notion of citizenship:

> Parents are responsible for the way that they raise their children, and they need to recognise that their children's well-being is not simply a private matter but impacts on the whole of society. In turn, parenthood is a role that society needs and values, and citizens who have chosen to become parents therefore have a right to expect support in this role.

His policy proposals include greater support (in the form of more stable funding) for the voluntary sector where its interventions are seen to have a positive impact, an expansion of the network of health visitors and midwives in order to create a comprehensive system of family support, integration of 'relationship education' into the new Citizenship classes and strong support for the Government's recent introduction of parenting orders. He also argues for changes to employment law which would offer parents the right to more flexible working hours and provide more paid parental leave along Scandinavian lines.

The chapter on pension reform draws a clear distinction between a 'Liberal', contributory model of welfare provision in the tradition of Beveridge, and the paternalistic model of the Fabians, latterly revived by Gordon Brown. The former is rooted in the notions of responsibility and empowerment, which are central to the ideal of citizenship. The latter has its roots in a collectivist tradition where the State is benefactor and welfare-recipients are its dependants. The Beveridge settlement has come under huge strain in recent years because of demographic change, but the

14

response to these pressures should not be to dismantle Beveridge, as Brown has sought to do, but to strengthen and revive it.

The central enhancement to Beveridge proposed in Chapter 10, in the form of a compulsory universal funded pension scheme, goes beyond existing Liberal Democrat policy; but it provides a bridge between the original Beveridge settlement of 1948, which first introduced the contributory principle into welfare, and the new politics of asset-based welfare, which will almost certainly gain ground as the new century progresses. Asset-based welfare has close kinship to the principle of citizenship, for whilst the traditional welfare model of income transfers does 'nothing to foster people's self-reliance or dignity (rather the contrary), giving people responsibility for their own assets would do much to further individual self-respect and instil a sense of citizenship.' The Labour Government is currently flirting with the idea of asset-based welfare, but its only policy initiative in this area (baby bonds) is half-baked and ill conceived.

It is a great irony that the modern Labour Party should now be toying with the language and philosophy of citizenship, for socialism has been one of the greatest enemies of a civil society, not least in our own country. Indeed, J. A. Hobson (quoted elsewhere by Edward Davey) actually used the idea of citizenship to distinguish Liberalism from socialism: 'Liberalism will retain its distinction from socialism in taking for its chief test of policy the freedom of the individual citizen, rather than the strength of the state.'[2]

Socialism introduced social class as the organising principle of political analysis. It substituted a distant monolithic state for the plurality of institutions that had hitherto been so essential to the vitality of civil society. It eroded the strength and self-confidence of the voluntary sector, turning it by the 1960s into what one commentator has described as 'little more than an amenity, a rung

15

on the ladder leading to the welfare state'. Labour colluded with the Conservative Party in the relentless centralisation of political life to Westminster and the corresponding atrophy of a local political culture, which had been so vibrant in the nineteenth century. And for all the benefits of the welfare state, the Fabian model of welfare, paternalistic and means-tested, has created a pattern of dependency that eats away at the heart of citizenship.

To be fair, some of the thinking on citizenship emanating from Labour circles (from Frank Field to David Blunkett) is not incompatible with Liberal traditions. But people are unlikely to accept leadership on the issue of citizenship from a party with such a statist heritage. It is more likely that the message will be lost or misinterpreted, as has indeed been the case; David Blunkett's reflections on citizenship have been interpreted largely as coded language for a more authoritarian approach to the justice and immigration systems – unfair perhaps on Blunkett, but not on the Labour Party and its traditions.

Labour's implausibility as advocates of citizenship only emphasises Liberalism's natural claims. In Labour hands, citizenship smacks of identity cards and the nanny state. In Liberal Democrat hands, it carries the flavour of democracy, civil society, voluntarism, self-help and self-government. Citizenship is the logical fulfilment of the New Liberals' quest for a more 'constructive' creed, in a century where the improvements in education, health and living standards should enable the vast majority of people, if they choose, not only to manage their own affairs but also to contribute in some way to the governance of their family, their community and society at large.

Citizenship can be the binding ingredient for the kind of policy commitments advocated by David Laws in Chapter 1. Laws reunites the key strands of Liberal tradition (economic liberalism, political liberalism, personal liberalism and social liberalism) and shows how they can be built into a coherent whole. The fundamental principles of Liberalism do not have to be invented or reinvented. They already exist. Each chapter of this book confirms their relevance in different ways. Taken together, they offer a strong and radical agenda for reform.

Notes
1. J. S. Mill, *On Liberty*, 1859.
2. Frank Prochaska, 'Schools of Citizenship: charity and civic virtue', April 2002.

1   Reclaiming Liberalism: a liberal agenda for the Liberal Democrats

David Laws

> We should, I hope, agree that there is no purpose in keeping a Liberal Party alive unless it promotes liberalism.
>
> Jo Grimond, 'The Future of Liberalism', National Liberal Club, 29 October 1980

Foundations of Liberalism

This chapter is primarily concerned with practical politics, not political philosophy. But its central argument is that in particular areas of policy the practical proposals of the Liberal Democrats have, at times, become disconnected from the philosophy and principles out of which Liberalism has developed. This is, therefore, an essay about how the agenda of the Liberal Democrat Party might be developed over the years ahead.

These coming years may well constitute a period of time during which our growing representation at Westminster will carry us into a major role in UK government, for the first time in many decades. But there is, for all political parties, a central question not just about how power is achieved, but about what purposes that power should be used for.

I believe that if the Liberal Democrats are to continue to play a creative and constructive role in British politics over the years ahead, then it will only be by revisiting and reclaiming some of the traditional building blocks of Liberalism, and using these to reshape and renew the policy agenda of Liberal Democracy.

The basic philosophical and practical foundations of British Liberalism have been a belief in personal, political, economic and social liberalism, combined with a strongly internationalist approach to extending these self-same freedoms across the world. Liberalism is, by every instinct, an internationalist creed.

It could be argued that in certain respects, over the past fifty years, Liberals and Liberal Democrats have sometimes lost sight of some of these fundamental principles of our Liberalism; now is the time to reclaim them.

I should start by explaining what I mean by each of these four essential strands of Liberalism.

Liberalism: personal, political, economic and social

By personal liberalism, I mean the freedom of the individual from all forms of oppression – including by the state; by the tyranny of majorities; and from ignorance, intolerance, prejudice and conformity. This means freedom under the law; freedom of expression; freedom from the nanny state; religious freedom; freedom to be different. This is the classic liberal belief in maximising the freedom of the individual, and protecting this freedom from all forms of coercion. The only condition is that the exercise of one person's freedoms cannot be allowed to seriously curtail those of other individuals.

The second key element of Liberalism is political liberalism – the belief that power should be exercised through account-able and democratic structures, as close to the people affected as possible, and therefore with the maximum possible decentralisation of power and decision-making. The great nineteenth-century political controversies over voting reform and Home Rule still have profound significance for liberals to this day.

The third strand of Liberalism is economic liberalism – which is the belief in the value of free trade, open competition, market mechanisms, consumer power, and the effectiveness of the private sector. These beliefs are combined with opposition to monopolies and instinctive suspicion of state control and interference, particularly in relation to the ownership and control of business.

Late nineteenth-century and early twentieth-century Liberalism was often dominated by the great parliamentary battles for free trade, with the Liberal Party as the defenders of free trade, and the Tory Party firmly positioned on the side of protectionism.

The final, essential, element of Liberalism, social liberalism, emerged towards the end of the nineteenth century, and clearly played a central role in the policy agenda of the great Liberal administration of 1906–11. Social liberalism brought to Liberalism itself an acceptance and understanding of the insight that personal, political and economic liberalism are not by themselves an adequate basis for securing for each individual a deeper and more meaningful sense of freedom.

Those who enjoy the benefits of personal, political and economic liberalism, but without a job, without enough food on the table, without education, and without access to adequate housing and healthcare, cannot be said to enjoy freedom in any sense that most people would understand.

David Lloyd George set out the basis for the 'new Liberalism' in a speech in Swansea in October 1908 when he urged: 'Let Liberalism proceed with its glorious work of building up the temple of liberty in this country, but let it bear in mind that the worshippers at that shrine have to live.'

This broader definition of the objective of Liberalism became

20

widely accepted across the Liberal Party. In October 1926, Asquith spoke of 'Liberty in its positive as well as in its negative sense. A man is not free unless he has had the means and opportunities for education.' Sir William Beveridge later declared war on the 'five giants' of want, disease, ignorance, squalor and idleness.

Finally, Liberalism's commitment to human freedom has always meant that it is an inclusive, not an exclusive, creed. Liberalism has always stood against narrow class interests, sectional interests, and purely national interests, and in favour of the general interest. Liberalism has an instinctively internationalist outlook, in which the value of each human being is given equal weight, whether in our own country and community, or overseas.

Liberalism is very definitely an internationalist creed – it stands for freedom for all people and for all countries. This was the philosophical outlook that undoubtedly underpinned W. E. Gladstone's striking speech, delivered in November 1879 during the first Midlothian campaign, in which he asked his audience to:

> Remember the rights of the savage, as we call him. Remember that the happiness of his humble home, remember that the sanctity of life in the hill villages of Afghanistan among the winter snows, is as inviolable in the eye of Almighty God as can be your own.

So these are, as I understand them, the fundamental philosophical foundations of Liberalism. They are as relevant to 21st-century Liberalism as they have been to the Liberalism of the past two hundred years.

How liberal are the Liberal Democrats?

But are today's Liberals, in the shape of the Liberal Democrat Party, sufficiently liberal? As Jo Grimond said in October 1980: 'We should, I hope, agree that there is no purpose in keeping a Liberal Party alive unless it promotes liberalism ... How often have we in the Liberal Party been told that we must be distinctive, even if the only distinct road leads away from liberalism?'

It is time to consider whether the Liberal Democrat Party of today is true to its Liberal traditions, and, if not, what we should be doing about it.

Personal liberalism

If we start by considering personal liberalism, we may well conclude that the Liberal Democrat Party has continued to speak up for freedom of the individual, and against oppression by the state and by majorities.

In the House of Commons and in the House of Lords, today's Liberal Democrats have been robust in defending the rights of the individual against the powers of the state, and against the tyranny of majorities and the oppression of prejudice. Some of the recent debates over criminal justice issues in particular remind us of the speech of May 1794 by Charles James Fox, in which he warned the House of Commons that a bill to suspend habeas corpus was:

> ... characteristic of those violent times when, instead of being guided by reason, we were to be put under the dominion of wild passion, and when our pretended alarms were to be made the pretexts for destroying the first principles of the very system which we affected to revere.

Liberal Democrats have helped to defend essential civil liberties against a succession of illiberal Home Secretaries for whom 'pretended alarms were to be made pretexts for destroying the first principles of the very system which we affected to revere'. Liberal Democrats have also robustly defended the rights of minorities, fought against discrimination on the basis of race, sex, sexuality and disability, and helped to promote a more tolerant and diverse Britain.

Consistently, Liberal Democrats have been willing at our conferences (to the frequent despair of our leaders and press advisers) to discuss and debate difficult issues involving the rights of minorities, and we have argued for measures to secure individual liberty against state and majority tyranny.

Liberal Democrats have, then, taken up John Maynard Keynes' challenge ('Am I a Liberal?', Liberal Summer School, 1 August 1925) to 'appear unorthodox, troublesome, dangerous, disobedient to them that begat us'. Indeed, some have made a career out of such activity. Such behaviour is sometimes difficult for the party, because defending minority rights from majority oppression is not always a popular, or populist, occupation.

In spite of the short-term adverse publicity about what are seen to be 'minority concerns', in the longer term, the party seems to have been notably successful in many areas in moving forward the national policy debate. On most subjects relating to 'personal liberalism', majority opinion eventually moves towards acceptance of the Liberal approach.

The recent Southport debate about voluntary euthanasia is a classic example of an uncomfortable and deeply controversial issue, which the party has debated in a manner consistent with its liberal principles. The party's persistent refusal to adopt politically-correct 'women-only short-lists' for parliamentary selection processes also shows that the bright light of personal liberalism – judging people on the content of their character, not by the category they appear to fit into – burns brightly. Long may it do so.

But there are a few occasions when some Liberal Democrats cannot convincingly claim to be on the side of liberalism, and against the nanny state.

23

Over the past few decades, we have also seen, alongside the strong, overarching commitment to personal liberalism, the development of a well-meaning 'nanny-state liberalism', in which respect for personal rights and freedoms has at times been compromised by the pursuit of other, no doubt well-intentioned, objectives.

This 'nanny-state liberalism' is really a 'liberalism à la carte', in which different liberals embrace different policies, not on the basis of whether these policies are truly liberal, but on the basis of whether or not their objective seems to be 'worthy' or well intentioned. But this is surely not what liberalism means. For example, because Liberal Democrats are concerned about our environment, we have at times allowed ourselves to be caricatured as being against the enormous extension of human freedom and opportunity that has come with wider access to the car and to cheap overseas travel.

Instead of concentrating on developing cleaner forms of transport and on containing pollution costs, Liberal Democrats have at times appeared merely to be in favour of trying to tax people out of their cars and away from their foreign holidays. To the extent that this can work at all – and the experience to date has surely not been very inspiring – it must work by pricing off the roads and out of the skies some of our poorest fellow citizens. Curbing opportunities for those on low incomes, while the affluent minority travel on regardless, does not seem a particularly good way to extend personal freedoms to the widest possible group of people.

These charging systems can only work effectively where the charge can be more accurately tied to the actual pollution or congestion costs imposed, and where money can be redirected into public transport and other alternatives.

Let us take another example of nanny-state liberalism. Many Liberal Democrats are rightly concerned about issues such as animal welfare, but are we always sufficiently rigorous in judging animal welfare policies in relation to our commitment to personal liberalism?

For example, a recent party conference approved proposals for the compulsory micro-chipping of dogs, a compulsory national dog registration scheme, compulsory animal welfare education in schools, compulsory bans on animals in circuses, and even a ban on giving goldfish as prizes at fairs. Whether these proposals strike the right balance between animal welfare and individual freedom seems to me to be highly questionable.

For example, why should a party which says it believes that central government should stop micro-managing the national curriculum, set down guidelines on compulsory animal welfare education in schools? This is 'liberalism à la carte' – picking and choosing which liberal principles we will apply, based upon our view of whether the end objective is well-intentioned or not.

If freedom means anything, it must surely include the freedom to engage in activities which others may consider unwise, provided the 'externalities' do not impose unreasonable costs on the rest of us. This includes smoking, overeating, not exercising, driving 'off road' cars in cities, even winning goldfish at fairs. A Liberal society is one in which people should be free to 'make their own mistakes'. The Liberal Democrats must surely be consistently rigorous in applying the principles of personal liberalism in the future.

There is a final issue of personal liberalism, which we must consider before moving on: the issue of crime.

Alongside our commitment to the rule of law and to protecting peoples' liberties under the law, the Liberal Democrats must address one of the biggest threats of all to personal liberty – the extraordinarily high levels of crime. Liberalism must mean not only the 'negative' freedom from oppression by the government, but also freedom from oppression and intimidation by other citizens. Freedom from fear and oppression by crime was not one of the five great evils identified by Beveridge, but it deserves a more central role in Liberal Democrat thinking and policy today.

In many communities across the UK, particularly in our most deprived communities, high levels of crime are today a far greater threat to liberty than the over-zealous activities of Home Secretaries. Liberal Democrats need to explicitly recognise this basic truth. Recognising such truths means confronting the fact that while prison is presently notably unsuccessful in reforming criminals, it is notably successful in protecting law-abiding citizens from criminal acts while offenders are in prison.

A liberal criminal justice policy must include a radical reform of our failing prisons system, and our over-stretched and failing systems of rehabilitation. But a liberal criminal justice policy must also ensure that sentences act as effective deterrents, and that criminals whose activities represent a persistent attack on personal liberty lose their own liberty in order to protect the law-abiding majority.

Liberals need to help make prison work, by strengthening its rehabilitative role. We also need to recognise more clearly the important role of imprisonment in deterrence, punishment and protection of the public.

Political liberalism

The Liberal Democrats (and their predecessor the Liberal Party) have consistently been at the forefront of steps to liberalise the political system in the UK. We have been strong supporters of more democracy, freedom of information, accountability and transparency. Liberal Democrats have also been consistent in their commitment to decentralising power within the UK – making a strong case for the passing of more power down from Whitehall and Westminster to the nations, regions and localities of the UK.

There is still much to be fought for in Britain's deeply centralised, and often secretive, state. But there is one major issue of policy in relation to political liberalism where we must consider whether the values and principles of Liberalism have always been correctly applied: European Union (EU) policy.

The Liberal Democrat commitment to political liberalism must mean a commitment to devolved and decentralised government – to power being exercised either by individuals themselves or as 'close' to them as possible. This is why Liberal Democrats have long argued for devolution within the UK, and for increasing the powers of local government at the expense of central government.

But when it comes to policy on the EU, two great liberal principles can at times come into collision – the commitment to internationalism, and the commitment to decentralisation. And when such a collision of principles has occurred, sometimes the commitment to internationalism and to the EU has overridden the commitment to political liberalism and decentralisation. Thus it has been that the great party of devolution in the UK has too often been wrongly perceived as being the party of centralism when it comes to matters European.

Of course, Liberal Democrats have been right to embrace some key opportunities opened up by the existence of, and our membership of, the EU. The EU, and before it the Common Market, has played a vital role in delivering stability and prosperity in Europe. Its achievements are too easily taken for granted. The EU is helping to liberalise trade and open up markets; forge greater cooperation on foreign policy and defence issues; and deliver better results by working together on genuinely cross-border issues such as international environmental pollution and international crime.

On all of these issues, a liberal (or Liberal Democrat) would robustly defend the role of the EU against the often ill-informed and over-hyped claims of the Europhobes. But in other policy areas, there is much less obvious justification, from a liberal point of view, for a role for the EU. For example, there is no obvious reason why much of social legislation needs to be coordinated on an EU basis. Too often, EU social legislation has been a way of bypassing national parliaments and avoiding serious debates about the balance between economic efficiency and greater social protection, which should be taking place in individual nation states.

Liberal Democrats should not only play a leading role in expanding EU cooperation, where this is necessary and beneficial, but we should also be unafraid to argue against the accretion of new powers by the EU, where these do not pass the basic, liberal, decentralisation tests. We should also be unafraid to argue for the repatriation of certain powers from the EU, where this is justified by the principle of decentralisation – for example, in the social policy field.

Liberal Democrats should use any constitutional agreement in relation to the EU to push for EU powers to be clearly defined – and clearly limited to those areas where international cooperation is necessary and desirable. This would be consistent with the principles of political liberalism.

Economic liberalism

In the late nineteenth century, Liberals could claim to be the proud defenders of economic liberalism, against the constant Tory calls for tariffs and protectionism. Liberals believed in the value of free trade and open competition. Liberals stood for consumer rights against producer interests. Liberals championed the market and the private sector; they were the bitter opponents of monopoly power. Gladstone condemned protectionism as a 'quack remedy'.

But over the decades from the 1930s to the 1980s, the Liberal commitment to these free market principles, and to economic liberalism, was slowly watered down. By 1980, Jo Grimond was warning of 'this new brand of politics, sometimes represented as democratic socialism, to which many liberals are addicted.' Grimond went on to warn that: 'The state-owned monopolies are among the greatest millstones round the neck of the economy ... Liberals must stress at all times the virtues of the market, not only for efficiency but to enable the widest possible choice.' And he went on to warn provocatively that: 'Much of what Mrs Thatcher and Sir Keith Joseph say and do is in the mainstream of liberal philosophy.' (Jo Grimond, 'The Future of Liberalism', National Liberal Club, 29 October 1980.)

Paddy Ashdown (Leader of the Liberal Democrats, 1988–99) used his last party conference speech to ask:

> Are we prepared to liberate the great institutions that deliver
> our public services – education, health, justice, welfare
> – from the clammy embrace of corporatism, whether local
> or national, in order to make them human in scale and
> responsive to the interests of the consumer, not the producer?

How did it come about that over the decades up to the 1980s the Liberal belief in economic liberalism was progressively eroded by forms of soggy socialism and corporatism, which have too often been falsely perceived as a necessary corollary of social liberalism?

There were three major causes of the decline in influence of 'economic liberalism' in the Liberal Party and its successor, the Liberal Democrats – though the belief in economic liberalism is now being strongly reasserted by the party, under the leadership of Charles Kennedy. The dilution of economic liberalism started in the early part of the twentieth century, and owes much to the common aspiration of both the Labour Party and the Liberal Party for broadly social liberal objectives, combined with confusion about how to secure those objectives.

Both the Labour Party and the Liberal Party came to the conclusion that the operation of free markets alone could not guarantee either the Labour Party's aspiration of 'social justice', or the Liberal Party commitment to 'social liberalism'. This conclusion opened the way to consider the different possibilities for state intervention to achieve social liberalism on the one hand, and socialism on the other.

The Labour Party's growing conviction was of the need for state ownership and control as a solution to underemployment, inefficiency and the apparently inequitable allocation of resources. The Liberal Party never shared this belief in state ownership and control, but the confusion between means and ends resulted in a progressive dilution of the traditional liberal beliefs in the benefits of markets, choice, the private sector and competition.

The belief in the value of free markets and competition was further undermined in the 1930s by the prolonged economic slump, which saw millions of people unemployed. The challenge then seemed to be how Government could intervene to deal with market failure, rather than how Government could prevent market mechanisms from being interfered with by monopolies and tariffs.

Keynes' work, *The General Theory of Employment, Interest and Money* (1936), was both an important influence in the Liberal Party, and in the wider press and political debate.

After the slump of the 1930s came World War II, in which the state took on a much greater role in managing and directing industry. World War II marked, perhaps, the highest point of state management and control of the economy in the history of Britain.

Suddenly, it was the state and not the market that seemed

to provide the necessary solutions to our social and economic problems, and free trade and free competition seemed like nineteenth-century relics in a brave new world of 'scientific' policy and benign political management. The invisible hand of the market was to be replaced by the more visible and apparently more benign direction of the man in the ministry – who, of course, knew best.

Sir William Beveridge was himself an example of someone who possessed many social liberal objectives, but who had at times a semi-socialistic view of how these objectives could be achieved.

For example, speaking in November 1944, he said:

> The way to cheapness of equipment is bulk buying. We do not
> want hundreds of different types of refrigerators or cookers,
> or electric washers, all needing different kinds of spares ...
> If we design a few main kinds of each for these and get them
> made in hundreds of thousands and millions, we can get
> them incredibly cheaper, while paying good wages ... Mass-
> production reconciles the need of the consumer for cheapness
> with the need of the producer for good wages.[1]

Beveridge went on to describe how good public services could only be secured by 'collective planning and social demand'.

Throughout the past fifty years there has been a tension in the Liberal Party and the Liberal Democrats between the heritage of economic liberalism and the tendency to reach for statist solutions to economic problems. For example, the 1945 Liberal Party Manifesto called for 'the State ... [taking] over all land which is badly managed or farmed', and went on to argue, somewhat confusingly, that 'Liberals believe in the need for private enterprise and large-scale organisation under government control ...'

The 1964 Liberal Party Manifesto called for 'a Ministry of

Expansion ... a national plan for economic growth', with Parliament 'weigh[ing] up the implications and deciding on a 4, 5 or 6 per cent rate of growth'. The 1979 Liberal Party Manifesto wanted to 'support attempts to synchronise annual wage settlements ... we would introduce a sustained prices and incomes policy...'

Contrast these views of the appropriate role of government and of economic policy with those of the 1950 Liberal Party Manifesto:

> Nationalisation for the sake of nationalisation is nonsense ...
> we recognise that the breaking of monopoly powers is one
> of the key problems of our time ... we would enact freedom
> of entry into trade, freedom from unnecessary controls and
> form-filling, and freedom for the worker from direction of
> labour.

Economic liberalism has waxed and waned in the party over the past fifty years, reflecting on the whole the state of contemporary political debate, rather than long-held and cherished Liberal convictions.

In all political parties, the 'philosophy in office' will inevitably be deeply influenced by the wider economic and social context, as well as by shorter-term political considerations. But it would be naïve to believe that there were not some fundamental differences of view in the Liberal Party/Liberal Democrats over some of these key issues of economic policy and organisation over the past few decades.

The confusion about means and ends was only exacerbated in the 1980s by the Conservative Party's decision to embrace the language, and some of the substance, of economic liberalism in their economic policies – which put competition, choice, the private sector and the market mechanism back on centre-stage. Since the embrace of this agenda by Margaret Thatcher and her government was not combined with a social liberal agenda of extending real opportunity and freedom to everyone in society, but was merely linked to cutting taxes to give choice to a minority, it was wrongly concluded by some Liberals that economic liberalism must be intrinsically part of a right-wing Conservative agenda, rather than a traditional Liberal commitment.

This outlook was underpinned by the merger between the Social Democratic Party and the Liberal Party in the mid-1980s, which saw many individuals who had believed in state solutions to economic problems participate in the new 'SDP-Liberal Alliance', and ultimately the Liberal Democrats. So, in the 1980s, only a few voices on the margins of the party were left to warn about the relative neglect of so much of the economic liberal legacy. Meanwhile, Liberals and Social Democrats were merely left arguing lamely that the boundary between the public and private sectors should be left undisturbed, wherever it happened to be at the time. The call for stability and moderation (for example, over the issue of nationalisation and privatisation), in an increasingly polarised political environment, was superficially attractive, not least with the public, but it papered over rather than clarified the tensions within the party in relation to economic policy.

Social liberalism

Liberals have been conscious of the limitations of the traditional concept of freedom from oppression from as long ago as the middle of the nineteenth century. Thomas Macaulay, in an early justification of state-funded education, argued that it was in the general interest of society that every person should be educated: 'The gross ignorance of the common people is a principal cause of danger to our persons and property. Therefore, it is the duty of the government to take care that the common people shall not be grossly ignorant.'[2]

33

But, later in the century, Liberals began to argue more significantly that it was not only Government's role to protect individual liberty, but also to extend liberty to the whole population by providing relief from extreme poverty, ignorance and ill health.

Perhaps unsurprisingly, this wider concern for the priorities of the lower income groups went hand in hand with the extension of the franchise. Liberty implied franchise extension, and franchise extension necessitated closer attention to the concerns of the newly enfranchised. In September 1885, Joseph Chamberlain spoke of his 'Radical Programme' in Warrington, and explained how the traditional Liberal commitments to free trade and individual freedoms were no longer, for him, sufficient:

> The great problem of our civilisation is unresolved. We
> have to account for, and to grapple with, the mass of misery
> and destitution in our midst, coexistent as it is with the
> evidence of abundant wealth and teeming prosperity. It is a
> problem which some men would put aside with references
> to the eternal laws of supply and demand, to the necessity of
> freedom of contract, and to the sanctity of every private right
> of property. But, gentlemen, these phrases are the convenient
> cant of selfish wealth. They are no answers to our question.

In the early twentieth century, Liberals competed to develop the 'New Liberalism', with its social liberal agenda. After his speech in Manchester in April 1908 in defence of free trade, David Lloyd George spoke on 'Social Reform' at the Welsh Liberal Convention in October 1908, setting out the new agenda of his party:

> Let Liberalism proceed with its glorious work of building up
> the temple of liberty in this country, but let it also bear in
> mind that the worshippers at that shrine have to live.

Winston Churchill and Herbert Asquith shared the new commitment to social liberalism, while being careful to mark out Liberal territory from that of the new socialist movement. At the Dundee by-election in May 1908, Churchill explained that:

> Socialism seeks to pull down wealth. Liberalism seeks to raise up poverty ... Socialism would kill enterprise; Liberalism would rescue enterprise from the trammels of privilege and preference. Socialism assails the pre-eminence of the individual; Liberalism seeks, and shall seek in the future, to build up a minimum standard for the mass ... Socialism attacks capital; Liberalism attacks monopoly.

Asquith, in December 1909, was calling for the state to 'lend a helping hand' to those affected by sickness, unemployment and invalidity, and in October 1926 he set out his vision of a Liberalism which would both defend individual freedoms and seek to expand the scope of liberty for all of the population:

> ... Liberalism means two things – the preservation and extension of liberty in every sphere of our national life, and the subordination of class interests to the interests of the community ... And Liberty ... means liberty in its positive as well as its negative sense. A man is not free unless he has had the means and opportunities for education. A man is not free unless he is at liberty to combine with his fellows for any lawful purpose in which they have a common interest.

Few Liberal Democrats today would argue with the key conclusion of the 'New Liberalism'; that Liberalism must be defined in a positive as well as a negative way. And this conclusion is surely as valid today, after a hundred years of unprecedented economic growth, as it was at the beginning of the last century.

Many of our people, even in a 'rich' country such as Britain, still today have their freedoms seriously curtailed by poverty, poor housing, poor schooling and second-rate public services. Freedom from unnecessary state interference, and freedom to trade, constitute vital freedoms, but limited freedoms. Most people today in Britain would define freedom far more widely, to mean a decent education, a home, a job, access to health services on the basis of need, a safe community, as well as security and opportunity in retirement.

These issues are rightly the central concerns of Liberal Democrats today, indeed the previous perceived 'obsession' of the party with issues of constitutional reform has been replaced today, certainly in campaigning terms, with a focus on social liberal issues such as education, health and pensions. Where there is, perhaps, less settled agreement, is how this wider concept of liberty should be delivered. To the present Chancellor of the Exchequer, Gordon Brown, public services should be delivered through a system of state monopoly provision, while welfare services should be delivered largely through a system of means-tested state monopoly. Should this be the Liberal Democrat vision, too?

A key question for the Liberal Democrats is to what extent we can draw on our heritage of economic liberalism to address some of the current problems in public service delivery. This categorically does not mean rejecting the social liberalism agenda, as some Liberal Democrats seem wrongly to fear. Economic liberalism does not mean shedding Liberal values in order to pick up Tory votes. The challenge instead is to ask to what extent we can utilise choice, competition, consumer power and the private sector to deliver a better deal for those on low incomes, as well as for those who can already fend for themselves.

Let us take just three examples. We will start with the National Health Service (NHS), which the current Chancellor has concluded is the most respected and cherished institution in the UK.

No doubt people who have had cause to rely on the NHS will be grateful for its existence, and for the dedication of its staff. But the NHS remains an organisation beset by failure – unacceptably long waiting times, too little capacity, outdated capital equipment and often poor standards of customer service. The patient has little power to shop around or insist on better service – he or she is left only with the choice of paying to 'go private', without reimbursement from the NHS, or sticking with what is on offer from the NHS.

Not long after I became MP for Yeovil, a lady came to one of my advice centres to complain about a waiting time for a consultation. It was September 2002 and she had been given an appointment date by the NHS at '9.30 am on 24 September 2004'! What organisation run with any real accountability to its clients would treat them in such a way? What organisation with any respect for customers would treat them in such a high-handed and thoughtless manner? So the question is surely whether another system of provision, founded on the same access principles, could deliver a better outcome.

When we look at many continental European health services, we see health services that deliver equality of access but without the appalling waiting times and often poor quality of treatment and care which sometimes scar the NHS.

It is incumbent on the Liberal Democrats to see if we can give the public a better choice than that offered by the other two parties. The Tory commitment to economic liberalism, but not to social liberalism, manifests itself in a policy of 'opt out', which will help the upper income groups to escape poor quality NHS provision, but without improving services for everyone else. The Labour commitment to 'social justice', without economic liberalism, leaves us reliant only on a second-rate, centralised, state monopoly service – customer-unfriendly, unresponsive and underfunded. The challenge for Liberal Democrats is to show how choice, competition and consumer power can deliver a better deal for all our citizens.

Our prisons system is another example of a failing state service, with only a small minority of prisoners held in private jails. Our existing prisons fail to reform and rehabilitate their inhabitants, who go on to commit millions of additional crimes as a consequence of our appalling rates of reoffending. Private prisons are in many cases delivering better value for money and can deliver better outcomes too. We should therefore be exploring in more depth how we can use private and voluntary providers to deliver better services to the public. This should also help to improve standards in public prisons.

Liberal Democrats also need to play a major part in reforming our state welfare system, not least our system of pensions.

The traditional Tory policy has combined a poor-quality basic state pension with generous tax breaks, with which the affluent minority can buy themselves private pensions. The Labour Government has introduced a pensions system that is so complicated that few people in Britain understand it. The system is also increasingly dependent on mass means-testing. As such, the new system erodes the incentive for people to take responsibility for themselves, and it leaves more and more people dependent on state handouts. The state is as likely to mis-sell its pensions as the private sector, as experienced with the short-lived earnings link and the State Earnings Related Pension.

It must be for the Liberal Democrats to help forge a new system of pensions, with a better-funded non-means-tested basic state pension to provide a minimum acceptable standard of living, but with an additional 'owned' second pension for every citizen, with choice built into the system.

There is a final challenge for Liberal Democrats when we consider what needs to be done to deliver freedom and challenge inequality of opportunity in our society.

It is increasingly clear that the problems of poverty, drugs, unemployment and crime are embedded in the experiences of a minority of children, but a sizeable minority, in the earliest years of their lives. Over the past few decades, the breakdown of the family and the increase in relative child poverty has led to a growing gap between the problems facing different groups of our young people.

In 1999, 39% of children were born outside marriage, compared with 6% in 1961. In 1999, 35% of children were living in relative poverty, compared with 10% in 1979. Britain has become the divorce capital of Europe, the teenage mums capital of Europe. A quarter of children in the UK live in one-parent families – double the European average.

These characteristics of our society are creating a vicious cycle of neglect, poverty and failure. These problems are a major threat to the freedoms of the children concerned and, through their effects on crime and anti-social behaviour, they are a threat to us all.

For Liberals, this is a difficult issue. We have tended to be non-judgemental about how people live their lives and manage their personal relationships. But can we afford to ignore the effects on young people that these developments are causing?

At a minimum, these problems necessitate a more active role for state and voluntary organisations in the early years – through assistance to children and through helping people to fulfil their responsibilities as parents. These developments also raise the question of whether the state has been right to seek to drive the single parents of very young children out of child-caring responsibilities and into work.

Where next for the Liberal Democrats?

The recent Liberal Democrat electoral progress at local government, Scottish Parliament, Welsh Assembly, European and Westminster levels opens up a real prospect of a breakthrough from the two-party system which has dominated British politics from the 1920s onwards, to a genuine three-party system.

If we can continue to make progress in increasing our seats in the Westminster Parliament, then it seems likely that in the years ahead the Liberal Democrats will finally be in a position to share power in UK government. But to achieve power, and to exercise power effectively, the Liberal Democrats must have a sharpened and defined policy edge, based clearly upon liberal principles. Such a policy agenda must, in my view, constitute a synthesis of the personal, political, economic and social liberalism, which is our bequest from earlier generations of liberals.

We must reject 'nanny-state liberalism'. We must reject the assumption that because we are internationalist we must always be in favour of 'internationalist' solutions that are offered to any problem, regardless of our decentralising beliefs.

We must continue to reclaim economic liberalism; and marry economic liberalism to our social liberalism, in order to deliver more opportunity and freedom to all of our citizens – particularly those on lower incomes who cannot opt out of failing state services.

A Liberal Democrat programme based on traditional liberal values would, at a minimum, imply a policy agenda including:

Personal liberalism

→ Respecting personal freedoms, and protecting individuals from state and majority oppression, whether unnecessarily coercive or well meaning. This means resisting 'nanny-state liberalism'.

40

→ Giving a higher priority to reducing crime, including recognition that prison presently works while offenders are incarcerated, but fails totally when offenders are released.

Political liberalism
→ Devolving more power within the UK, reducing the power of central government and abolishing a variety of Whitehall departments to devolve more power locally and regionally.
→ Reforming Europe, by repatriating powers which should be exercised at a local or national level, agreeing a constitution if it clearly defines and limits EU powers, ending the Common Agricultural Policy, and working to extend EU cooperation in areas such as the single market, foreign policy and the environment.

Economic liberalism
→ Accepting that competition, consumer power and private sector innovation offer the best prospect for increasing wealth and reducing poverty – including in the developing world. We should press for the reduction of international trade barriers, including those that hit the developing world producers.
→ Simplifying the tax system to create a more logical and comprehensible system, with less 'breaks' and lower tax rates; abolishing regressive taxes such as council tax, and taking more low earners out of income tax.
→ Reducing the state's role in the economy, including investigating the case for privatisating the Royal Mail – with employees being given a generous disbursement of shares in the new, private, company.

Social liberalism
→ Introducing more choice, competition and consumer power

into public services such as health, while preserving the principle of access for all on the basis of need, not ability to pay.

→ Reforming our welfare system to give people more control and involvement in their own security, in exchange for more personal responsibility.

→ Breaking the cycle of deprivation, which is caused by family breakdown, poor parenting and child poverty; improving the standards of our education system to help address inequalities of opportunity.

Conclusion

The Liberal Democrats have a proud liberal heritage and a distinctive and popular philosophy.

We must ensure that we remain consistent in relation to the four strands of Liberalism – personal, political, economic and social.

We need to continue to embrace our social liberal agenda, while demonstrating that it is not incompatible with our economic liberal heritage.

We must reclaim Liberalism in all its forms and with all its mutually reinforcing strengths, and continue to resist a nanny-state liberalism or 'liberalism à la carte', which would be no more than a philosophy of good intentions, bobbing about unanchored in the muddled middle of British politics.

If we can reclaim our Liberal heritage, we will not only increase our chances of exercising power in British politics, but, much more importantly, we will ensure that we are exercising power with, passion, purpose and effect.

Notes

1. Sir William Beveridge, 'Liberalism with a Radical Programme', Newcastle-upon-Tyne, 1944.
2. Thomas Macaulay, House of Commons, 18 April 1847.

2   Liberalism and localism
Edward Davey

Localism after the centralists' century?

Liberals have long argued for stronger local government, with power being devolved from central government. Our case has been largely pluralist, resting on grounds of enhancing democratic accountability and maximising opportunity for innovation and experimentation.

However, Liberals did not win the political argument in Britain during the twentieth century. Britain became one of the most centralised democracies in the western world, as both socialist thinkers and conservative forces saw central state power as the best way to impose their order. On the left, the Fabians in particular saw national government as the only way to promote equality and redistribution, with the state grappling with the capitalist forces they opposed. On the right, central power was seen as necessary to tame nationally organised labour and other opponents such as 'loony left' councils that challenged national public spending controls. External forces such as world wars, the end of Empire and the Cold War all helped to legitimise the century of centralism.

Now there are signs that the ground is shifting. The ideas dominating the domestic and international controversies of the 21st century require the British State to take a new, more classically Liberal, shape. As the main battlefield has moved away from the economic and industrial sphere towards public services and quality of life, the all-powerful Westminster-Whitehall model is under strain. Nor does the modern external threat of international terrorism or the new challenges posed by relationships with modern supranational bodies such as the European Union, United Nations and World Trade Organisation, lead to the need to retain a leviathan state.

Pressed to its limits under the targets, initiatives and task forces of New Labour's first term, the Westminster-Whitehall model has not delivered. Both Labour and Conservative parties have already recognised this, as they have begun to embrace gingerly the decentralist agenda. While the Conservatives have yet to propose anything significant, New Labour has, imaginatively, proposed something called 'new localism'.

Labour's new localism has one main problem: it continues the existing system of central-local relations. Rather than acting as a guiding principle for public service reform, new localism can appear to mean anything to anyone at any time – all within the current constitutional centralism. The Treasury's vague talk of managerial decentralisation completely avoids democracy. Concepts such as 'earned autonomy' reveal that no power shift is envisaged. An agenda of 'freedoms and flexibilities' is set in terms of Whitehall's own targets, inspections and judgements.

Yet at least the debate is moving our way. The challenge for the New Liberals of the century is to update and refresh our notion of the Liberal state.

The arguments for decentralisation must be remade and robustly tested. To win the case for a Liberal localism, we must, for example, show that social justice will not be harmed, but actually enhanced. We must show that stronger local government and new regional assemblies are not just reinventions of bureaucracy at a lower level, but can instead be mechanisms for checking state power and for promoting quality and choice in public services for the individual. By shifting the balance of power away from the centre, we must meet the J. A. Hobson measure: 'Liberalism will retain its distinction from socialism in taking for its chief test of policy the freedom of the individual citizen, rather than the strength of the state.'[1]

Overcoming local-scepticism

The centralists' century has left a difficult inheritance for localism. Any grand restatement of Liberal commitment to localism must be grounded in that political reality, to have any real impact. Many commentators and voters do not have a rosy picture of local government. Just as pro-Europeans face eurosceptics, pro-localists face local-sceptics.

Both species of sceptics have some roots in the reactionary right. Both species have successfully propagated their views to influence more moderate opinion. Both oppose change with remarkably similar arguments.

Local-sceptics believe town halls, like Brussels, are filled with meddling bureaucrats. They see crackpot schemes down every council corridor, and perceive local councillors as being as corrupt as the 'Johnny Foreigner' national politician.

Unfortunately, such bar-room stereotyping has gained a certain legitimacy. Like euro-myths of straight bananas, the local-myths of council-sponsored knitting lessons for disabled goldfish may not actually be believed, but there are too many quarters of public opinion that ignorantly nod in agreement. Winning the political argument for localism will be tough.

Even more challenging for localists, just as for pro-Europeans, is that the public's experience of local government is not uniquely positive. Tabloid caricatures aside, there is much wrong with local government today – just as there is in Europe and, for that matter, Whitehall. A New Liberal advocacy of localism needs to understand

45

the stronger arguments of local-sceptics, whilst debunking their myths.

Any honest audit of local government across the UK would include a range of negatives. The quality and competence of local councillors and local council officers is not always high. Strategic decision-making capability is often particularly weak. Partisan politics and personality feuds can sometimes infect the local political debate, obscuring the really important issues. Such an audit could be backed up with a host of examples where different councils have wasted money, taken daft decisions and delivered poor services.

Of course, such findings and examples could easily be more than countered with a wealth of success stories. The Audit Commission's recent exercise, the Comprehensive Performance Assessment of England's 150 largest councils, is reputed to have disappointed Number 10 as it revealed a much higher degree of competence across councils than the prejudices of Prime Ministerial aides had wanted to find.

Perhaps part of the problem is that councils have been poor in selling themselves. Perhaps it's just a few poor councils that give the rest a bad name. Perhaps things have been improving, yet press and public perceptions have not yet caught up.

Whatever the reality, the case for a Liberal localism must address the need to reform local government, as well as merely praise it.

The localist case

Strong, reformed local government will come up with better ideas for running public services and spending taxpayers' money more efficiently than Whitehall ever has or will.

While there are many ways of restating the case for decentralisation, this statement concentrates on two of the core issues in modern political debate – public services and taxation. If New

Liberalism can make localism, as one of its core tenets, directly relevant to these key debates, the political prize could be great. Though these arguments of hard cash and entrepreneurialism are the strongest we localists have, they need to be explained carefully, as they are no longer self-evident truths after the century of centralists.

Ideas: innovation and choice

Freedom to experiment has proved to be one of the greatest attributes of free-market societies. Yet Britain's centralised state is not well designed to mirror the private sector's ability to innovate. From monolithic structures in the NHS to national pay-setting across the public sector, the Whitehall model looks increasingly inflexible and unable to embrace difference.

The localist case is that decentralisation provides a democratic alternative for improving services. More freedom for stronger local government offers the chance for public services to import at least some of the flexibility of the private sector.

Different authorities could have the freedom to make their own choices about the best way to deliver services. Diversity would be actively encouraged as one proxy for competition within the state sector. Allowing councils to experiment brings the opportunity to discover and disseminate best practice. The slaying of national 'sacred cows' becomes more feasible, with local politicians and public service managers freed up to find the best solution for their communities.

The acceptance of difference

The critical political decision to unlock such entrepreneurial energy in the public sector is the explicit and public acceptance of difference.

While some progressive commentators feel such acceptance

would be a betrayal of our commitment to equality and poverty reduction,[2] the reverse is actually the case. Yet it is important to understand why centralists feel this, if we are to secure consensus for the localist alternative.

The British centralist state came about partly because of the desire to end inequality. As the original welfarist responses to nineteenth-century poverty were spurred by local initiative, with no underpinning national framework, it is not surprising that by the late nineteenth century there were grotesque variations in welfare provision in different parts of the country.

It was perhaps not unreasonable, therefore, that national government stepped in, to address the hotchpotch that had evolved, not least to deliver on basic social priorities such as access to free education and healthcare.

From such beginnings, national control of all social policy has therefore come to be seen as vital by centralists. The progressive centralists fear the re-emergence of significant inequity if Whitehall hands over power to local councils, and they believe the battle to end remaining inequality would effectively be lost. Such arguments were, for example, voiced by many on the Labour left in the debate over foundation hospitals. Misguided fears of 'two tier' services and of 'postcode lotteries' drives much of this critique.

Yet the centralist argument has a serious weakness: its reliance on history.

First, no one arguing the localist case wishes to see core public services withdrawn or seriously undermined in any area of the country. The modern acceptance of difference is primarily about a desire to raise standards, not reduce them. Most models proposed for decentralisation envisage national minimum standards, to protect against the unlikely situation of a local decision to dismantle a public service.

Second, there are few localist calls for the decentralisation of the social security system of benefit payments. Certainly, most Liberal thinkers would defend a basically national system of benefits. This distinction is important when considering the lessons of history. For one of the main tensions that occurred in the development of the early welfare state was that between the local ratepayers and the demands for more financial help for the poor of their own area, particularly in relation to the discredited Poor Laws. As income redistribution at the local level not surprisingly proved unpopular and difficult, a key driver of central intervention in the late nineteenth and twentieth centuries was the understandable desire for national safety-net systems.

Thus, the guarantees of national minimum standards, for example, of free access to health services, plus the stout defence of nationally organised income redistribution, are vital elements to winning widespread progressive commitment to localism.

There will remain centralists who worry about different quality levels of public services in different parts of the country. Yet centralists' arguments about varying services' levels are flawed. For the truth is that decades of central management of public services have not brought territorial uniformity and equality. New Labour's concern about the so-called 'postcode lottery' is a concern about the failures of a centralised system to deliver equality. Moreover, the criticism that localism would produce more postcode lotteries is simply wrong: there would be postcode differences, but those differences would be through more transparent, democratic choices, not through a national lottery.

Indeed, public services are unlikely ever to conform to common standards across a country as large as the UK, and much money is likely to be wasted by attempts to impose national uniformity. The localist answer of legislating for national minimum rights and standards for individuals, whilst allowing local authorities and communities the freedom to decide what actually to deliver, is the best way to prevent unacceptable inequalities within a framework of dynamic service improvement. Nor is such an approach theoretical. Countries such as Sweden and Germany are decentralist, yet are much more equal than Britain.

The opportunity for local choice models

One of the most exciting elements of the localist case is the opportunity for more choice, within a more pluralist state. Freedom to innovate and to do things differently brings with it the opportunity to embrace the choice agenda, so crucial to the reform of public services.

The lack of choice in public services has produced much of the recent public disquiet. Yet it will always be more difficult for a national government to implement choice across national services because of the varying needs and priorities of different parts of the country. In comparison, locally-driven choice has the potential to develop more appropriate models.

Of course, devolving power and budgets to local government by itself will make no difference at all to the choices service users face. The criticism that one would simply be swapping one bureaucracy for another would have merit, if the localist agenda ended at mere devolution.

Far more has to be put in place to realise the potential of local flexibility. A whole host of models and options must be developed, so individuals and communities can pick and choose, finding out what works best for them.

Many of these models exist already. Elsewhere in this book, Liberal colleagues are developing new ones. New research projects are finding a whole host of choice models for local services in housing, social services and education.[3]

The key advantage for such ideas in a localist world is that, sooner or later, one authority might decide to implement a new idea, without having to wait for a Whitehall missive or a new Act of Parliament. Localism can thereby unlock the energy and creativity of policy experimentation.

There are various families of choice models that liberated councils could build upon and develop. They differ from a private market model of choice in one basic sense, namely that the democratic body is the ultimate provider of the funding. Yet, that aside, they could provide the pluralist approach to public policy evolution that Britain has lacked for so long.

Some local authorities will opt for the individual to choose the provider. As happens quite often already, the individual could have the direct right and funding stream to choose his doctor, his place of further education or his care home. By working with multiple providers, the authority could choose to enhance the choice of provider and service quality directly and/or allow members of their community to do that for themselves with direct payment and voucher-based systems. Further education for 16- to 19-year-olds could, for example, easily be delivered through a voucher-based system.

Other authorities, for different services, would opt for the collective choice of provider – with the collective voice operating not through the council, but through specific groups of users. Here, the council facilitates the collective choice of its community in reaching better service decisions. Thus, disabled people in a community could be involved in periodic decisions on selecting specialist transport providers. Or tenant housing cooperatives could hire and fire their estate's management. Or councils could help streets or neighbourhoods to form consumer mutuals to buy their electricity and gas on more favourable terms.

Even more traditional models of service provision could be adapted to provide users with meaningful choice. Local authorities might decide that one provider of a service is more efficient, but that this provider should be contractually required to offer users different levels of service, for example by age, time of the year or by top-up payment options.

Efficiency in experimentation
Indeed, by seeing the local authority as a liberated, empowered, accountable funder of public services, one can begin to envisage a whole range of reform options being tested.

Some would, of course, fail. Just as many national policy experiments fail now. Yet that only confirms one more advantage of the localist way forward: efficiency in experimentation.

The localist critique of centralisation is not that national government fails to change. Recent UK governments have been impressive in their pace of change, and their willingness to experiment. From privatisations, poll tax, national curriculums, internal health markets, public service agreements, tax credits and foundation hospitals, it is impossible to argue that central government has been slow in coming forward with new ideas.

The localist critique is that central government tends to experiment on the whole country at once. Political timetables rarely allow for piloting or for learning lessons from piloting, whilst political machismo rarely allows for the admission of error. So dynamic national government has been responsible for many expensive mistakes, for which the whole country has had to suffer or pay.

A localist structure of innovation might at one level seem less exciting and dynamic. Many authorities might decide to do nothing until a new policy idea had been trialled elsewhere. Yet, if it provides both extra stability and more long-termism in policy thinking, that could be yet another benefit.

Cash: better financial accountability
The localist case normally starts with the potential for improving

democratic accountability. Most people can readily see that decentralising power will produce more democracy and more opportunity to question their politicians. The passing of power down to local communities is something that many will instinctively favour.

But, in truth, this is hardly a chief concern for voters. Accountability may be seen as important, but it means little to most people. It is not a strong basis for building a political coalition for localism. That's why the advantages in terms of taxpayers' cash need spelling out. If people believe there are cash benefits for dismantling chunks of Whitehall in favour of the town hall, that might change people's perspectives. So it is financial accountability on which we must focus.

Theory and practice: the failure of Parliamentary accountability
So why should a power shift from central to local government lead to more efficient government, based on better financial accountability?

Explanations can be theoretical. If the job of government is to raise and allocate resources for those things society does in common – from parks to police, from emergency services to education – then democratic structures are supposed to be one discipline for demanding improved service levels and overall efficiency. Where markets cannot operate with full force, whether for reasons of efficiency or equity, then the elected public custodians hold sway – in deciding levels of taxation and spending, in building systems for audit and improvement, in designing quasi-market structures to focus public services on their customers.

So the localist-centralist question turns on which tier of government can best fulfil these roles. Theory may not provide a conclusive answer, but arguments such as information costs, transparency and contestability would tend to favour more local

53

democratic structures to promote efficiency.

Thus, on a very basic, practical level, it will normally be far more difficult for politicians and bureaucrats in Whitehall to judge the quality of a service and the capability of local providers, from audit reports and data, than for the local politicians and civil servants on the ground.

Yet, to focus empirically on financial accountability, and the relative record of local and central politics to perform this key function, we need to recognise the virtual absence of national democratic involvement in financial accountability in Britain today.

This may surprise some. Yet, at present, Parliament plays almost no meaningful role in examining the budgetary decisions of the Government and Britain's Civil Service, except in the most general terms, or several years after the money has already been spent. The capability of the UK's national Parliament to hold the Executive to account for how it spends taxpayers' money has never been high, but is probably now at an all-time low. In terms of information, resources and procedures, the British Parliament is arguably the weakest national legislature in performing budget scrutiny of the entire OECD community. There is, for example, no parliamentary office to provide independent advice to MPs and select committees about government spending and taxation proposals.

Members of Parliament appear to have no interest in changing this. Even if they did, MPs would almost all need complete retraining if they were ever to try to exercise any active role in financial accountability. While ideas for reform are made from time to time,[4] the failure of the modest Cook proposals for reform of the Commons shows the extent of the addiction to financial subservience of most British national politicians.

Moreover, even if Parliament were radically reformed and at last tried to perform its theoretical role as watchdog of the purse-strings, it would be an impossible task for it to monitor all government spending. National politicians examining the cost and financial performance of locally delivered services are unlikely to produce much improvement on the attempts of Whitehall civil servants to do this – though one would hope they might start to scrutinise the budgets of large Whitehall departments more effectively.

A local democratic alternative

In contrast to Parliament, in local government today there are an increasingly large number of politicians playing active roles in real budget decisions and real budget scrutiny. Councils with strong oppositions may face probing amendments to their budgets. Local communities – from head-teachers and governors to residents' associations – are likely to be far more informed about details within their local authorities' budgets than they will ever be about distant national plans.

Yet financial accountability at the local level cannot work properly in the current system. With councils dependent for most of their budget on a central grant, and with the plethora of Whitehall controls, such as ring-fencing, passporting and capping, local authorities are not masters of their budgets. Small changes in central grant levels decided by ministers can lead to large changes in local taxes or local services. This is the so-called 'gearing effect', as a result of which a 1% cut in central grant requires, on average, a 4% increase in local council tax to offset it.

The Government's current 'Balance of Funding Review' between local and central government may produce some solutions to this problem. Some of the research undertaken by the review and published on the website of the Office of the Deputy Prime Minister suggests a real understanding of these difficulties. Yet indications from ministers to date suggest the review will not produce radical solutions. There remains a prevalent view in Whitehall that the level of central control via grants and the 'gearing effect' is a good thing, because it reduces local freedom. Labour's professed new localism seems so far to have had no impact on such views.

The net effect of weak financial accountability in Parliament and the inflexibility of local government finance mean Britain has produced an unusually bizarre system. Nationally, few MPs take budget scrutiny seriously. Locally, some councillors do, but don't work within a rational financial framework.

Moreover, this system wastes huge amounts of money because of the paranoia of Whitehall. Bred in a political culture which distrusts local government and believes only Whitehall can spend efficiently, successive governments and their civil servants have devised increasingly costly systems of audit and regulation that simply duplicate many existing local financial control systems. The focus on targets and statistics itself has led to the creation of new armies of bureaucrats whose sole task is to collect data to feed the demands of the leviathan machine.

Of course, both Parliament and councils could and should be reformed, so these democratic assemblies could work harder and more practically for their taxpaying constituents. Irrespective of any power switch from central to local government, the Commons should be radically reformed to be an activist legislature. The central regulatory burden on councils could be reduced. Taking existing responsibilities alone, the balance of central-local funding could be shifted. All this could happen within the current framework, without any further decentralisation.

Yet the current parlous state of affairs reveals the danger of excessive centralism and what it can mean for financial accountability. Rather than relying purely on reform of national institutions and improvements to the current framework, the case for relying more on local democracy for scrutinising state spending is strong.

How much of the current budget that could be devolved for this heightened scrutiny is open to debate and analysis? Yet if the principle was that centrally retained cash was solely for equalisation purposes alone – to protect poorer areas primarily – then one might envisage a reversal of the current 75/25 split, whereby the average council now receives about 75% of its revenue in the form of a central grant. An important part of this proposal would be a significant reduction in national taxation, to offset the shift to more tax-raising at a local level.

In short, to make sure the extra resources going into public services are well spent, we need the control of more of those budgets to go to local authorities. Rather than considering taking school funding out of the hands of councils, as Downing Street's Policy Unit has floated from time to time, we should be looking at greater freedoms for councils to manage their existing responsibilities more effectively in partnership with local providers. Indeed, the agenda needs to be looking forward to examine what other locally-delivered public services would be better financially managed at a local level, with primary healthcare services an obvious candidate.

Since this is the reverse of the received wisdom in Whitehall and Fleet Street, proponents of such a shift need to build a convincing case.

Local government would, above all, have to rise to this challenge. Handling more cash, overseeing new budgets, and dealing with more financial autonomy, would be too much of a culture shock for some councils; all of these changes couldn't happen at once. Capacity building would be important, from improving existing financial management expertise, to training more councillors to understand the budgets prepared by officers. Yet much of this is already happening, through the work of the Improvement and Development Agency and the Audit Commission. Existing work to improve procurement across councils is engaging elected members at levels rarely seen before.

A localist agenda, based on spending tax more wisely, through enhanced local financial scrutiny, may not of itself sound politically engaging, but its policy implications could be dramatic. In national policy terms it might mean:

→ radical cuts in national income tax and major reductions in Whitehall spending;
→ abolition of central targets and Whitehall-led inspections for most councils;
→ the creation of 'The Office of the Taxpayer' (Oftax) to advise MPs on the budget.[5]

For local government, the policy options could include:

→ a local income tax to replace council tax, as the foundation for tax decentralisation;
→ redundancy or redeployment for all council staff involved with council tax and target-related data-gathering for Whitehall;
→ a Local Government College to improve training opportunities for all councillors and council officers.

Making localism happen

Reversing Britain's centralised state is likely to take a political generation. As Mrs Thatcher's government took three terms to roll back the central economic state she inherited in 1979, it would take even a well-prepared Liberal Democrat government two or three terms to roll back the central political state.

Political liberalism, like economic liberalism, would be a huge culture shock to society. Current British polity is addicted to the notion that national government is responsible for everything. When some tragedy or crisis erupts, the gut instinct of MPs, the media and much of the public is to demand Prime Ministerial action, even when the issue ought to have nothing to do with Downing Street or indeed any Cabinet minister.

Whilst the adoption of territorial pluralism is challenging culturally, perhaps the toughest task will be re-engineering the political classes and the Civil Service. For localism will require a different breed of local and national politician. Local politicians will have to be more professional, while national politicians will have to learn to stop interfering. Localism threatens a wholesale revolution for Whitehall. Departments will need to be merged and abolished. Fewer civil servants will be London-based. Careers will be made 'in the sticks', as the social status of senior local government officers is transformed.

All this has to be done in the face of local-sceptics, discussed previously. So, detailed preparation for such an ambitious political programme of change will be essential, changing both people and structures.

People change: local politicians and civil servants
British local government has a large number of superb local councillors and local government officers. Yet there are too many councillors and local government officers who are, frankly, second rate.

If we are to have an expanded, vibrant, local politics, we have to be sure there are no barriers or disincentives to prevent people of talent entering. We have to face up to the problems of recruitment and retention. We have to change the image of being a councillor and working in local government.

Fortunately, the whole process of localism should do much of this work for us. If political power shifts, people will shift with it. Many people have been put off local politics in recent decades as local government's powers have been stripped away. Some areas have witnessed a vicious circle, whereby people of talent moved out of local politics, as it was no longer the vehicle for them to put something back into their community. There is every reason to suspect that a significant and public reversal of this trend will have the opposite effect, creating a virtuous circle of responsibility and active, participatory, citizenship.

Certain initiatives by Labour have begun the process needed for the rejuvenation of the local political class. More full-time councillors, experiments with Cabinets and mayors, and the Improvement and Development Agency (IDeA) are tackling the bleak inheritance of the Conservatives. Yet more rapid progress is needed.

The drive to raise the status and quality of local councillors is essential. If councils are to have more financial freedoms and more responsibilities, the type of people attracted to local politics and their skill base will almost certainly need to change. Given that we already need more diversity amongst councillors than at present, this poses some real personnel challenges, in and outside political parties.

The balance to be struck is between creating more professional politicians, which is certainly necessary, and retaining roles for people from all walks of life, so politics does not become even more elitist and unrepresentative. After all, councillors fulfil a range of functions beyond simply running the council. All councillors need to be representatives of their communities and some need to be outside the ruling group of councillors, both as the formal Opposition and as councillors free to ask the difficult questions. Inevitably, policies to develop the role of councillors will create tensions between these different roles.

Labour has sought to square this circle with the new Cabinet structure adopted by most councils. A minority of councillors serve on the Cabinet, often as full-time politicians, with full-time salaries, while other councillors perform a scrutiny role. Yet they have not chosen to go for purely full-time councillors only.

It is early days to test whether the new system has worked generally, or even in the narrow terms of attracting a different type of council candidate. Evidence, such as it is, suggests that new tensions have been created between 'the backbenchers' and the 'executive members'. Moreover, there is no evidence of a new rush of talent for local political office. Even in the most high profile of changes designed to attract new blood – the introduction of mayors – the results have been mixed.

Two different, though not mutually exclusive, conclusions are possible.

The first is that such reforms take time to yield results. After all, politics does not have a good name and the local-sceptic message has put down deep roots in parts of the target groups for recruitment. A new generation of local politicians cannot be born overnight.

The second possible conclusion is that such reforms were simply not bold enough. By avoiding tougher political decisions about the total number of councillors, Labour missed the opportunity for more radical reform. The option of reducing councillors in a large number of authorities would be extremely contentious, but could enable *every* remaining councillor to be at least part-time if not full-time.

The counter-argument – heard within all parties – is that we have too few politicians, and that, if anything, we should have more councillors, not less.

Such a proposition – to keep or increase the current number of councillors – is, in truth, fundamentally flawed. To begin with, it assumes there are queues of people wanting to be local councillors. We live in a different type of society – fast-moving, complex and demanding, where the political classes will never, thankfully, regain the type of deference they once received. Local politics will never again be like some extension of the local golf club or union branch.

Any political activist who has tried to organise a slate of candidates for an all-out local election will immediately recognise the problem. It is astonishingly difficult to find enough candidates, let alone enough keen, talented candidates. If we are going to re-empower local government, we cannot continue on the basis of so many press-ganged, unprepared people.

With fewer candidates to find, and greater incentives in terms of power and pay, the chance of reforming the local political classes will be a very real one. Local political parties will begin to see regular internal elections, as members compete to win the nomination to stand. Coupled with reforms to the electoral system (see later), the forces of competition could be unleashed to drive up the competence and commitment of local politicians.

If the politicians are to be reduced but enjoy better terms of service, what of the humble local government officer?

The Government, working with the Local Government Association and others, has fortunately been giving this aspect some serious attention. Graduate recruitment programmes have been improved, and the attempt to sell local government within and outside the Civil Service has received much needed attention. Training from the IDeA is now well-thought of – especially as it includes training of elected members – and bodies such as CIPFA (the Chartered Institute for Public Finance and Accountancy) continue to provide a high level of professional support.

Yet even this welcome attention will not be enough in a new full-blown localist world. Even on the training front, we need the equivalent of the Civil Service College, for local government, both to signal the step change and to make it actually happen.

Moreover, there are some serious challenges remaining. In high cost areas, the ability to recruit and retain is now one of the leading obstacles to performance improvement. Good officers achieve and leave, as the ability to pay attractive packages is hampered both by national agreements and by limits on resources. Whilst the financial freedoms of localism could make a difference, national government working with local government have to persuade the unions to accept more local and regional pay bargaining, both in the form of housing and travel allowances and in terms of weightings.

Structural change: political competition and entrenching localism

Given the ambition of the localist agenda, it would be surprising if it were not accompanied by some structural change. Whilst it is important to avoid unnecessary restructuring, the centralists' century will not be reversed without some pain. So the objectives must be focused on ensuring the decentralisation package tackles the weakest parts of local government, builds in the right creative tensions and creates longer-term stability.

The most significant structural changes must inevitably focus on making the electoral process work better – so there's more competition and more democracy. Reducing the ability of any area to become an uncontested monopoly fiefdom for any party must be a priority, whilst tackling the quango state must be another. For stability, local government must, above all, move from being a statutory creation of Parliament to having its own constitutional status and position. Coupled with a complete reorganisation of the way central-local inter-relationships work, with the abolition of the Office of the Deputy Prime Minister, localism would become entrenched and much harder to shift.

Intensifying political competition at local government level inevitably requires electoral reform. The case for proportional reform is at its strongest at local government level. For under 'first past the post', parties have been known to win all or almost all of the seats on little more than 50% of the vote, destroying the ability of Opposition parties to undertake their vital role.

Over time, the inability of Opposition parties to win many seats, let alone challenge for power, can totally undermine both the forces of direct political competition and the wider civic culture. In parts of the UK that have been one-party states for generations, the extent of voter apathy and the tendency towards corruption is significantly greater.

The desire to maximise the forces of political competition is part of the traditional attraction Liberals have always had towards the Single Transferable Vote (STV) system of proportional representation. Since it reduces the power of parties, and increases the power of voters who can choose between candidates of the same party, it has real potential to energise local democracy.

The (misguided) opposition some politicians show to proportional representation at national level because it could produce coalition government is also a rather redundant argument in the local government context. Not only have many councils operated successfully without one party having an overall majority for many years, but the notion of local political groupings being elected on clear mandates is even more far-fetched than at the parliamentary level.

Indeed, the achievement of Liberal Democrats to negotiate STV for Scottish local elections from 2007 should eventually provide UK evidence of the benefits of the competitive power of STV proportional representation locally.

Finally, local government's role in tackling the quango state has often been overlooked, partly because so many quangos operate on a national or regional basis. Yet if a main part of the localist rationale is financial accountability, strengthened councils have a major role to play in opening up some of the more closed parts of Britain's quango state. Some councils will be large enough to do this in their area alone. Others may need to operate jointly. Yet the capacity of local democracy to reduce the cost and opacity of many of Britain's unelected state bodies ought to be a strong argument for localists.

Conclusion

The New Liberals of the century have a historic task to turn round the centralist political inheritance of successive Conservative and Labour governments. It is a daunting task, not least because the core building block of local democracy is in far from robust health and the centrifugal forces of Whitehall, the national media and the dominant political culture of ubiquitous Prime Ministerial responsibility support an insidious local-scepticism.

Yet, paradoxically, New Labour has prepared the ground for a full-blooded Liberal localism by its own mistakes. First, its early adoption of a centralised target-based approach to government quickly revealed the political and practical limits of managerial centralism. By attempting to reform public service delivery through the most centralised methods ever seen in peacetime, the absurdities and weaknesses of the model became obvious to all, even to its creators. Second, New Labour's belated volte-face, with its rhetoric of 'new localism', is moving the terms of the key political debates on to Liberal territory. While this was unavoidable for the Labour hierarchy, they come to the debate with no developed philosophy, no shared acceptance of the logic of decentralisation and with little policy substance. Just as the Healey–Callaghan recognition in 1976 of the limits of economic centralism softened the way for the Conservatives' more enthusiastic embrace of market economics, so the dawning acceptance by Brown and Blair of the inadequacy of political centralism will assist the credibility of the Liberal Democrats as the advocates of more radical political reform.

Therefore, in this chapter I have begun to sketch out some of the localist reforms that must form key elements of the programme of the first Liberal Democrat administration. Devolving power to local government may be a prerequisite, but it has to be delivered through coherent and carefully designed pathways, beginning with efforts to improve the capacity and average quality of local politicians and the local civil service.

More competition in local politics is the key. Competition between parties and within parties. If we are to give more power to local authorities, that should attract new people in, but they must compete to earn the right to wield that power. Thus, two key proposals are a reduction in the number of councillors linked to improving their terms and conditions, plus a more competitive electoral system based on STV proportional representation. The first proposal should force politicians within local parties to compete within their party for selection. The second proposal will both enhance internal party competition, and, most significantly, end one-party monopolies on power in many local authorities.

Many other initiatives will be needed to refine this new competitive model – for example, a Local Government College to provide the best possible training and the encouragement of a more participative civic society beyond the party political realm – but a change in the culture of national politicians will be needed to embed them.

Thus, a Liberal localism will necessitate radical reforms at the centre, too. The most significant will include a new basis for central-local relations, with local government gaining a constitutional status rather than a mere statutory status. Yet the practical policy changes will perhaps be more shocking for people used to the current model. These must include the reduction and even abolition of major Whitehall departments, the ownership transfer of national bodies relating to local government from Whitehall to joint local authority control, the democratising of quangos and the promotion of regional and local pay bargaining solutions in the public sector.

Parliament and central government should simultaneously take on very different roles to facilitate this shift in power and political culture. Parliament needs to find, for the first time in its history, a more proactive role in the scrutiny of central government, particularly in relation to the budget. A start could be made with the establishment of an Office of the Taxpayer, in Parliament, aimed at helping MPs to scrutinise the draft budgets proposed by ministers. Ministers themselves should refuse to answer questions on issues that are devolved to local and regional authorities, and start to focus on running their own departments more effectively.

Whitehall's role in relationship to local government becomes a more enabling, supportive one, focusing on spreading best practice and providing the comparative information and case studies that local policy-makers will need. Top of its priorities under a Liberal Democrat government should be the development of choice models for the delivery of local public services, to nurture a climate of experimentation across councils, with new options for individual and collective choice.

Developing and articulating this highly ambitious agenda should be a top priority for New Liberals. Above all, we need to show that this is the only programme that can deliver the best possible public services at sustainable levels of taxation.

Notes

1. J. A. Hobson, *The Crisis of Liberalism*, London, P. S. King and Son, 1909.

2. David Walker, 'In Praise of Centralism', a Catalyst Working Paper, November 2002.
3. Dr Adam Lent and Natalie Arend, 'Making Choices: How Can Choice Improve Local Public Services?', New Local Government Network, 2004.
4. See, for example, the author's 'Making MPs Work for Our Money: Reforming Parliament's Role in Budget Scrutiny', Centre for Reform, 2000.
5. See above for details, and for other proposals for reforming the House of Commons' role in financial accountability.

3 Europe: a Liberal future

Nick Clegg

Introduction and chapter overview

The British debate about Europe has long been disfigured by intellectual fundamentalism. On no other issue of public policy are positions quite as polarised or as vitriolically expressed. The wording used to categorise people's views is uniquely rigid: you are either 'anti-European' or 'pro-European'. This is a debate resistant to shades of grey, to the middle ground, to the multitude of subtleties that exist between two extremes.

The public is subject to an unremitting diet of press misinformation about the European Union (EU). The Government, led by arguably the most instinctive pro-European Prime Minister in a generation, has lost its way. A failure of nerve on the single currency, internal dissent between Tony Blair and Gordon Brown, and a strategic blunder in Iraq, have left New Labour's promise of leadership in Europe unfulfilled.

Making matters worse, the EU itself has experienced a prolonged period of turbulence. The bitter divisions about Iraq, about a new EU constitution, about the rules of the single currency, exacerbated by the challenges of a dramatic expansion in the EU's membership and persistent institutional shortcomings, have conspired to make the EU a bewildering and unattractive proposition to voters.

The danger of such fundamentalism to pro-Europeans is that they are compelled to join the argument in rigid, extremist terms in order to be heard. Since the critics of the European Union usually express their views in highly emotional terms – 'superstate', 'conspiracy', 'bureaucratic monster', etc. – it is difficult to resist the temptation to return fire in similar terms. The result is a debate that is both hysterical in tone and dishonest in content. A false choice is presented to the public: one of two extremes in which an almost theological choice needs to be made about whether you are 'for' or 'against' Britain's entanglement with Europe.

If the Liberal Democrats want to be heard in this debate, it is essential we set ourselves apart from such black-and-white discourse. It is highly convenient to the opponents both of the Liberal Democrats and of the European Union to characterise pro-European Lib Dems as doctrinaire, fanatical, foot-soldiers of the European cause – willing to trample all domestic considerations underfoot. Those pro-European politicians who pander to this stereotype by proselytising on Europe in excessively strident terms do their own cause much damage.

For years now, opinion polls have told the same story about public attitudes in Britain towards the EU. Whilst the minority with fixed, hard-line views against the EU is larger than the minority with fixed, hard-line views in support of the EU, the vast majority of the electorate is both confused and undecided on the big European questions. For this great swathe of the British electorate, Europe is not an issue of overriding importance, and has instead become an area about which they naturally reflect the sceptical twist of much media and political comment, but on which their opinions are essentially fluid.

It is to this pivotal audience that the Liberal Democrats must address themselves. Importantly, such opinion is rightly distrustful of claims that the European Union is either all good or all bad. Most people, most of the time, will accept that the EU, much like any other political endeavour, has virtues and vices. For this reason, above all else, it is essential that Liberal Democrats demonstrate that being pro-European is perfectly compatible with the legitimate doubts and quibbles which many people harbour about the EU. Someone who has general reservations about, say, the transparency of EU decision-making, or the impact of EU regulation, or the effects of the Common Agricultural Policy, must be encouraged to believe that their views are consistent with a generally positive approach to the EU.

I have lost count, as a former Member of the European Parliament (MEP), of the number of times I have met constituents who assumed that, as a Liberal Democrat, I would be unable to accept or share their concerns about the way in which the EU is run. This is dangerous, since it suggests that, for reasons largely beyond the party's control, the Liberal Democrats are not perceived as speaking the same language as many voters on Europe. The moment any political party is perceived – even if unjustified – as being 'out of touch' with widespread public sentiment, it becomes more urgent than ever to rediscover a new means by which to communicate with voters.

Liberal Democrats, then, must urgently explain, and explain again, that to be pro-European does not require an abandonment of basic critical faculties. A true pro-European stance should be creative, innovative and bold in proposing reforms to the way in which European integration is pursued. It represents the height of political pessimism to believe that pro-Europeans must automatically cede all ground on the reform and improvement of the EU to anti-Europeans.

This chapter will analyse the acute difficulties in making the case for Europe in a domestic political debate which has become ever more hostile to reasoned argument, by distinguishing the key facts about EU governance from the widespread myths which have taken root. It will suggest how Liberal Democrats should reassert themselves in this debate, by adopting a clear stance that addresses the need for EU reform whilst promoting the simple and over-whelming case for EU integration.

It will then turn from the domestic arena to the European Union itself. It will analyse the unique psychological and polit-ical conditions in which the UK joined the EC in the first place, conditions that still shape the awkward attitude of the UK towards the EU today. The key principles of a reformed, liberal European Union are then set out. They include political stability (possible only if a moratorium is introduced against further institutional changes once the present draft EU constitution is agreed), the need to strengthen the legitimacy of EU procedures (both in Brussels and in all national Parliamentary systems), and the urgent task of streamlining the present mishmash of EU powers (trimming some existing EU powers whilst developing others). These prin-ciples are applied in a detailed critique of the EU's institutions and its policies.

Finally, the conclusion will illustrate that a combination of events and political logic are, in fact, pushing the EU in precisely that liberal direction. The evolution of the European Union in a more open, decentralised, accountable direction is exactly what Liberal Democrats have always advocated. Now that the drift of history is moving in the right direction, it is essential that Liberals everywhere reap the political dividends.

Reform where reform is due

The essential logic of the European Union is simple and plain enough: by doing things together, EU member countries are able to shape their own societies and the world around them more effectively than if they were to so on their own. International commerce, environmental protection, cross-border crime, the regulation of cross-border business, aspects of foreign policy, aviation, energy supply ... the list goes on. In none of these policy areas is it possible for the UK, or any EU member state, to exercise the same reach as when the EU acts in its collective interests. In contrast to the familiar accusation that the EU inhibits the 'sovereignty' of its member governments, the reality is that pooling formal decision-making authority has allowed all its member states to extend the scope of their policy-making sovereignty well beyond national boundaries.

Far from becoming outdated, such supranational EU governance represents the most fitting response to the modern challenges of globalisation, in which economic and political sovereignty has become increasingly disjointed. It is worth noting that in continents as diverse as Latin America and South-East Asia, the European Union is being held up as a model for nation states struggling to cope with the challenges and uncertainties of globalisation.

But in promoting these contemporary virtues of European integration, it is essential to maintain a focus on the way in which European integration can and should be improved. A widespread and particularly misleading caricature of Liberal Democrat policies on Europe suggests that the party is short of ideas on how to reform the EU. Yet, even a cursory glance at the record of Liberal Democrat politicians active in Europe reveals that reform is a prominent theme.

→ Lib Dems have been at the forefront of recent efforts in Brussels to screen all draft EU regulation in a way which will significantly reduce unworkable 'red tape';
→ Lib Dems have led debates on the economic liberalisation of key economic sectors such as financial services, telecoms and energy;
→ Lib Dems have been most outspoken in attacking the way in

which government ministers persist in legislating in secret in
the Council of Ministers;
→ Lib Dems were at the forefront of the criticisms which led to
the mass resignation of the previous, discredited European
Commission;
→ Lib Dems have a long-established policy of antagonism
towards the key tenets of the Common Agricultural Policy;
→ Lib Dems have consistently voted against excessively
parternalistic EU regulation in areas such as social and public
health policy.

This list is neither exhaustive nor perfect – there are no doubt
areas where the Lib Dem position could have been bolder or clearer
– but the underlying point is obvious. There is nothing inconsis-
tent between an advocacy of European integration and a highly
reformist approach to policies, institutions and procedures.

The great problem is that the British electorate is largely ignorant
of these efforts, and remains unduly susceptible to the view that
to support the Liberal Democrats is tantamount to accepting
untrammelled direct rule from Brussels. The balance between
advocacy of European integration and reform of EU policies and
procedures has, at least in the imagination of the public, swung too
far in favour of the former.

Dispelling myths

The other major obstacle to the clear expression of a reformist,
pro-European stance is the apparent complexity of EU issues. In
reality, there is nothing especially convoluted about the Brussels
decision-making process compared to those in London, Washington or any other centre of political activity. Bureaucracy, depart-
mental infighting, Parliamentary shenanigans, waste, duplication,
hierarchies and a blizzard of incomprehensible acronyms are not

unique to Brussels. Even a cursory attempt to explain to an uninformed visitor the Byzantine peculiarities of Westminster, or the vicious backstabbing between Washington government departments, is enough to suggest that complexity is endemic in most modern governing systems most of the time.

The real problem is lack of familiarity. Since the growth in EU governance is recent, and the subject of much public polemic, it is not surprising that it should be branded as unduly complex. A lack of familiarity with how the EU operates merely fosters the ill-defined feeling that it must be up to no good. Lack of knowledge about EU procedures aids and abets those who harbour an agenda of general hostility towards them. A lack of precision about the way in which the EU works actively assists those wishing to spread false concerns about EU institutions.

The laughable tabloid caricature of the EU Commission as some rampant bureaucratic leviathan empowered to snuff out the remaining embers of plucky British independence would not, for instance, be sustainable if it were more widely appreciated that: the Commission is half the size of Birmingham city council; that Gordon Brown, the Chancellor, has added 23,570 civil servants to Whitehall's payroll in just one year up to April 2003, a total greater than the entire staff (22,453) accumulated by the European Commission in more than fifty years; and that the Commission has no autonomous power to pass or impose EU legislation. The preposterous, if widely held, belief that the EU is awash with taxpayers' money would evaporate if more people appreciated that the EU's total budget is a mere 1% of total EU income, whilst the British Government alone commits just over 40% of the UK's income to public spending. Even the notoriously flawed controls on EU spending would be the subject of less shrill comment if it were more clearly understood that up to 90% of all EU expenditure is the responsibility of national governments, and that the total fraud in the EU budget is significantly less than the annual fraud in the budget of the UK's Department for Work and Pensions alone (which now stands at roughly £2 billion out of a total £100 billion budget – the department has not had its accounts signed off for the past fourteen years).

Curiously, it is highly doubtful whether most voters are any better informed of the detailed ins and outs of Whitehall and Westminster procedure. Ask anyone to describe precisely how a law is passed in the UK, and an array of imprecise guesses ensues. Quite right, too. It is hardly necessary for all citizens to know how the internal mechanics of Britain's somewhat untidy non-constitution operate. What is important, however, is that they should feel that the system is generally accountable, transparent, and merits their trust and confidence. As long as that minimal trust and confidence can be maintained, the demand for a forensic understanding of how the system works is unnecessary. Indeed, it is interesting to note that as confidence in politics generally declines in the UK, so interest in hitherto invisible internal parliamentary procedures has steadily increased (MEPs' pay and work conditions, voting records, Westminster working hours etc.).

Ironically, it is precisely the messiness of much EU decision-making that guarantees that it could not possibly pose the mortal threat to British sovereignty and independence often feared. One popular perception is that the EU is governed by disembodied institutions, largely unaccountable to anybody, capable of foisting new-fangled Euro regulations on to an unsuspecting (and uniquely law-abiding) British citizenry. In truth, the EU possesses far more checks and balances on the abuse of executive power than the Westminster system, in which governments are free to impose their will on the back of the thumping parliamentary majorities they invariably enjoy under our eccentric electoral system.

By contrast, the EU executive, the European Commission, has

the formidable power of setting the legislative agenda through a monopoly right of initiative, but remains entirely dependent on the support of two separate legislative branches, the European Parliament and the Council of Ministers, in order for any of its proposals to reach the statute book. The European Parliament, in turn, subjects the Commission to a degree of political scrutiny unheard of in most national parliamentary systems. The Council of Ministers remains the most powerful legislative body, and possesses far-reaching executive powers too, many of which have significantly strengthened in recent years.

The greatest failing in this system is not the degree of unaccountable technocratic EU power, but the concentration of unaccountable power amongst national bureaucracies and ministers in the Council of Ministers. Until recently, ministers continued to legislate on behalf of 375 million citizens in secret – a practice found only in two other legislatures in the world, in Pyongyang, North Korea, and Havana, Cuba. Officials who represent EU governments in Brussels possess a degree of political freedom and authority matched only by the more senior members of a government Cabinet.

The truth, then, is both more mundane and more unsettling than the normal stereotype would allow. It is more mundane because the guiding dynamic of European integration remains a messy compromise between EU institutions dedicated to promoting the wider European interest, and the formidable residual powers of national governments represented at all levels in Brussels. This is no superstate, and it was never designed to be. The EU is a carefully calibrated constitutional fudge between competing forces, in which national interests collide continually with each other and with the European Commission and Parliament. The European Union represents a permanent tug-of-war, a game of shifting alliances and interests. Far from extinguishing national differences and interests, it is a system that provides the means by which those differences and interests are articulated and, most of the time, resolved.

It is more unsettling because the grip of national bureaucracies on the principal levers of EU decision-making persists in a political vacuum. Civil servants exchange political trade-offs in the great negotiating bazaar in Brussels without the same level of scrutiny that would be attached to their activities at home. Ministers often affect boredom or indifference to much EU business, and collude in a process where they are expected to do little more than rubber-stamp deals fixed by their officials in Brussels beforehand. National parliaments, with the notable exception of the Danish and Finnish parliaments, remain woefully weak in monitoring what national ministers are up to when they disappear to Brussels for their regular meetings with their EU ministerial colleagues.

The challenge of keeping the EU simple, and encouraging a growing sense of familiarity and trust in it, must be channelled through a relentless focus on a few key facts:

→ the EU does not decide things for us. We decide things in the EU with others;
→ if we don't like what the EU does, blame ourselves, not others;
→ ministers get away with a lot behind closed doors. We need to hold them to account;
→ the EU bureaucracy is tiny;
→ the EU budget is tiny, just over 1% of EU income;
→ we need stronger parliaments, both in Europe and at Westminster.

Repeating these simple facts, coupled with an equally repetitive focus on reforming the EU, should be the touchstones for all political communication on Europe by Liberal Democrats. Given that

Tony Blair seems to have attached himself limpet-like to the foreign policy priorities of Washington, it is also worth repeating that the UK is likely to exercise far greater influence abroad if it exercises intelligent leadership in the European Union. The prospect of persistent subservience to US objectives is deeply unattractive to British voters, making it all the more necessary to demonstrate that the UK can retain greater autonomy and shape wider events more effectively by way of its membership of the EU.

Of course, such emphasis does not exclude a more sophisticated, nuanced debate within relevant policy circles on EU policy and institutions, especially in Brussels. But the task for the Liberal Democrats as a political party is pressing: how to reconnect with a domestic electorate which, in large part, either ignores or misinterprets what the party has to say on Europe. Reform and simplicity are the essential ingredients.

The British dilemma

The speed with which the European Union (and, before it, the European Community) has evolved is breathtaking. In little more than four decades, what started as a sector-specific experiment in joint decision-making in the coal and steel industries in France and Germany has evolved into the world's most elaborate system of supranational governance, touching on everything from monetary policy to asylum and immigration.

The UK has always had a uniquely uncomfortable attitude towards this burgeoning political and economic club. The lofty dismissal of the first steps towards European integration in the 1950s by the British foreign policy establishment is well documented, as is the humiliating rejection of UK membership by an equally lofty Charles de Gaulle a decade later. Even when Britain joined, in the early 1970s, it was an anguished step that soon required yet another convulsive referendum campaign to settle the issue in 1975. Since then, matters have hardly improved. With each important step in the development of the European club, from the creation of the single market in the late 1980s and early 1990s, to the launch of the single currency, to the present debate about the 'threat' of mass migration as the EU expands into Central and Eastern Europe, the British have consistently reacted with a unique mixture of dismay, fear and hostility.

It is important to consider why, as a nation, we are so singular in our fraught attitude towards our European vocation. There is no other member country of the European Union that suffers remotely the same intensity of emotion and fear, even now as attitudes towards the EU are taking a significant nosedive in almost all member states. Whilst it is difficult to identify all the various strands which make up Britain's complex European attitudes, one pre-eminent fact stands out: the circumstances in which the UK joined the European Union were different to those of all other member nations.

For the six founding members, especially for France and Germany, launching the EC was a supreme act of peaceful cooperation over military conflict. Their motivations were formed entirely by the trauma of two bloody conflicts on the European mainland within a generation. For the founding fathers such as Jean Monnet and Robert Schuman, there might have been plenty of technical justification for the creation of a new framework for economic cooperation, but the enduring political inspiration was to create a guarantee against further military bloodshed. By tying the founding nations together in an increasingly dense web of economic interdependence, the objective of preventing war between these nations from recurring was secured.

For those states who joined from the southern reaches of Europe in the 1980s – Greece, Spain and Portugal – the overriding political motivation was clear, too. All of these countries had suffered prolonged domestic conflict and military rule. Joining the European Community was, for them, a symbol of the modernisation of their societies, a confirmation that democracy had finally uprooted fascism for good. Again, whilst the immediate economic benefits of membership were well appreciated, the principal motivation was a political one, steeped in the specific domestic circumstances of each country.

The UK stands out as the only nation in which the decision to join the EC was taken out of a sense of weakness and defeat, rather than achievement and success. Having shunned European integration at first and then been rejected twice, there was little heartfelt enthusiasm for the enterprise. Rather, a creeping feeling of inevitability was the prime motivation behind the reluctant drift 'into Europe'. Whilst the political underpinnings of European integration were not hidden from voters, for the vast majority of the British electorate the prospect of joining the EC was sold in terms of money saved, jobs secured, prosperity guaranteed – as if the nation were buying a mortgage in a financial marketplace. These were the only terms in which a people accustomed to empire and international pre-eminence could be persuaded to countenance joining a European club in which they would enjoy no more than level pegging with other European peoples recently considered either economically inferior or militarily hostile.

The rapid disappearance of Empire, the threat of Soviet communism, the emergence of the German economic miracle, Britain's sickly economic record, the active support for European integration in Washington, and the prospect of economic benefits, all these factors and more conspired in the 1960s and 70s to create a sense that there was no alternative but for the UK to join a club towards which it had always harboured much ambivalence. This was a decision taken with a collective shrug of the shoulders, rather than a jump for joy. A decision taken because of necessity, rather than aspiration. A decision taken because of Britain's relative decline, rather than relative success.

Much the same latent grumpiness can be seen in the debates today about the possible UK membership of the single currency. Whilst a large majority of voters do not wish to join at any time in the near future, opinion polls show that there is an overwhelming sense of inevitability in which a sizeable majority also thinks that entry into the euro will be unavoidable. In other words, the reluctant dragging of feet that accompanied Britain's initial decision to join the EC still governs the approach taken by the nation to contemporary moves towards further European integration.

The only other members of the EU who display a similar sense of caution are to be found in Scandinavia. It is no coincidence that Sweden and Denmark (Finland has a different historical trajectory, not least to do with its proximity to Russia) both remain outside the Eurozone. For both of these nations, joining the EC was also an indication of relative weakness rather than strength, of something that was unavoidable rather than positively desirable. For decades, both countries, especially Sweden, revelled in their reputations as leading welfare societies, based on traditions of generous welfare support, active state intervention and great social equality second to none in Europe.

For them, joining the European club was a painful admission that the facts of economic reality could not be ignored any longer. The demands of international economic competitiveness required greater borderless integration with the rest of the European continent. The great welfare state could not be sustained in splendid isolation. No wonder, then, that the EU is still regarded with great suspicion in both Stockholm and Copenhagen as an agent of uncaring economic competition that threatens the sanctity of the Scandinavian welfare model. It is not a little ironic that British eurosceptics believe precisely the reverse – that the EU is an agent of sclerotic European welfarism threatening the virility of Anglo-Saxon entrepreneurialism.

But even by the standards of Scandinavian euroscepticism, the level of vitriol and venom aimed at the EU in the British political debate is of a unique character.

A Liberal Europe: three principles
Principle 1: stop perpetual revolution
Set in this historical context, it should be obvious that a process of relentless institutional revolution within the EU is guaranteed to inflame passions within Britain. If the overwhelming need is to foster a greater sense of familiarity and trust in the EU amongst the British electorate, then the cycle of restless treaty changes which has engrossed the EU for the last decade or so poses significant risks. It is extremely difficult to coax a sceptical public to confer greater loyalty towards the EU if it is in a constant state of flux. A fearful electorate needs the reassurance that the EU is a stable, transparent and accountable apparatus, not an amorphous process that continually changes shape.

Whilst the intellectual case for continuous institutional and legal tinkering in the EU may be strong, the political case is more difficult to justify. The degree of institutional churn that has occurred in the EU, as one intergovernmental conference has flowed into the next without pause since 1992, risks appearing self-indulgent.[1] Whilst the need for constant institutional reform and revision is objectively justified, not least in order to adapt the EU to the challenges of a much enlarged membership, the unsettling effect on Europe's voters, especially but not exclusively in the UK, has been profound. No wonder, then, that the latest attempts at the drafting of an EU constitution have been as captivating to a small political elite as it has been perplexing to the vast majority of voters which that elite purports to represent.

There is a powerful argument, then, for a prolonged pause in the institutional development of the EU. This is where the constitution presents an important opportunity. This is not the place for an exhaustive analysis of the pros and cons of the constitution. What is significant, however, is that in terms of the evolution of the EU's powers, it is a conservative document that broadly enshrines existing EU powers whilst strengthening EU capabilities in only a few areas, notably in the field of asylum and immigration policy. The main innovations in the constitution are generally of an institutional and procedural character, such as the abolition of the rotating presidency of the European Council, the restructuring of the Commission, and the role of national parliaments in scrutinising draft EU legislation.

Those who claim that the constitution represents a qualitative change in the nature of the EU are as misleading as those who claim that it is a full-blooded federalist blueprint. As ever, it is somewhere in between, important in its success in mustering a broad consensus on how an enlarged EU should operate, yet not nearly as significant as previous treaty revisions which introduced many more changes to the scope and powers of the European Union (notably the launch of the single market and the single currency).

Valéry Giscard d'Estaing, Chairman of the Convention that drew up the first draft constitution, claimed that he hoped the text would survive without major revisions for up to fifty years. This may be another case of grandiloquent overstretch, for which Giscard d'Estaing is well known, yet the sentiment is right. The constitution, if properly debated and accepted by the peoples of Europe, could serve as a great opportunity to instil much-needed stability into the European Union. That is one of the many reasons why a referendum on the draft text is desirable. If the text were to be submitted to a nervous electorate as a durable settlement, one that would avoid the need for further treaty revisions for the foreseeable future, then there may be a chance that many popular fears could be dispelled and a sense of familiarity fostered.

In other words, Liberal Democrats should embrace the acrimonious debate on the constitution as an opportunity to explain the limits to EU action, the numerous checks and balances in EU policy-making, and the prospect of political stability that the text offers. One possible innovation might be to insist that were the UK to ratify the constitution by way of a referendum, it would be accompanied by an obligation on British governments to refrain from further treaty negotiations for a period of, say, ten years. This would provide a simple, transparent commitment by which a much-needed degree of finality, of tranquillity, could be introduced into the anguished public debate about Britain's role in Europe.

Principle 2: make all power accountable

It is one of the enduring principles of Liberalism that excessive concentrations of power, both in the political and commercial realms, should be broken up, and that all power should be exercised in an accountable fashion. This principle is so widely accepted as to appear almost trite. Yet its full application offers Liberal Democrats real scope to take a distinctive approach to the way the European Union is governed.

The Conservative Party, at least in its present form, has vacated the battlefield of ideas as far as EU governance is concerned. The party, which has done so much to promote international economic liberalisation, remains bizarrely enthralled to an atavistic notion of political sovereignty. A party that seems incapable of accepting the basic tenets of supranational governance – which it blindly rejects as a threat to British identity – is simply not in a position to think creatively about the way in which the countless regulatory and political decisions taken at levels above the nation state should be organised.

The Labour Party, meanwhile, is full of good intentions. Indeed, some opinion polls suggest that Labour Party members are the most strongly pro-European of the membership of all three parties. Yet it is also a party wedded to a highly dogmatic approach to policy-making, in which the existence of alternative poles of power is regarded with deep suspicion, in which political pluralism is not naturally encouraged. The consistently aggressive stance taken by Gordon Brown to almost all new EU initiatives is perhaps the clearest expression of this tendency. Whilst the UK Treasury has a long history of myopia and irrational condescension when dealing with EU affairs, the level of animosity directed at the EU has sharply increased whilst Gordon Brown has been Chancellor. His public antipathy towards the European Commission and his infamous habit of delivering high-handed lectures to his colleagues in the Council of Finance Ministers is part and parcel of an approach to policy-making which cannot tolerate the influence of those beyond his immediate control.

That is why a Liberal approach to the exercise of power in the EU, which insists on checks and balances, on diffused centres of power and on the greatest degree of parliamentary accountability, offers an attractive and fresh alternative.

Such an approach has a number of obvious consequences. Most notably, it underpins the trenchant criticisms that the party has long made of the unaccountable manner in which decision-making power is exercised by national governments within the Council of Ministers, which still remains the dominant legislative forum for EU business. Whilst some efforts have been made recently to make the activities of officials and ministers within the Council more transparent, there is still a very long way to go until this body conforms to the most elementary norms of democratic and accountable decision-making.

But a Liberal approach to the exercise of power leads to two other conclusions that are perhaps more surprising. First, it should encourage a natural scepticism towards the European Commission. The Commission is a remarkably effective organisation, notwithstanding its notorious internal management failings. Without the Commission, the European Union simply would not have got off the starting blocks in the first place. It was designed to act as an engine room for EU integration by counterbalancing the individual powers of national governments and fostering a wider sense of common European purpose.

However, this effectiveness has been secured by conferring on the Commission a peculiar constitutional status. It is at once a political, legislative, judicial and executive body. It is an institutional hybrid that runs roughshod over the normal divisions of labour that exist in a modern democratic system of government. It possesses a monopoly right of legislative initiative, yet is governed by commissioners with a tenuous democratic mandate. It can compel member governments to abide by EU law by taking them to the European Court of Justice, yet can be partial in the application of this executive power. It has extensive responsibilities in everything from the application of the EU's monetary and fiscal rules to the implementation of development projects in sub-Saharan Africa, yet remains woefully short of much of the expertise necessary to fulfil such a bewildering array of tasks.

In short, whilst the Commission is an indispensable tool in the evolution of the European Union, it merits sustained scrutiny from all those who value the importance of transparent and accountable government. That is why, contrary to all the stereotypes applied to Liberal Democrats in the domestic UK political debate, it was the Liberal Group in the European Parliament which took the most outspoken attitude towards the wrongdoings in the Commission presided over by Jacques Santer, and which recently led the calls for the resignation of individual commissioners in response to the accusations of financial mismanagement in the EU's statistical office.

This stance highlights an important point: that whilst Liberal Democrats may be pro-European, the party must be seen first and foremost to advocate accountable government at all levels. An admiration for what the European Commission has achieved for the EU as a whole should never obscure the need for constant scrutiny of a body that, in some important respects, still does not adhere to key principles of modern governance.

The second conclusion that a Liberal approach to power yields when applied to the EU relates to the basic concept of democratic legitimacy itself. Again, it is a view not normally associated with the false stereotype applied to Liberal Democrat attitudes towards Europe. Liberals believe that accountability can only be most fully exercised when there is a strong, vibrant democratic culture under-pinning the exercise of power. In other words, for those in power to be held to account, the collective choices of voters affected by the decisions taken in their name must be clearly expressed via the ballot box. A community of voters, a *demos,* must be empowered to exert effective pressure on those wielding authority.

Yet the problem for the EU is that there is no cohesive pan-European *demos* able to animate such normal channels of accountability. Whilst much decision-making authority has rightly gravitated towards the EU, supranational democracy is still in its infancy. Voters do not generally vote on pan-European issues. The democratic cultures of EU member states remain stubbornly fixed within national and local borders.

There is, then, a persistent legitimacy gap created by the distance between authority exercised at EU level and the democratic process

EUROPE: A LIBERAL FUTURE

played out at subsidiary levels. The most logical response to this
legitimacy gap is that espoused by leading European federalists,
namely the creation of pan-European parties aimed at fostering
a pan-European *demos*. The Green party in the European Parliament, for instance, has recently announced that it will fight the
2004 Euro elections on a common pan-European platform, in
which campaign themes and messages will be applied in the same
manner across the whole of the EU. The French UDF party, an
avowedly federalist party, has expressed the hope that it might
regroup with like-minded parties across Europe to campaign on
an identical pro-European platform.

Yet, whilst the logic of such a federalist approach is impeccable,
the reality reveals serious shortcomings. For a start, it is notoriously difficult to iron out the significant policy and ideological
differences that exist between parties from different countries,
even when they are members of the same pan-European political
family. The German Greens, for instance, are ardent advocates of
the single currency and the constitution, yet they are expected to
campaign together with Green parties from the UK and Scandinavia who are equally ardently opposed to both.

A more profound difficulty, however, lies in the reaction of
voters themselves. The dismal turnout at European Parliamentary
elections speaks for itself (though it should be stressed that falling
turnout is a problem for elections at almost all levels, especially
local elections). Whilst a minority of voters may have strong views
about Europe, one way or the other, the vast majority is more
inclined to vote on issues on which the European dimension is at
best indirect, such as local public services.

The European Parliament is the embodiment of the federalist
impulse, of the attempt to create a pan-European *demos*. Whilst it
has been strikingly successful at exerting meaningful Parliamentary
authority in the EU's political and legislative agenda, it has not

89

yet been able to inspire coherent loyalty or support from Europe's voters. European Parliamentary election campaigns are invariably run along national party lines, with domestic political issues dominant, in which candidates are selected by national parties rather than according to a pan-European mandate. The result is a hotchpotch of parliamentarians with a bewildering mix of motives, backgrounds and specialisms, all of which are rooted in their own home political terrain. The hope that MEPs could distil and represent the interests of Europe's electorate as a whole is, for now at least, stillborn.

This has important implications for the way Liberal Democrats view EU governance. In the absence of a European *demos*, it must be accepted that the primary source of meaningful political legitimacy in the EU remains the nation state, at least for the foreseeable future. This does not mean that power cannot be accountably exercised at the EU level, but it does mean that an exclusive emphasis on the European Parliament as the sole source of legitimacy at the EU level is not sustainable. This makes the work to improve the transparency and the accountability of the Council of Ministers all the more important, and confers an even greater responsibility on national parliaments to improve their own scrutiny of EU affairs and of the way in which their own governments act within the EU.

It also places a heavy burden of proof on those wishing to expand the powers of the EU. Since the normal channels of accountability will remain imperfect as long as there is no European *demos*, the allocation of authority at EU level must only ever be countenanced if there is an overwhelming and compelling reason to do so. Relocating powers to a supranational stage when voters are still trapped in local or national political cultures must be done with great caution. The very real risk is that powers gravitate to the EU precisely to avoid the normal channels of accountability that operate at national level. Such a development would exacerbate the legitimacy gap that already exists, and open up the possibility of an abuse of public authority. The scandalous manner in which decisions have been taken in the field of police and judicial cooperation at EU level in recent years, escaping any meaningful European or national parliamentary scrutiny, serves as a clear warning.

Making all power accountable in the EU, then, leads Liberal Democrats to some surprising conclusions. Far from leading to a blithe assumption that EU institutions such as the European Commission and the European Parliament are always well equipped to discharge their political duties, it leads to a healthy caution about the legitimacy and mandate of those bodies, whilst still supporting their important functions. It calls for an aggressive attitude towards the tendency for national governments and bureaucracies to monopolise the EU decision-making process to push through decisions without proper political scrutiny. In accepting that our democratic communities remain rooted in national cultures, it places a serious onus on national governments to modernise their often antiquated methods to match the modern challenge of supranational EU governance. If Liberal Democrats are not starry-eyed about the EU institutions themselves, they must be unrelenting in pushing for radical reforms in the way in which our own parliamentary system, designed to suit the needs of a nineteenth-century imperial government, operates to meet the needs of a borderless 21st- century Europe.

Principle 3: streamline EU powers

One of the most illogical beliefs held by some ardent pro-Europeans is that the value of the European Union must be expressed through a constant accretion of new powers. In policy circles in Brussels, there is a widespread view that the EU must retain 'momentum' by developing new responsibilities in an ever-wider range of public policy areas. The comic-book analogy of the EU as a bicycle – it must keep moving to avoid falling down – has taken root in the minds of generations of EU policy-makers.

This entrenched policy activism is, of course, enshrined in the institutional design of the European Commission. It is a body primarily dedicated to exercising its monopoly power of initiative. Commissioners and officials judge their worth according to the new initiatives launched in their areas of responsibility. It is an institution naturally drawn towards thinking about the future. At best, this can give it a refreshing, forward-looking character; at worst, it leads to a cavalier approach in which a blithe support for new policies supplants attention to the application of existing policy and law.

This institutional bias towards policy activism has been exacerbated by the uneven manner in which the EU's powers have evolved in response to national political pressures. The EU's notorious Common Agricultural Policy (CAP) is a good case in point. Objectively, it is difficult to understand why the early stages of the European Community, in the 1950s and 1960s, should have been dominated by the creation of this wasteful and economically perverse support system for Europe's farmers. Yet the CAP was part of the founding bargain struck between France and Germany at the inception of the European Community: Germany would secure greater access for its competitive exports, whilst France would receive substantial support for its important farming constituency. Memories of wartime food shortages also made the prospect of European self-sufficiency in agriculture especially attractive.

Equally, the single market itself, the brainchild of Jacques Delors, was in large part shaped by his insight into what would be acceptable to Margaret Thatcher. Whilst he clearly understood that the single market represented a huge increase in the pooling of decision-making sovereignty in everything from industrial standards to environmental and consumer protection, he also had the intelligence to sell the proposal to Thatcher as a bold experiment in economic liberalisation across Europe.

In other words, the powers enjoyed by the European Union are not the result of some perfectly formed blueprint setting out a coherent approach to the circumstances in which supranational authority is justified. Rather, the rag-bag of EU powers represents a step-by-step evolution shaped by the activism of the EU institutions on the one hand, and the limits and preferences imposed by national governments on the other. Whilst this may represent an effective accommodation between the competing forces of supranationalism and nationalism, it does not necessarily yield the most logical division of labour between nation states and the EU.

Indeed, the EU's powers remain curiously lopsided. Why is it, for instance, that the EU possesses detailed legislation on the precise design of a bus, or the use of seatbelts in cars, or the time worked by junior doctors, or vibration and noise levels in the workplace, or the energy efficiency of public buildings, and yet remains invisible as an entity in the UN, ineffective in promoting peace in the Middle East, toothless in tackling international crime and terrorism. It is as if the EU has decided to micromanage those areas of economic and social life for which it has some responsibility, whilst leaving great swathes of public life crying out for supranational cooperation untouched. The reason, of course, is essentially political. For various reasons, national governments are happier to accept EU legislation that penetrates into the minutiae of domestic economic and social life, whilst insisting on maximum freedom of action on the international stage or in the fight against criminality.

This illogical, lopsided allocation of powers to the EU should be vigorously criticised by all Liberal Democrats. A Liberal approach to the allocation of responsibilities to the EU should be founded

93

on a rigorous application of the principles of subsidiarity and proportionality. Whilst there is much disagreement about what these terms mean in practice, for Liberals they must be rooted in a belief that the EU must only act if there is a clear cross-border issue at stake, or when collective EU action brings obvious benefits to all member states that they would not be able to secure on their own.

Those areas which are beyond reproach if such a simple test were to be applied consistently are obvious enough: the lifting of barriers to the free flow of goods, services, capital and people; the setting of standards to tackle cross-border environmental problems (an area in which the EU has been perhaps more successful in recent years than in almost any other policy area); the regulation of cross-border business activity to avoid monopoly or the abuse of dominant position; a common asylum and immigration policy; foreign policy coordination in those areas where common EU interests prevail; a single commercial policy in which the EU negotiates as an integrated trade bloc; standard setting for the trade in goods and services to guarantee high standards of consumer and public health protection; the promotion of cross-border infrastructure links, notably in transport and energy; monetary policy for those states participating in the currency union; a common fisheries policy managing shared marine resources (notwithstanding the profound flaws of the present Common Fisheries Policy).

As it happens, the areas listed in the new constitution as those areas in which the EU enjoys 'exclusive' competence are much narrower in scope, which should provide reassurance to those who falsely claim the draft constitution arrogates great swathes of new exclusive powers to Brussels.[2] So far, so good. The problem arises, however, where the necessity for supranational decision-making is not entirely clear, or where the implementation of supranational decision-making is blighted by serious shortcomings. The Common

Agricultural Policy, for instance, is deeply flawed. Whilst there are clear cross-border imperatives – agricultural products move across borders within the EU more readily than almost anything else – the unwieldy manner in which the EU and its member states administer CAP subsidies has conspired to foster unsustainable farming practices, penalise taxpayers and consumers, and boost unnecessary agricultural production. In theory, it would be more logical for the EU to wield strong powers in the manner in which agricultural products are traded across Europe, especially to guarantee high quality and animal welfare standards, whilst leaving much of the system of production support to national governments themselves, subject to EU rules on subsidies and fair competition.

Similarly, there is a danger that the system of EU regional subsidies has reached a point of such excessive complexity that the value added of collective EU funds is being undermined. The founding logic of the EU's so-called structural funds remains compelling – that the richer parts of the EU should help provide resources to those parts in dire straits, especially in helping to cover high infrastructure investment costs. Yet, in practice, regional funds are still being channelled to all member states, even those such as Britain, France and Germany who are the main contributors in the first place. Logically, those governments should take full responsibility for the channelling of funds to their own deprived regions, rather than depend upon the recycling of funds via the EU.

Naturally, local and regional administrations in those countries have become attached to the largesse of EU structural funds. Understandably, they are not confident that national governments would be as forthcoming in allocating public funds to them. Yet that is essentially a domestic political debate that should be left to domestic politicians to fight out amongst themselves. EU structural funds should not displace the normal tug-of-war between competing claims on public resources in those member states who could easily replace EU funding to their own regions from domestic budgets. That, in turn, would allow the EU structural funds to concentrate wholly on those countries where the economic need for financial assistance is overwhelming, such as in almost all the new accession states of Central and Eastern Europe, or on those infrastructure projects which are of a clear cross-border interest within the EU.

A final example is social policy. There seem to be two principal motivations for those in favour of an extensive EU legislative programme in social and labour market regulation. The first, felt keenly by politicians from the left, is that the EU must set high social and labour-market standards in order to match the cross-border liberalisation of business within the single market. The belief is that in a borderless single market, businesses will inevitably gravitate towards those economies with the most lax social standards and the lowest labour-market costs. In order to avoid such 'social dumping', the EU must set high minimum standards so that businesses and investors cannot play one member state off against another. The second motivation is more simple: in those member states, such as Britain, with a tradition of loose social and labour-market regulation, there is a widespread feeling that the EU can be relied upon to introduce progressive social legislation which otherwise would not be adopted by domestic governments. The present debate about draft EU legislation on temporary (agency) workers is a good case in point. Those who advocate the law in Britain do so because they believe it is the only way in which the exploitation of agency workers in Britain can be stopped, given that the UK government itself is reluctant to take action.

Both reasons are profoundly misguided. There is no empirical evidence that business investment is rushing to exploit loopholes in social and labour-market regulation. International investment has, in fact, been sharply increasing in France, a country with famously rigid labour-market regulations, whilst it has been plummeting in Britain, a country often accused of presiding over Dickensian working practices. The reasons why investors invest are complex: language, location, infrastructure, an educated work-force, and monetary policy have as much, if not more, bearing on those decisions than social policy alone. As for those who look to the EU to do their bidding in social policy in the face of domestic political reluctance, the danger is an obvious one. Whilst it is, of course, entirely understandable to support EU measures because of their beneficial effects – working time and parental leave legis-lation spring to mind – doing so in order to supplant the normal domestic policy-making process risks undermining the basic tenets of democratic accountability. If the EU were to be used systemati-cally as a means to bypass domestic political debate, voters will be even more perplexed about who is responsible for what, and EU institutions will foolishly arrogate to themselves a political role that should be the preserve of elected national governments.

However desirable it may be, for instance, that the EU has set legislative limits to the time worked by junior doctors, there is no conceivable cross-border justification for this measure. The scandal of excessively long working hours for junior doctors is entirely a problem of the UK government's making, and it should be UK ministers who are made accountable for that failing. It disrupts the key relationship between voters and those elected to public office if domestic issues with no obvious EU dimension are arbitrarily shuffled off to Brussels for resolution.

For these reasons, there is a compelling case to curtail the EU in its responsibility in the social policy sphere. There are other areas, too, where a similar audit of EU powers would lead to a more logical division of labour. The multitude of small and dispersed EU budget lines, in everything from youth programmes to tourism, for instance, should substantially be reduced. It is highly doubtful whether their marginal benefits to EU citizens justify the scarce personnel resources in the European Commission allocated to them.

The message, then, is clear. Liberal Democrats should push for the reallocation of certain existing EU powers – much of agricultural, regional and social policy, for instance – whilst arguing for the elevation of new powers in areas such as foreign, asylum and immigration policy, where the value of collective EU action is compelling. Importantly, such a stance could not possibly be construed as 'anti-European'. It has nothing in common with the facile claim made by many Conservatives that the EU should be summarily dismembered. What it does represent, however, is a robust attitude towards the powers enjoyed by the EU, so that those powers that are either ill justified or ineffective are dropped, and those requiring new EU action are taken up. This would help correct the lopsided nature of the EU and so make it more logical and comprehensible to British voters.

The shape of things to come

These three principles, which can help guide the evolution of a liberal Europe – free of constant institutional revolution, significantly more accountable, and with streamlined powers reflecting contemporary needs – may seem like a tall order. There is a profound pessimism in the political debate within the UK that assumes that the EU is incapable of being reformed. The depiction of the EU painted by eurosceptics suggests that it has hardly changed in several decades.

In truth, however, the EU is a highly dynamic arrangement that is undergoing almost constant change, reform and renewal. Indeed, one of the key arguments in this chapter is that the EU has evolved too fast without pause for too long, and now requires a period of stability.

It is in this context that there are good reasons to believe that the EU will evolve in precisely the direction set out in this chapter.

There are four prominent factors that suggest that the drift of the EU in the coming years will be in increasing conformity with the principles set out above.

First and foremost, there is the impact of the enlargement of the EU in mid-2004 to a total membership of 25. It is impossible to exaggerate the significance of this change for the future of the EU. Undoubtedly, the short-term effect of an enlargement of such magnitude will be highly disruptive. The established patterns of doing business within the EU, the web of relationships between existing governments, the power play between the institutions, all will be significantly altered by the sheer complexity of reaching agreement amongst so many members. The unsettling effect on those nations traditionally at the apex of the EU pecking order, notably France, is already apparent. The potential for promiscuous deal-making in a club of 25 makes the familiar hierarchy between established members that much more uncertain.

More specifically, it will dramatically reduce the attraction of repeated treaty revisions in the future. The prominent role played by Poland in the failure of the European Council to agree a new constitution in December 2003 has served as a timely warning of the risks of repeating such fundamental debates once the present constitutional talks are concluded. That is why many of those involved in drafting the constitutional text attach so much importance to the insertion of new provisions that would allow for a lighter method of treaty revision in the future, avoiding full-blown intergovernmental conferences. But even if such provisions are included in the constitution, the pace of treaty change is set to diminish rapidly. As advocated in this chapter, the appeal of settling the present constitutional wrangles for a prolonged period of time will become overwhelming.

Equally, the assumption that the EU's powers should continue to evolve and expand at the same pace in the future as they have in the past couple of decades will bump up against the practical constraints of making the present set of EU responsibilities workable in an enlarged EU. In a larger EU club it is inevitable that it will become progressively harder to forge consensus in controversial policy areas. That, in turn, will compel the EU to focus its most productive energies in those policy areas where there is greatest agreement that the EU should act. In other words, an enlarged Union may, in practice, lead to a certain contraction in policy focus.

Second, the European Union's political leadership is undergoing a generational change. Gone are the days when the union was captained by leaders who professed a strong ideological attachment to the identity of the Union itself. Helmut Kohl, François Mitterrand and Jacques Delors created a triumvirate dedicated to the rapid growth of a stronger, deeper Union. Their successors – Gerhardt Schroder, Jacques Chirac, Tony Blair et al. – represent a more pragmatic, less ideologically driven approach to European affairs. Germany, in particular, has witnessed a shift towards a more introverted politics in which the enthusiasm for national self-sacrifice in the cause of European unity has waned considerably.

This shift in generational perspective will, again, lead to greater caution when contemplating grand new treaty revisions, and will focus debates on a narrower policy base where pragmatic consensus can be more readily achieved.

Third, the European Union is suffering from much angst about Europe's relative economic underperformance compared to the USA. This is particularly acute in Germany, where public opinion, traditionally accustomed to Germany's reputation as the continent's pre-eminent economy, is struggling to come to terms with deep-seated structural economic problems. Similar debates are raging in France and Italy, too. British policy-makers, aided and abetted by much misleading self-congratulation in the press and from Gordon Brown, seem convinced that the UK is somehow exempt from unflattering international comparisons. Yet a cool look at key indicators of economic well-being – such as productivity, gross domestic product (GDP) per head, infrastructure performance – quickly reveals that the UK has stubborn economic problems of its own, many of which place the UK behind most of its European partners, let alone the USA.

Such a climate of economic uncertainty will also serve as a break on excessive institutional tinkering in the EU, or on excessively adventurous new EU policy initiatives. An awareness of the impact of EU decisions on the competitiveness of European economies has already intensified in the context of the so-called 'Lisbon process', which has set the EU the increasingly unrealistic target of becoming the world's most competitive knowledge-based economy by the end of the decade. This gap between aspiration and economic performance will, again, compel policy-makers to focus their efforts on those policy areas where value-added benefits from EU action are indisputable, rather than get sidetracked into new or risky undertakings.

Finally, the dramatically altered international scene will make its presence felt on the internal business of the EU for many years to come. The threat of terrorism, of failed states, the deepening crisis in relations with the Islamic world, will force the EU to improve its effectiveness in precisely those areas where it has been lacking for too long – in foreign policy, in tackling cross-border crime, and in dealing with the mass migration of peoples from outside Europe's borders. Whilst, as already explained, there will be an increasingly conservative bias to much EU policy-making as the focus returns to the implementation of the EU's core responsibilities, these three areas will be notable new growth areas in EU activity. This, in turn, will force the EU to rebalance the lopsided flaws in its present menu of policy competences, in favour of these new pressing demands that require supranational responses and to the detriment of those policy areas that do not have a clear rationale for EU action. Over time, this will result in an EU more fully equipped to deal with contemporary international challenges and will force the EU to become less introverted in its general outlook.

Conclusion

The challenges facing a pro-European party such as the Liberal Democrats in the febrile and distorted political debate on Europe in the UK are acute. But a relentless emphasis on the way in which the EU can and must be reformed, coupled with clarity and simplicity in advocating the case for European integration, should over time allow the Liberal Democrats to reconnect with the large body of undecided opinion amongst British voters.

Equally, Liberal Democrats should espouse a straightforward approach to the development of the EU that promotes greater constitutional stability, enhanced accountability and a rebalancing of the EU's powers to match the contemporary needs of Europe as a whole. Such an approach would help reassure a nervous electorate, make the EU itself more comprehensible, and guarantee that the EU delivers benefits to Britain's citizens in those areas where it is obvious that supranational responses are required.

Such an approach will not be easy in the face of the systematic distortion and introversion of much of Britain's political and media debate. But it has the virtue of running with the grain of the changes that are already being unleashed in the European Union because of its enlargement, its economic difficulties, the generational change in Europe's political elite, and the challenges of a more insecure international setting. With persistence and clarity, such a Liberal vision for the European Union will no longer seem to be outlandish or out of touch with everyday fears and anxieties. Rather, it will emerge as the only positive, compelling vision for Britain's wholehearted commitment to its European vocation, responding as it does to the real needs of Britain and Europe in the early decades of the 21st century.

Notes

1. Treaty of Maastricht, signed 7 February 1992; Treaty of Amsterdam, signed 2 October 1997; Treaty of Nice, signed 26 February 2001.
2. Paragraph 1 of Article 12 of the draft constitution reads: '1. The Union shall have exclusive competence to establish the competition rules necessary for the functioning of the internal market, and in the following areas: monetary policy, for the Member States which have adopted the euro; common commercial policy; customs union; the conservation of marine biological resources under the Common Fisheries Policy.

4 Global governance, legitimacy and renewal

Christopher Huhne[1]

This chapter discusses the failings in the current system of global decision-making. It first looks at the key determinants of globalisation, namely transport and communications technology and a political willingness to be open to global opportunities. It then examines the consequences of globalisation, both good and bad. Globalisation needs to be managed politically if its good aspects are to be encouraged and its bad ones repressed. But, at the same time, decisions taken at international level are removed from the democratic structures and debate that continue to work at national level, and are the only structures that are truly effective in conferring legitimacy. This chapter argues that, for Liberals, there is therefore a modern paradox of global governance and legitimacy. We need global governance, and yet we have not yet found an effective way of connecting that governance to the popular will. Moreover, the current structure of international governance is creaking, even if it is assessed by technocratic standards. Too often it addresses yesterday's problems: war between states rather than within them, trade protectionism rather than threats to the global environment. But change is particularly difficult, and is complicated by the dominant role of the USA within the international system. The chapter sketches out some of the key changes in global governance that might make it more effective, democratic and legitimate.

Why globalisation happens

Globalisation depends on two things. The first and necessary condition is the development of communications and transport technology. The second is the political will, in the countries affected, to remain open to world opportunities. In economic history, perhaps the most dramatic illustration of the need for both of these factors – opportunity and openness – took place in the 1870s and 1880s when the introduction of the steamship on the Atlantic opened up dramatic trading opportunities between Europe and North America. The price of a quarter of American wheat landed at Liverpool dropped from 625 pence in 1870–74 (annual average) to 356 pence per quarter in 1895–99.[2] Until this shift, the effects of free trade in Europe were modest because transport costs were relatively high and gave natural protection to home markets. Europe was relatively open: there was even free trade between Britain and France.

The episode is still a cautionary tale in how to handle – and how not to handle – global opportunity. France and Germany, where landed elites were still politically important, introduced agricultural protectionism and pretended that nothing had changed. By contrast, Britain already had a tradition of free trade and a powerful middle class prepared to defend it. The British economy adjusted brutally. Farming was plunged into a prolonged crisis. The flight from the land caused great hardship as people moved to the cities and higher paid work. Only Denmark pursued what, in retrospect, was a classically successful response to a major trade change: it moved from being a grain producer to being a livestock producer, importing cheap feedgrains from North America to fatten pigs for export to the UK market. Denmark therefore provides one of the first successful examples of boosting living standards through an adjustment to changes in the terms of trade.

Despite these differing reactions in the agricultural sector, the forces of globalisation proceeded apace until they stalled with the conflicts of 1914–18 and 1939–45. Since then, globalisation has accelerated, with the further falls in communications and transport costs. World merchandise exports now exceed 17% of world output, more than three times the proportion of 1950, and more than double the previous peak on the eve of the 1929 crash.[3] International investment has also exceeded its pre-World War I peaks. The only measure of internationalisation that is still more modest than during the passportless Edwardian era is migration: 60 million Europeans headed for the new worlds in the century before World War I.

The consequences of globalisation

As with any such far-reaching phenomenon, both good things and bad things have globalised. Increased trade in pharmaceuticals, among other factors, has helped to extend average world life expectancy by a half since 1930,[4] and there has also been a sharp decline in the inequality of life expectancy. Increased trade has stimulated growth, which has lifted an ever-higher share of the world's population out of absolute poverty. The proportion of the world's population living in extreme poverty on less than US$1 a day declined from almost half in 1950 to less than a quarter in 1992.[5] Cross-border investment has boosted pay levels in many economies, since foreign companies tend to pay more than domestic ones. Some countries have taken spectacular advantage of world markets: South Korea had the same level of income per head as Sudan at the beginning of the sixties, and has now caught up with middle-ranking EU countries such as Greece or Portugal.[6]

There have also been significant political benefits from the spread of ideas through global media and travel. On one estimate, the proportion of the world's population living in partial or liberal democracies rose from 32% to 74% in the twenty years to 1995.[7] Nearly half of the world's population now live in regimes that can be changed through the ballot box, that respect basic norms of civil rights and an open society. In addition, it is arguable that the traditional political argument in favour of free trade made by Liberals has also been right. The greater degree of commercial exchange and interdependence makes conflict less likely than it is between autarkic countries. Trade is only undertaken if there are benefits to both parties from the exchange. Therefore an interruption to trade causes losses to both sides in proportion to its importance. High levels of trade provide a key economic incentive to good neighbourliness.

However, globalisation may also have accentuated the trend towards greater inequality of incomes. Those who fail to grasp the opportunities of the world market are left behind, while those who have special skills or talents may be rewarded globally with a munificence that their purely national forebears could never imagine. Thus David Beckham, Paul McCartney or Paul Smith are as big in Tokyo as in Manchester, and now receive star payments from both places. They are only the most conspicuous examples: corporations want the best researchers, management consultants, accountants and advisers. They will pay vast amounts to get them because the cost of second-rate performance – in a winner-takes-all marketplace – may be higher. Nor is the decline in poverty an unalloyed success. Though the proportion in poverty has fallen dramatically, the total numbers in world poverty have only edged downwards fractionally: the population explosion means that the shrinking proportion of the very poor is still a vast number. More than a billion people live in absolute poverty, as they did in 1929 and in 1950.[8]

Perhaps most crucially of all, the increasing sum of global economic activity and population growth is imposing grave costs on the global ecosystem, a fact recognised by almost every advanced government except that of the USA. According to the Intergovernmental Panel on Climate Change, the global average surface temperature increased during the twentieth century by about 0.6 degrees Celsius[9] and this trend is projected to accelerate alarmingly through the rest of this century. The potential effects include increased droughts in many agricultural regions and flooding in low-lying areas. The regional effects, however, are relatively slight (particularly in vulnerability to flooding) in North America even though the continent is the largest contributor to greenhouse gases. The case for policy change for the Americans may rest on an appreciation of the absolute costs that they will pay in climate change, together with an understanding of the second-order effects such as threats to US global security interests, as highlighted in a recent report for the Pentagon.[10] Growth and population pressures are also placing strain on natural resources such as water, timber and fish: every major world fishing resource is now being depleted at unsustainable rates.

The fall in communications and transport costs benefits organised crime – people traffickers and drug-runners – as much as legitimate traders and investors. Communications make it easier for small groups sharing eccentric interests to link up – it is good news for steam enthusiasts, curlew watchers and Inuit food aficionados – but it is also easier for potential terrorists to identify others with a similarly extreme outlook. The same forces that have done so much good in spreading modern medicine have also done harm in making lethal weapons available to small groups: whether al-Qaeda in the airborne attack on the Twin Towers, or the less successful attempt of the cult Aum Shinrikyo to spread sarin through the Tokyo subway system. The late nineteenth century was marked by a wave of terrorist attacks, often perpetrated not by the poor and dispossessed but by tiny fanatical groups of well-educated and privileged young people. The potential for damage today, given the creation and spread of deadly technologies, is far greater. The dilemma for Liberals continues: the counter-measures that civilised societies must take to defend themselves in turn threaten to undermine many of the freedoms we have fought to preserve.

The classical challenge to internationalists also remains: war between states and within them, which remains perhaps the most significant underlying cause of poverty and disease. However, the classical responses have withered. Whereas the Liberal imperialist would happily have tried to sort out a failing state (and some not-so-failing states) – annexing it to the empire as an incubator for civilised self-rule – there is now no easy solution to failing states. There is no list of candidates willing to pay taxpayers' money to put them back on track. Yet the disorder in failing states – in Cambodia, Rwanda, Bosnia-Herzegovina, Kosovo, Sierra Leone, Colombia and Afghanistan – has been the most significant cause of abject human misery in our times. Indeed, wars between states have become relatively few and far between. Wars within states are more frequent and, if anything, more destructive of well-being. In small wars, it is not state-of-the-art weaponry that counts, but the availability of small arms.

Rules or raw power: the role of the USA

Faced with these issues, there is a glaring clash of policy attitudes. On one side, there are the heirs of Thomas Hobbes who believe in projecting force unilaterally, if necessary, and building up the ramparts: broadly the position of President George Bush. With the hegemony of the USA (and the campaign contributions of Texas oil), Mr Bush rejected the Kyoto protocol to control greenhouse gases, repudiated the 1972 Anti-Ballistic Missile Treaty and instituted a National Missile Defence system, shunned the new International Criminal Court, imposed steel import tariffs (subsequently found in breach of the World Trade Organisation), and opposed enforcement of the 1972 Biological Weapons Treaty and an international agreement on small arms.[11] Most crucially of all, President Bush went to war on Iraq in a pre-emptive strike designed to avert threats from weapons of mass destruction (whatever the reality). The 'coalition of the willing' that backed the President – the governments of the UK, Spain, Italy, Denmark, the Netherlands and the central Europeans – was only a cloak of respectability for the failure to secure UN Security Council approval. Few doubted that the USA would have acted alone if necessary.

In the USA it is at least possible to believe in the continued capacity of the nation state to meet threats and problems. It is arguable that the USA is unilateralist because it can be – as the French and the British were with the Suez invasion as recently as 1956 – while the Europeans are multilateralist because they have no other option.[12] As the uncontested global military power – with an increase in defence spending in one recent year equal to the entire annual defence budgets of the two largest European states – the USA has a capacity to project state power that makes it the most influential of countries even in Europe's Balkan backyard. The USA now accounts for nearly half of all military spending on the planet.[13] Every other country's foreign and security policy is defined in relation to the USA. Moreover, the attack on the World Trade Center on September 11, 2001 has given the USA the will to use that power in defence of its homeland, a will that unites every strand of mainstream US politics.

At the same time, the USA faces political difficulties that other nations do not face in committing to international obligations. Any treaty negotiated by the executive must be ratified by the US

Senate by a two-thirds majority, but that body is formed of two senators for each state, regardless of the state's size: Rhode Island with a million people and California with 30 million have equal representation in the Senate. The consequence of this disproportion is that a relatively small part of the US population may have veto power over a treaty. The senators from seventeen states are enough to block a treaty, and the seventeen smallest states account for just 7% of the US population. The list of unratified treaties is a long one, spanning the governance of the St Lawrence seaway, the League of Nations and the Kyoto protocol. A small number of people – and their interests – may have a disproportionately important impact on the definition of US interests as a whole.

This disproportion, combined with the absence of any limits on campaign spending, makes the US political system alarmingly responsive to specific corporate interests. A typical example was the 1999 battle of the Clinton administration, which had received campaign contributions from the large banana-ripening combine Chiquita with interests in Central America, to erode the preferential treatment given by the EU to the Caribbean and African producers (some of which were highly dependent on banana exports). Indeed, the extent of corporate influence – particularly on environmental matters such as limits on carbon emissions and other pollutants, and the opening up of wilderness to commercial exploitation as recently demonstrated by the Bush administration in Alaska – makes the USA a special case among industrialised democracies.

However, there are limits to unilateralism, even for the USA. Not only do territories have to be pacified after the war has been won – a process that remains painful for the USA and its allies in Iraq, and which is certainly harder for the lack of international approval for the invasion – but the unilateral use of force may have a cost in international (and public) opprobrium. Many problems are not amenable to the use of force, and remain intractable without international cooperation. In the security field, this applies to intelligence-sharing about terrorism and the proliferation of weapons of mass destruction (which remains a real threat whatever the imagined threat in Iraq). It applies to the 'hearts and minds' campaigns necessary to detach social groups and peoples from the terrorists they tacitly support. But it is even clearer in the environmental and economic areas.

True, the US administration can seem breathtakingly unilateralist in economic matters, too, not least because a continent-sized economy is relatively insulated from the pressures that afflict smaller economies. In an earlier period of dollar weakness, the then US Treasury Secretary, William Simon, told the complaining Europeans: 'It may be our dollar, but it is your problem.' However, this attitude is hard to sustain for long, even with an economy as strong as the USA. The Reagan administration performed an abrupt U-turn on its dollar policy with the Plaza accord in September 1985. By capping the dollar, the USA agreed to resist domestic protectionism and rectify its substantial and growing trade deficits. Less than two years later – in February 1987 – the Louvre accord signalled support for the dollar following a dramatic fall that threatened financial confidence and inflation within the USA.[14] Now that US deficits are larger than they were then, it is not difficult to predict similar changes in Washington's policy.

Nor is the appetite for unilateralism merely conditioned by interests and circumstance. In any open society founded on the rule of law, the natural instinct will be to project similar behaviour into the international arena. The US constitution was a flower of European enlightenment thought, with its belief in the rule of law and in checks and balances. One consolation in the recent attitudes of the US administration, for a European liberal, is that much of President Bush's foreign policy agenda has outraged American liberals as well. 'America First' unilateralism will not necessarily remain US policy.[15]

A multilateralist order and its problems

The alternative is a more optimistic search for a world political system that is not only ruled by the power of the strongest, but by conciliation, contract and law. In macro-economic matters, the case for multilateralism was most persuasively made by the beggar-my-neighbour protectionism that aggravated the thirties' recession. There has long been a strong case for institutions to support countries that find themselves in temporary financial difficulties. Indeed, the USA has been keen to push relatively relaxed International Monetary Fund support packages for its own allies in Latin America, as was the case for Argentina in 2003 or for Mexico in 1994. There is financial contagion as certainly as contagious diseases. There is also the whole new range of global problems for which there can be no unilateral solutions, such as the AIDS pandemic, global warming, the combating of international crime and terrorism, or the creation in Europe of consumer safety and environmental standards and of a single currency that enables a continent-wide marketplace in otherwise segmented national markets.

All such problems require some measure of continuing public decision-taking, and therefore require institutions with at least a regional and generally a global scope: the United Nations (UN) to promote security, the International Monetary Fund to combat financial and economic instability, the World Bank to encourage development, the European Union to create a single market and tackle cross-border problems in a continent of small states, the World Trade Organisation to promote multilateral liberal trade rules, the International Labour Organisation to promote accepted employment rights, and the World Health Organisation to combat

113

infectious diseases. This is not an exhaustive list (particularly of UN specialised agencies)[16] but they are all to some degree responses to the internationalisation of problems for which there is at least some expectation that there can and should be a public policy response.

There are, though, distinct problems with the capacity of the world community to face common problems. The first is that the legitimacy and credibility of these institutions is hard (if not impossible) to establish. Some have come under unprecedented public challenge: the meetings of the WTO in Seattle in 1999 and of the International Monetary Fund in Prague in 2000 were both disrupted by violent street demonstrations. The IMF, far from being seen as a safety-net for governments buffeted by capital flight, has itself become the whipping boy for non-governmental organisations and Church groups in much of the developed world. The United Nations remains an important source of legitimacy for international action (as the US and UK efforts to seek approval for the invasion of Iraq in 2003 show), but even this legitimacy is flawed. The UN does not look behind the principle of state representation, regardless of whether those states broadly represent their peoples (the democracies) or merely an unaccountable regime (China). The only international institution that has a directly elected component is the European Union (in the European Parliament), and low and falling turnouts bear testimony to the difficulty that the parliament has in establishing itself in each of the vibrant national political debates that it covers.

Most electorates, even in the better educated of the industrial democracies, have only a frail grasp of the economic and environmental trends that have so undermined the effectiveness of the nations with which they identify. Almost every electorate is also instinctively suspicious of globalising trends: a survey of public attitudes in 24 countries in the developed and developing world found majorities in every country against immigration, and majorities in all but two (Netherlands and Japan) in favour of limiting imports.[17] For those nation states with a strong sense of democracy and a combative media – both France and Britain – this is a particularly painful transition. The result is an alarming paradox. Globalisation increasingly requires international policy responses, but those policies are difficult to legitimate in the eyes of public opinion. Problems are increasingly global, but politics remains local.

Nor is it easy to adapt essentially post-war institutions to a changing environment. The world has lived with *de facto* or *de jure* systems of incipient global governance for only two hundred years. In that short historical span, the only time that the framework for relations between states, or institutions, has been renewed is during or following a period of immense and destructive crisis: the Congress of Vienna in 1815, the peace conference in Paris in 1919 and the Bretton Woods conference in New Hampshire in 1944. In the interim periods, the world's powerful players settled with their institutions into a kind of stasis. At any point, the checks and balances that had been built into the international system to secure initial agreement also became impediments to anything other than the most marginal and incremental renewal and change. Therefore, a further problem is the chronic difficulty of changing the institutional status quo. First and foremost, this concerns the UN system.

The United Nations system shows its age

In theory, the United Nations ought to be coming back into its own after many years when its proper functioning was blocked by Security Council vetoes on one or other side of the Cold War. As a pre-cold war institution, it was designed with the failures of the League of Nations in mind. It was meant to deal with intra-state conflicts of the sort that had occurred between the wars. The writers of its charter restricted its purview to the relationship between states, as it was essentially seen as a bulwark for existing borders; any intervention in another state's internal affairs was not contemplated. The vetoes in the Security Council were designed to ensure that the UN did not tackle more than it could handle, but this was the feature that caused deadlock during the Cold War. Since the fall of the Berlin Wall in 1989, it has passed as many Security Council resolutions as in its entire previous history, and has deployed more than half a million troops in blue berets.[18]

However, the UN shows its age by comparison with current world problems, particularly those of civil conflict, humanitarian outrages and failed states. It has to change its approach to domestic sovereignty, which is set out in Article 2, paragraph 7 of the charter[19] forbidding intervention in the internal affairs of its members. UN members must have the collective capacity to challenge the sovereignty of other members for gross and persistent abuse of human rights, the denial of the right to peaceful coexistence of nations and communities, or wilful and widespread environmental damage.

This should certainly not be an invitation to intervene. Any such intervention needs to be in a framework that is clearly set out beforehand, and which might be judged against criteria such as the exhaustion of diplomatic avenues of progress, firm evidence of the breach of international law or the Universal Declaration of Human Rights, the compromise of regional stability through large numbers of refugees or widespread environmental damage, the flouting of UN resolutions, the practicability of intervention, and the commitment of intervening powers to commit resources to peace enforcement in the long term. This necessarily requires the reform of the Security Council and the General Assembly (in which each member, regardless of size, has one vote) and the strengthening of the UN's finances. The most practical means of instituting reform of the UN would be to call a constitutional convention to draft a new charter more in keeping with the security challenges that the world now faces. At the same time, the UN might appear less wilfully prolix if it were to embark on an audit of its existing resolutions, weeding out those that have not stood the test of time.

In the security field, the European Union can do much to strengthen the multilateral system by creating its own rapid reaction force, and being prepared to commit that force to UN tasks. The USA bears too high a share of the burden of global security, and focuses too little on economic and diplomatic channels of influence. Europe cannot expect to have the influence it would like when its own contribution to global order is so feeble. Since this weakness arises principally from the extraordinary inefficiency of European defence spending – on one estimate, the EU countries spend nearly half the US total on defence, but get less than 10% of the firepower – much can be done by procuring in common.

Different armed forces insist on different tanks, rifles and helicopters. Even where there is cooperation, it is often half-hearted and flawed. Projects like the Eurofighter have traditionally overrun because suppliers are faced with divided procuring authorities, each attempting to get slightly different specifications for their own armed forces. As a result, economies of scale cannot be reaped, and it is also difficult for purchasers to threaten to stop the project if overruns get out of hand. A single budget holder would have much more power, particularly if the holder could also insist on common specifications and large production runs. In November 2003, the EU defence ministers agreed to set up a European Defence Agency, and it remains to be seen whether this will prove more effective than previous efforts to tackle the same problem. If the EDA succeeds in making substantial savings, the highest priorities for Europe should be more effective forces for humanitarian intervention and state reconstruction, priorities almost wholly ignored by the USA.

Perhaps the greatest weakness in the present global system is the failure to address environmental problems with the same will and credibility as security or economic problems. The United Nations Environmental Programme (UNEP) has a number of achievements to its name, not least the monumental works published by the Intergovernmental Panel on Climate Change in collaboration with another UN specialist agency, the World Meteorological Office. But global institutions in the environmental field are far weaker than those dealing with trade, finance and security. A more influential and better-resourced environmental organisation within the UN family is overdue, both to initiate and oversee conventions on environmental degradation. Moreover, international pressure has utterly failed to persuade the largest source of carbon emissions – the USA – to implement fuel tax policies that might sustain a cutback in use, and this is a bipartisan policy, not a quirk of President Bush. After all, the US Senate rejected the Kyoto protocol in 1997 by 95 votes to nil. If governments are to create a global consensus for action on climate change, a greater effort will have to be made to persuade the USA that there are other ways of meeting Kyoto commitments than higher fuel taxes, which are not likely to gain political support soon. An alternative would be intensified research and development into non-emitting technologies. This would, of course, happen naturally with higher taxes on carbon fuels, but it could also occur through direct subsidy.

Whether solutions to global environmental sustainability involve taxing and regulating 'bads', or encouraging 'goods', a strong international framework such as the Kyoto protocol is essential to limit the incentive to take a free ride while relying on the efforts of others. UNEP should be established as a UN agency with assigned funding, so that it is no longer reliant on variable donations. The Global Environment Facility (GEF) should be better resourced, and there should be a big effort to develop the same sort of compliance mechanisms for environmental agreements that exist for trade.

Economic governance: poverty and instability

Turning to changes in the system of economic governance, there is a substantial unfinished agenda of debt and poverty relief that the European Liberal Democrats and the EU should champion. The Heavily Indebted Poor Countries (HIPC) initiative launched in 1996 has begun to deliver more substantial debt relief for the poorest developing countries, but poverty criteria should be given the same level of importance as economic criteria by the World Bank and the International Monetary Fund when they administer the scheme. The developed world should be much more ready to cancel unsustainable debt, conditional on the debtor country's commitment to poverty eradication and human rights. Nor should unilateral help be confined to debt: opening up markets for developing country produce – particularly for agricultural goods that are the first rung on the export ladder for so many countries – is just as crucial.[20] The 'Everything but arms' initiative – under which the EU is set to open its markets to free access for all goods except arms to the 48 least developed countries – was an imaginative departure. The real test is now to extend that access further up the development ladder so that developing countries have similar access to developed markets as other developed countries.[21]

For middle-income countries that have substantial amounts of commercial debt, either in the form of bonds or bank lending – countries like Argentina, Brazil, Thailand and Malaysia – the international system is still exceptionally brutal and has become more so (as the Asian crisis in 1997–8 showed). The International Monetary Fund (IMF) retains its traditional role of providing support to countries when market confidence evaporates – as it may through no fault of a particular country, but merely through contagion from a neighbour's crisis. But the failure over many years to maintain the IMF's lending resources in line with international trade flows (let alone capital flows) means that it is able to provide less support than hitherto. The result is that the pace of change for the countries concerned, as they have to bring their domestic spending and import levels into line with available resources, is far greater than it was.

Compare, for example, the pace of change for Britain when we suffered a sterling crisis in 1976. The package of support from the IMF at that time scarred a generation, and was one of the defining moments that ushered in a Conservative government determined to break with the post-war muddling through. Yet that package was, by the standards of recent packages for developing countries, generous. It allowed a slow adjustment so that the balance of payments deficit – the excess of imports over exports – had to move into surplus by just 2.1% of the economy over the two years to 1978. By contrast, the turnaround in Mexico in just one year in 1995 was 6.6% of gross domestic product. In Korea in 1998, the improvement in the current account from deficit to surplus in just one year was 14.4% of gross domestic product (GDP). With such wrenching changes, the country must inevitably curb imports sharply, which it is only able to do through a general crackdown on spending in the economy, which hits activity and jobs.

There should be a review of the IMF's financing needs to bring it into line with what is required to support a number of crisis-hit countries, and this amount should be determined by an open discussion of modern needs. It must take into account the appropriate pace at which it is reasonable for a country to adjust to the withdrawal of private finance without damaging its society and its economy. At present, IMF finance is determined by past

IMF finance, regardless of the change in the world. It is therefore entirely arbitrary, and increasingly inappropriate. The system needs to be examined, starting with what is an appropriate pace of adjustment, and then determining the mechanisms necessary to deliver this pace of adjustment. In other words, we need to start by analysing the extent of the problem, and then ask about the means necessary to deal with it.

This adjustment process need not require cash, but instead might involve sanctioning a reduced flow of debt service. An alternative to a rapid IMF bail-out is the renegotiation of existing debts, but the proposals floated by the IMF's economics team for a standstill arrangement for sovereign nations have run up against US opposition. The case, however, is compelling. When a company fails, it is given a period of administration or receivership in which its assets and liabilities can be assessed, and as much of the concern saved as possible. This avoids a rush by creditors to attach any particular assets of the business, whatever the damage that may do to its future performance (and the chances of repayment of other creditors). The same principle could, and should, apply to countries: a standstill authorised by the IMF (or a similar body) would give countries facing a crisis time to reschedule debts (reducing and prolonging payments) and work its way out of cash-flow difficulties. In addition, the big countries should set an example by introducing so-called 'collective action' clauses into their own bonds: these allow a majority of bondholders to accept renegotiated terms without a recalcitrant minority holding out for special treatment.

There is also a role for prevention rather than cure. The international financial system would become more stable if both the IMF and borrowing countries took greater care to collect and disseminate relevant data, particularly concerning debt that comes due in a short period of time. This short-term debt is a key source of vulnerability, since it is like an overdraft that may be called in by the bank. In normal times, it will not be called in. But the bank may do so just when the overdraft is most needed. In theory, a Tobin tax – a small tax on exchange rate transactions – might also introduce frictions into capital flows, and hence reduce vulnerability to speculative attacks by the market, but the result might also be the opposite since less liquid markets (with fewer buyers and sellers) tend to be more volatile. Moreover, it is hard to see how a Tobin tax could be practically applied in a world where foreign exchange trading can be shifted so easily to an alternative centre – say, Singapore or Hong Kong – that did not levy the tax. A measure with more predictable effects of the type favoured by advocates of the Tobin tax would be the type of capital controls operated by Chile to ward off short-term speculative capital from coming into the country: Chile has run a deposit scheme whereby investors buying short-term instruments in Chile have to put a similar amount on deposit, effectively reducing the interest rate for short-term money.

Trade and corporate controversies
Trade liberalisation has been one of the great post-war successes, and has been rewarded with greater imports and exports than ever before. However, there has been much concern that the legal framework for liberalisation – the World Trade Organisation's disputes procedures – militates against developing countries. This is mainly because of their relative lack of access to the official and legal back-up that the developed countries can muster – a problem that could be addressed with selective support from the developed countries. In addition, it would make sense to allow non-voting and amicus interventions in disputes by non-governmental organisations, together with greater transparency about the whole dispute resolution process. However, the criticism of

the WTO also reflects the wider focus (since the Uruguay round of trade talks) on services, agriculture, Trade-Related Intellectual Property (TRIPs) and Trade-Related Investment (TRIMs). There needs to be a tilt in favour of the developing countries, too, in the framework of rules, particularly in subsidies and infant industry protection.

The UN system also lacks a clear capacity to monitor and regulate excessive concentrations of corporate power. Much of the criticism of multinationals is wide of the mark and over the top: they do not possess the monopoly use of force, as any effective state does. They have no taxing powers. And the comparison of their sales figures with the gross domestic product of countries is implausible propaganda, since it is not comparing like with like. Even the world's largest corporations have little power compared with developed states.

However, there are exceptions where the contest is less equal. The first is where developing countries are keen to attract foreign direct investment and are prepared to waive environmental or other standards to attract it, or where they are simply too undeveloped to have appropriate regulatory and supervisory frameworks. This is the case with many developing countries that host multinationals in the primary and extractive industries: forestry firms may ignore the needs of sustainability in the interests of a quick return. The second case where the contest between companies and countries is less equal is where corporations are involved in anti-competitive activity in markets where there is no strong competition authority. Since the vast majority of multinationals are public companies quoted in the three major developed blocs – the USA, European Union and Japan – much can be done by improving reporting of corporate activities through listing requirements. Codes of good corporate governance can, and should, specify a ban on bribery, a commitment to high environmental standards, and a respect for core labour standards enshrined in International Labour Organisation conventions.

Although the extension of multilateral trade rules to investment was one of the most controversial aspects of the breakdown in trade talks at Cancun, the idea can, in principle, have merit if countries voluntarily opt in. Any such comfort for investors is likely to encourage investment and benefit the countries swiftly. It might also open the way to a new type of development aid, namely subsidies paid to direct investors to offset perceived political risk. It would also enormously simplify the current mesh of bilateral treaties on investment, which have leapt from about 400 in 1990 to 1,300 with more than 160 countries participating in more than one treaty by 1997.[22] An agreement should also set out responsibilities for investing companies, perhaps modelled on the provisions in the Organisation for Economic Cooperation and Development's (OECD's) guidelines on multinational enterprises.

On competition, there has been a closer collaboration between the anti-trust division of the US Department of Justice and the EU Commission's competition directorate-general, although they are still capable of coming to different conclusions on major issues. Moreover, neither competition authority is at all bashful about defending its own region's interests even if the two companies involved are both domiciled outside it. For example, the Justice Department cleared, but the EU Commission blocked in 2001, the proposed merger of the two big US companies, General Electric and Honeywell, a controversial decision that is still subject to appeal in the European Court of Justice. But a formal agency within which competition authorities could discuss criteria would make sense, and would also provide a resource whereby developing countries could begin to establish their own competition authorities.

The limits of legitimate tax competition

It is possible, of course, that international competition may lead to a race to the bottom on environmental and labour standards, and on taxation. Companies may shop around to find the laxest regimes in which to do business, and invest in areas with the lowest tax rates. However, the evidence for such practices is much less strong than popular mythology holds. Multinationals run serious reputational risks with their developed-country customers if they are seen to exploit third world workforces, as Nike found to its cost in Indonesia. Far from being cut, corporate taxation has been stable or gently rising in many developed countries.[23] Overall, the tax burden of most developed countries is higher today than it was either ten or twenty years ago, which suggests that tax competition has not required countries to impoverish their exchequers. Any country that sets out a very low level of corporate profit tax – like Ireland at 12.5% – may soon face demand pressures and the risk of higher inflation. There is a self-correcting mechanism in any such competition.

The experience within the USA, with no tariff barriers, a single currency and free capital flows, is that no federal rules are necessary to establish minimum tax rates. Vermont levies an income tax seven cents in the dollar higher than neighbouring New Hampshire, but this does not lead to wholesale flight because Vermonters believe that their public services compensate them for the tax payments. As David Landes has persuasively argued,[24] competition between the small states of Europe was a fundamental reason why Europe developed in the past few centuries more quickly than China. If rules became too oppressive, business people could move to a more friendly and commercial jurisdiction. In centralised China, that was never an option. Competition between systems may also be a useful spur to public sector efficiency.

There is, though, a strong case for tougher international action

125

against tax evasion – the illegal hiding of taxable income – which has been made much easier by global capital flows. The clamp down has already begun within the European Union, with the attempts to exchange information on non-resident interest and dividend payments or with the application of a minimum with-holding tax. Other countries are gradually being brought within the system. Though some are cynical about the likelihood of success, it is worth pointing out that there has been a widespread attack on money laundering through the application of new 'know your customer' rules by banks. Offshore banking centres that failed to cooperate – like the Seychelles – found themselves threatened with a cessation of money transfers from the main centres, and soon came to heel.

Migration can be reverse aid

Migration remains, of course, a nationally determined issue. But migration has become a fact of life for many millions of people. Some commentators have argued that it is time for a conven-tion on minimum rules for the treatment of migrants, who often provide temporary labour services.[25] So far, the UN convention on migrants' rights has been signed only by developing countries that export workers. Developed countries appear to fear domestic reaction to the extension of familial rights of residence. However, this leaves a gaping void in many receiving countries. Discrim-ination against migrants is rife. Often, contractual relations are exceptionally poor, and there are few, if any, grievance procedures for migrants, especially in middle-income countries like the Gulf States. There is also an ethical issue when developed countries – including the UK in recent years – rely heavily on the training undertaken in much poorer countries like South Africa to provide nurses and doctors for their own public health services. This flow deprives developing countries of the most precious resource needed for development, and involves a serious loss. It is surely time to open a debate on appropriate means of compensation for this reverse aid, including handing over some of the tax revenue paid by the migrant to the host country.

Conclusions

Our political and economic systems of global governance are creaking. They have not been updated to deal with either the security, environmental or economic challenges that the world faces today, but the desirable changes are not so radical that they are unattainable. For any institutional change, there should perhaps be three guiding principles.[26] The first is that the institution should be able to deal with the cross-border problem it is designed to tackle. The second is that the institution should be as democratically accountable as possible, and at the very least should be open and transparent. The third is the old Liberal principle that decisions should be taken as closely as possible to the people affected by them (now dignified with the ungainly description of subsidiarity). Any liberal international system will apply these principles to achieve a balance between competition and order. There needs to be a light enough touch to ensure that countries and companies can compete economically, but a strong enough framework to ensure that economic competition does not spill over into political competition and conflict. Above all, there must also be enough rules to control unwanted environmental side effects.

In sum, the political reforms require a renewal of the UN charter to make explicit the terms on which national sovereignty may be overruled; namely the fundamental and persistent breaches of human rights in failed states. Small arms are now as great a problem as major armaments, and much more can, and should, be done to limit small arms exports to fields of conflict. Europe needs to reshape its military to make a substantially greater contribution to the keeping of global order, particularly for humanitarian interventions and the reconstruction of failed states. The biggest lacuna in international organisations is a champion for global sustainability: a more effective world environment organisation is crucial.

On the economic side of global governance, the World Trade Organisation needs to tilt more towards the developing world through changes in its procedures and help for poor countries in legal representation. The International Monetary Fund needs once again to become the crisis manager of the system, but it should have the resources and the mechanisms to manage change at a socially acceptable pace. Competition between political systems on taxation, public spending and conditions of work beyond core standards is legitimate and healthy, and does not involve a race to the bottom. But determined international action needs to be taken to disrupt tax evasion and money laundering. Migration is an issue where there needs to be minimum standards to protect temporary workers, and compensation to poor exporting countries whose investment in human skills disappears.

Globalisation can bring great benefits to countries that grasp its opportunities. The nations that have, at times, closed themselves off from the world marketplace are, in general, a salutary warning of how not to proceed: Cuba, North Korea, Libya and the former Soviet system. But globalised benefits also bring globalised costs, and the political institutions necessary to tackle those costs need to be stronger and more agile than their current incarnations are now.

Notes

1. I am grateful for the comments on earlier drafts of this paper from Duncan Brack, David Laws, Paul Marshall and William Wallace (Lord Wallace of Saltaire). They have much improved it.

2. See page 21 of Michael Tracy, *Agriculture in Western Europe*, London, 1964. Tracy's classic gives a full description of differing European reactions to this seismic change, and this short discussion draws heavily on it.

3. Angus Maddison, *The World Economy: a Millennial Perspective*, OECD, 2001, p. 363.

4. From 38.5 years in 1929 to 61.1 years in 1992, according to Bourguignon, Coyle et al., 'Making Sense of Globalisation: a Guide to the Economic Issues', Centre for Economic Policy Research (CEPR), paper no. 8, July 2002.

5. In terms of constant 1990 dollars. See ibid.

6. See 'The East Asia Miracle', World Bank, Washington DC, 1993.

7. David Potter et al. (eds), *Democratisation*, Cambridge, 1997.

8. Table 1 in Bourgignon and Morrisson (2001), cited in CEPR, op. cit.

9. A report of working group 1 of the Intergovernmental Panel on Climate Change, United Nations Environmental Programme, 2001.

10. See Peter Schwartz and Doug Randall, 'An Abrupt Climate Change Scenario and its Implications for US National Security', commissioned by the US Department of Defense from Global Business Network, 2003 (www.gbn.org).

11. See John Dumbrell, 'Unilateralism and "America First"'? President George W. Bush's Foreign Policy', *Political Quarterly*, Blackwell, Oxford, 2002.

12. See Robert Kagan, *Paradise and Power: America and Europe in the New World Order*, London, 2003.

13. See p. 238 of *The Military Balance*, International Institute for Strategic Studies, London, 2003. US spending in 2002 was $362 billion compared with a global total of $843 billion.

14. The effective exchange rate of the dollar fell by 28% between the annual average of 1985 and 1987 on the IMF measure (reported in *National Institute Economic Review*, 3/1990). For a full account, see Yoichi Funabashi, *Managing the Dollar: from the Plaza to the Louvre*, Institute of International Economics, Washington DC, 1988.

15. The tables are turned since the arrival in Paris in 1919 of US President Woodrow Wilson, bearing his fourteen points to underpin the new order and bemusing the world-weary Europeans, Georges Clemenceau and David Lloyd George.

16. Such as the United Nations Conference on Trade and Development, the various United Nations regional organisations and others.

17. O'Rourke and Sinnott, 'The Determinants of Individual Trade Policy Preferences: International Survey Evidence' (forthcoming), quoted in CEPR, op. cit.

18. According to Robert Cooper, between 1946 and 1990 there were 683 Security Council resolutions; in the thirteen years after that, the number more than doubled. R. Cooper, *The Breaking of Nations: Order and Chaos in the Twenty-first Century*, Atlantic, London, 2003, p. 57.

19. This states: 'Nothing contained in the present Charter shall authorise the United Nations to intervene in matters which are essentially within the domestic jurisdiction of any state or shall require the Members to submit such matters to settlement under the present Charter; but this principle shall not prejudice the application of enforcement measures under Chapter VII.' However, there are some countervailing texts in international law such as the prohibition of genocide in the 1948 convention.

20. This access, even for off-season fresh produce, is vulnerable not just to deliberate protectionism but to a sudden zeal in application of consumer protection measures. Currently, many sub-Saharan exports of fresh vegetables are threatened by new and tough European phyto-sanitary measures where the cost of compliance – requiring scarce capital – has a disproportionate impact on poor developing country producers.

21. The General Agreement on Tariffs and Trade – superseded in 1995 by the World Trade Organisation – has introduced a more liberal trade policy between the industrial countries than at any other time, with average tariffs below 4% in both the USA and EU. See M. Bordo, B. Eichengreen and D. Irwin, 'Is Globalisation Today Really Different than Globalisation a Hundred Years Ago?' National Bureau of Economic Research Working Paper 7195, June 1999. www.nber.org

22. See E. M. Graham , *Fighting the Wrong Enemy: Antiglobal Activists and Multinational Enterprises*, Institute for International Economics, Washington DC, 2000, quoted in Martin Wolf, 'Globalisation and Global Economic Governance', *Oxford Review of Economic Policy*, Vol. 20, no. 1, 2004.

23. See answer by the EU Commission to a parliamentary question from the author, number E-1394/2001, which showed that, on average, corporation tax as a percentage of GDP in the EU had risen from 2.1% in 1980 to 3.2% in 2001. There was no member state that recorded a fall in corporation tax revenues as a share of GDP.
24. See David Landes, *The Wealth and Poverty of Nations*, Abacus, London, 1998.
25. See Wolf, op. cit.
26. See Vincent Cable, 'Globalisation and Global Governance', Royal Institute of International Affairs, 1999.

5   Liberal economics and social justice

Vince Cable

Introduction and principles

After the ideological battles of recent decades, today's are somewhat tame. Labour no longer even pretends that there is some alternative economic organising principle constructed around public ownership and government controls, and ministers use the vocabulary of the market without evident embarrassment. Conservatives have been much less adroit in ideological repositioning, but their more intelligent spokesmen recognise that the evangelising Thatcherite belief in raw, uncompromising, capitalism has to be allied to the language of fairness and commitment to public service. Except on the wilder political fringes, no one seriously pretends that fundamental, systemic, economic upheaval is called for, or that integration with the global economy can or should be stopped and reversed. There is now a reasonably settled consensus that the task of modern government is to manage an open market economy, providing macro-economic stability allied to micro-economic flexibility and, alongside this, to try to achieve a sense of equity across social classes and generations.

This is easier said than done, of course, especially in times of economic and political stress. Moreover, the existence of such a broad consensual framework poses both problems and opportunities for Liberal Democrats. The problem is congestion: too many politicians and parties with essentially the same message. The temptation is to head off into vacant political territory on the left and into the anti-capitalist, anti-globalisation fringes. But such territory is largely unoccupied for good reason; that the remedies are fundamentally implausible and, in any event, totally alien to Liberal Democrat traditions.

Our opportunity lies precisely in those liberal traditions. From the Liberal beginnings in the nineteenth century to the modern alliance with the Social Democrats, there have been consistent threads: a commitment to a liberal and open economy inter-woven with a concern for social justice. Indeed, the tradition goes back earlier; Adam Smith described how a benevolent society combined 'self-love' or self-interest, with sympathy for fellow citizens. In dealing with the central preoccupations of modern British politics, Liberal Democrats have no need for the elaborate contortions which are necessary to accommodate them within something called 'socialism', with its lingering distrust of markets, entrepreneurs, property rights and decentralisation. Nor, like true Conservatives, do we have an instinctive disdain for the collective provision of services for those in society who are less successful and less affluent (and we are, in any event, clearly demarcated from the Conservatives by their inability to transcend the xenophobia and social authoritarianism of many of their core supporters).

But there are also some new or emerging areas where the Liberal Democrats have to define or redefine their position.

An open economy and mercantilism
The origins of liberal economics lie in an era long before modern political parties were created. But the arguments advanced by Adam Smith and other thinkers in favour of free trade and against mercantilism reverberate to this day.

Free trade revisited

The main contemporary challenge is a new international division of labour that involves rapid, and sometimes painful, integration into the world economy. The 'free trade' agenda relates, these days, more to the European Union than to the UK itself. Indeed, Britain no longer has an independent trade policy. As the party which, more than any other, advocated British membership of the EU and, then, defended it against 'anti-Europeans' of the left and, now, the right, the Liberal Democrats have a special responsibility to defend economic liberalism within the union, working with the other liberal parties like the German and Dutch Liberals.

There is a lot to be proud of. Arguably, the European Union, with its gradual enlargement, has been the biggest single stimulus to liberalising trade creation since World War II. The single market, clearing away regulatory barriers, has intensified competition and generated more trade, both in goods and services, and, increasingly, cross-border investment. The euro will gradually deepen the single market by intensifying competition and making prices and costs more transparent. The establishment of a cartel and monopoly-busting competition policy, and strong rules outlawing distorting state aids, are further positive steps, as will be the extension of the single market to energy, postal services and other areas dominated by state monopolies. The state aids regime, for example, is the strongest potential safeguard against such expensive follies as the 'bail out' of Britain's nuclear power producer, British Energy, or the French Alsthom. The inability of today's British Conservatives to identify with this impressive creation (to which Mrs Thatcher, no less, made a major contribution through the Single Market Act) and the EU's liberalising achievements and potential is one of the more bewildering aspects of the Conservatives' odyssey in the political wilderness.

The early worries that the EU would become a closed, inward-looking bloc have also been largely unfounded. In the language of customs union theory, the union has been primarily a force for trade creation rather than trade diversion. It played a constructive role in the last Uruguay round of trade negotiations, leading to the establishment of the World Trade Organisation (WTO) with its rules-based system of dispute settlement. Indeed, the European Union (EU) could – at least until the breakdown of the latest negotiations in Cancun, which it partially caused – claim to have become the main champion of global, multilateral rules and a strong WTO, in the face of capricious, unilateralist and protectionist behaviour by the USA. Indeed, such a commitment to multilateral rules has recently proved its worth in forcing the USA to retreat over steel tariffs.

There are, however, two major problems with the European Union from the standpoint of liberal trade, and Liberal Democrats and their allies in Europe should pull no punches in combating them. The first is the baleful influence of the Common Agricultural Policy (CAP). Its system of production subsidy, import levies and export subsidies causes immense damage, way beyond the agricultural sector. It helps explain the waste and imbalances in the European budget. It is a massive roadblock in multilateral trade negotiations and, in particular, does immense damage to developing countries' agricultural exporters. It is regressive in its impact on European consumers and rewards rich landowners disproportionately. And it damages the environment by artificially intensifying production to land ratios. In short, the CAP is an economic, environmental and moral disaster.

To assert this is not some liberal or British heresy. Various well-intentioned, if ineffectual, EU reforms, latterly those authored by Commissioner Fischler, have sought to remove production subsidies, albeit on a glacial timescale. But they have made only modest headway in the face of the powerful vested interests involved in large-scale agriculture. The cynical concordat between France and Germany to obstruct reform is doing great harm. Economic liberals cannot endlessly temporise over this issue, not least because multilateral negotiations, and even the future of the WTO, are in peril. If the other EU countries refuse to reform more rapidly (or to allow CAP opt-outs to countries that wish to pursue more liberal policies) then the UK should be quite obdurate, resorting if necessary to a prolonged veto over future budget negotiations. But the immediate UK priority is to build on the agreement to decouple subsidy from production and to ensure that foot-dragging in Europe over agricultural reform does not derail multilateral trade regulations.

Regulatory protectionism

A second problem lies in the fact that, increasingly, arguments about free trade have less to do with old-fashioned tariffs and quotas, which have largely disappeared, than with the use of regulation as a barrier to free exchange. The use of harmonised regulation, particularly social and environmental standards or food safety standards, is being used not as a market opening, liberalising, measure but as a protectionist device to raise costs and thereby create barriers to services and products from other EU members (and non members). The insidiousness of this approach lies in its apparently benign character. It is difficult, for example, to quarrel with the proposition that workers should be protected from unscrupulous employers who abuse their position in the labour market to impose hours of work that are damaging to health and family life. Most economic liberals should have no difficulty with establishing rights for employees to balance the property rights of employers, provided it does not create serious disincentives to hiring new workers. There are, also, occasions where European remedies may be called for, as with long distance, cross-border lorry drivers. But European directives are currently being imposed on member states regardless of whether any market abuse is involved, whether there is a cross-border issue or whether national (or local) remedies can be achieved.

Such interference by European institutions is often justified in the name of 'level playing fields' or, more crudely, 'social dumping'. Such arguments are economically very questionable and, by failing to respect different democratic preferences and characteristics, violate the whole concept of subsidiarity. The same issues are involved in environmental standard setting; there is a legitimate role for European institutions in preventing cross-border pollution but not, for example, in dictating standards of local pollution.

Whether protectionist in intent or simply motivated by a centralising culture of harmonisation for its own sake, much European regulation has become intrusive, costly and unnecessary. It is time for economic liberals to take a stand and to reassert some simple principles: that all that is necessary for trade, investment and cross-border movement of workers is for different standards to be mutually recognised and that there is merit in competition between different standards (as there is between different tax systems). In practice, the union should not be setting legally binding social standards at all. New environmental standards are helpful in dealing with genuine cross-border pollution issues – sulphur emissions ('acid rain') and CO_2 – or protecting common resources like the Rhine basin or the North Sea. But many do not involve genuine cross-border 'spill-overs'. There is a legitimate but more modest role for the union in setting out aspirations and also for setting comparable benchmarks; thus, it may be sensible and helpful to consumers to be able to find out easily how local bath water, or drinking water, or air pollution, compares with European equivalents but not to legislate on these matters. A broad liberal principle is to require producers to identify the origin of their products so that informed consumers can choose whether they wish to indulge lower social and environmental standards – but not to impose higher ones.

A tougher, more sceptical, approach to European institutions and legislation may seem an unfamiliar posture for the 'pro-European' Liberal Democrats, but it is precisely because the Liberal Democrats and its antecedent parties have unimpeachable European credentials that they have an opportunity – indeed, a duty – to speak out forcefully against illiberal and damaging European measures. They should do so not on grounds of British exceptionalism but to save Europe from itself. Helping to shape a developed and decentralised European Union will be a key challenge for the Liberal Democrats over the years ahead.

The industrial welfare state and the new mercantilism

These days, traditional protectionism and import controls have few advocates. Nor is there much nostalgia for the crude industrial intervention of the 1970s – 'picking winners' and bailing out 'lame ducks', though it persists elsewhere, notably in France. What has begun to emerge is a more subtle approach to intervention in the traded parts of the economy (mainly manufacturing but including those services like banking which are increasingly international in character). In the interests of so-called 'national competitiveness', governments implicitly or explicitly subsidise 'national' producers – to the extent that this is at all meaningful in a world of cross-border share ownership and alliances. The favoured techniques are the use of government procurement to skew orders towards favoured companies, notably through defence and other public sector contracts, or aid tying (seen at its most mercenary and corrupt in the Bush administration's allocation of contracts in post-war Iraq); the use of export credit guarantees for weapons sales and other capital goods; intervention to favour 'national' producers where 'strategic' interests are identified, usually very loosely defined; active 'trade diplomacy' to persuade overseas governments to buy items they would probably not buy on grounds of price and quality alone or (as with airlines and access rights or overseas investment in banking and insurance) to use discretionary regulation to favour 'national' companies; tax breaks to subsidise investment or research and development where export subsidies are forbidden by international rules; and largely random, selective intervention (like the £3.8bn recently approved by the UK Parliament for unspecified future industrial assistance).

The degree of intervention in the form of what the late Harry Johnson called the 'new mercantilism' has little to do with traditional alignments of left and right. The most aggressive and shameless exponents of this policy are Bush 'neo-Conservatives' and French Gaullists. But Blair's Britain has seen its share. Motives are several: a misguided, non-economic belief that government salesmen and taxpayers' money 'save' or 'create' jobs; the insatiable appetite of politicians to wrap themselves in national flags in trade no less than in sport or military conflict; the seductive potential of the word 'security' when used by 'national champions' to justify favours; and sometimes outright corruption or cronyism when the government help is a quid pro quo for past or expected political support. A more pragmatic reason is that other governments also help 'their' producers in different ways, generating calls for a 'level playing field'. For a combination of the above reasons, some enterprises have been extraordinarily successful in persuading the British Government to underwrite their shareholders' risks and secure commercial advantage overseas.

Economic liberals should look at these activities with a very jaundiced eye. It is entirely predictable and understandable that business should seek favours; but not that governments should naively concede them, particularly if taxpayers' money is involved.

The response should be essentially twofold. The first is to be strongly supportive of multilateral initiatives designed to get rid of mercantilist behaviour – like the EU rules on state aids; the WTO rules on public procurement and trade-distorting industrial subsidies and investment measures; and the (voluntary) Organisation for Economic Cooperation and Development (OECD) 'gentleman's agreement' on export credit.

But there is a case, too, for unilateral action in some areas. The government has already dropped aid tying to UK exports: a brave and sensible decision, which has inflicted no obvious damage on the British economy and considerably increased the value of its aid. Given the many other calls on government funding, many of the industrial support functions of the Department of Trade and Industry (DTI), like the DTI itself, should be dismantled. The Export Credits Guarantee Department (ECGD) could be privatised (short-term export credit insurance already has been) and operate in an environment where firms pay the full cost of risk insurance. And as long as the ECGD operates with government backing, it should cease to underwrite armaments exports altogether with the implicit subsidy involved (the risk premiums do not fully cover the risk of default to the tune of £200 million a year). The International Monetary Fund (IMF) has set out the wider economic (and moral) case for governments to desist from promoting arms exports, not the least being that it is wholly unproductive and commonly associated with corruption. If, however, willing commercial sellers can find willing buyers who satisfy the human rights, sustainability and other tests required in the export control regulations then, of course, that is a matter for the market (and there is a – quite separate – argument for military assistance in some cases).

New challenges: the Asian giants

However, other issues are emerging that will test the traditional Liberal commitment to free trade. One is the rapid emergence as trading partners of the giant Asian economies, China and India. Overall, this development must be seen as highly positive. On a purchasing power parity basis, these are respectively the second and fifth biggest economies in the world (with Britain the sixth). Their growth is becoming a key factor in sustaining global growth, especially if the USA should falter. But the development of Indian software and corporate systems services, followed by international call centres, has sent frissons of alarm through the service sectors of the UK economy, which has hitherto not been internationally traded or subject to the same compulsions of competition and specialisation that have long constrained manufacturing.

The current calls to stop offshore subcontracting are fundamentally no different from the angry (indeed, violent) protests in London over three centuries ago against 'unfair' imports from India of calico made by 'coolie labour', and are equally misguided; or more recent antipathy to East Asia manufacturers of products of varying degrees of sophistication. So far, the response of British ministers has been robustly sensible, as it has to 'globalisation' more generally, but as the process becomes more intense, particularly if less favourable employment conditions return, it will require some courage for economic liberals to assert the strong mutual benefit to be derived from such trade and to resist the clamour for protectionist measures (such as stopping the use of international outsourcing in the public sector). The role of the government in such circumstances should be to help the workforce adjust to change (be it change originating in demand, or technology, or trade) through continuing education, access to training and ensuring that local agencies can provide competitive infrastructure to attract new investment. The old liberal (and Liberal) precepts of 'free trade' apply just as much to this new challenge as to more deeply rooted obstacles to trade, such as agricultural protectionism.

One of the most difficult and growing issues for all economic (and social) liberals is immigration. On the positive side, there is a lot of evidence from economic history and wider international experience that a relatively liberal approach to immigration boosts not just growth, but also income per head – since migrants fill gaps in the labour market. Those who are educated, skilled or entrepreneurial bring their talents with them. Migrants are also likely to be more adaptable and energetic than the host population to justify the costs and risks of moving from one country to another. They help to keep public services going at affordable costs. Their remittances are perhaps the most cost-effective form of foreign aid.

On the debit side, migrants add to pressure on infrastructure. They arouse fear in the host population, because the supply from poor countries is virtually infinite in practice, and at some point worries about 'identity' come into play in a major way. Governments can try to reassure their native population that immigration is being 'managed' but, inevitably, in a reasonably open society with large numbers of overseas visitors, it is impossible to stop illegal migration. And, however necessary, immigration control inevitably carries with it all the bureaucracy, arbitrations, rough justice and inefficiency associated with other economic controls.

The issues are, in practice, complex and problems of asylum and immigration are intertwined. The role of economic liberals in these debates is to resist panic and xenophobia and to stress that there is an upside to maintaining a relatively open system; that other sources of labour also have costs as well as benefits (pressure on older workers to postpone retirement and pensions; pressure on both parents of young children to work); and that there are wider advantages of living in a society which is not afraid of, and which is receptive to, people from overseas with energy and new ideas.

Deregulating the regulatory state

There is an increasing concern, sometimes anger, among many firms, especially small firms, that the cost, complexity and inconsistency of government (and EU) regulation is severely undermining their ability to adapt to change and function in an entrepreneurial manner. To a degree, there is the obvious – Mandy Rice Davis – response: 'they would say that, wouldn't they'. Producers will tend to be repelled by government controls, as they are often attracted to protection and subsidy. But there may be a deeper problem. Not just the Institute of Directors and the Federation of Small Business but even the think-tank Demos has argued that 'the regulatory state is on the brink of crisis'.

The problem, however, is that the issues are extremely complex. It is tempting to create a simple dichotomy between less regulation (good; liberal – and 'right wing') and more regulation (bad; illiberal – and 'left wing'). But the issue is not fundamentally one of principle. Regulation is sought because there is a market failure. The real world is full of market failures: local, as well as national, monopolies; asymmetries of information between suppliers and purchasers; externalities from networks or negative externalities from pollution or congestion. An almost infinite amount of regulatory intervention can be justified in these terms. The issue is more a practical one of whether the government failures associated with regulation, and the cost of regulation, outweigh market failures and, more fundamentally, destroy the entrepreneurial and competitive impulses on which the private enterprise system depends.

In practice, the British regulatory structure has come from two (perhaps three) different sources with opposing motivations.

143

First, the main infrastructure regulators were part of a liberalising move away from 'command and control' structures based on nationalised industries and Whitehall central control. Regulators were created to ensure that privatised network monopolies (the electricity and gas distribution grids; the rail system; water; fixed wire telecommunications) or companies privatised as monopolies (airports) could be constrained to act within the public interest, notably through price control, at least until competing companies or systems emerged. But, in practice, these regulators have grown in scale and scope.

Second, firms in competitive markets have been subject to increasingly demanding social, environmental and other regulation. Within the past few years, firms have acquired legal responsibility for minimum wages, maximum working hours, flexible working, paternity and maternity leave, avoidance of discrimination on grounds of sex, race and disability, immigration control in respect of overseas employees, increasingly stringent emission controls, welfare benefit administration, data protection, elaborate checks on money laundering, checking criminal records for sex offenders as well as more traditional company law, audit, (employee and public) insurance, planning, fire, consumer protection, anti-cartel and health and safety regulations. Many of these measures, it must be said, are desirable, have long been fought for by reformers (including Liberal Democrats) and reflect a broad social consensus. The problem is that what often seem desirable measures in isolation are becoming, cumulatively, very onerous.

There has been some regulatory traffic in the opposite direction – the ending of price, wage and exchange controls; weaker union recognition – but not much.

Regulatory overload
There are numerous technical, political and intellectual issues

thrown up by regulation in its many forms. Moreover, many structures are not yet settled. The Post Office is still nationalised – a hybrid of the Royal Mail and the Counters' network – but also regulated and also subject to growing competition. The network monopoly underlying the bank clearing system has not, so far, been made subject to a threatened regulator, PayCom. The new competition watchdog, the Office of Fair Trading, appears to be acquiring some regulatory functions overseeing networks (newspaper distribution; pharmacies; credit cards).

As argued earlier, there is no scientific basis for judging whether there is 'too much' regulation in aggregate or whether there is some 'tipping point' beyond which the economic costs outweigh the benefits. International comparison is not too helpful either. The world's least regulated economies – anarcho-capitalist countries like Nigeria or post-Soviet Russia – are deeply inimical to serious, long-term, private investment. Apparently free and successful capitalist economies have extraordinarily fussy and detailed regulation of many aspects of life (Switzerland or Singapore) or (as in the USA) have displaced regulatory action into the courts, where the costs appear in legal fees. Some apparently highly regulated economies (such as Italy and India) are highly entrepreneurial, perhaps because corruption and systematic non-compliance make regulation ineffective.

But, this said, there are many examples of how excessive regulation is having negative consequences in the UK. The cost of operating systems of complex regulation for the financial services sector has meant that the industry can no longer profitably market simple, low-cost products for low-income consumers. And while a 'command and control' system of regulation has created a small and expensive army of financial regulators ticking numerous boxes, the same army has been caught wholly unprepared for a succession of disasters overtaking millions of investors (of

145

endowment mortgages; split capital investment trusts; precipice bonds; Equitable Life) and currently seems totally blind to the dangers presented by unrestrained debt promotion and spiralling personal debt.

In other sectors, badly needed care home capacity has been lost because of demands placed on marginally profitable suppliers by a radical tightening of standards; the railways are suffering years of chronic disruption caused in part by a tightening of safety regulation to a standard which reduces risk far below that in competing modes of transport, notably motoring; dredging companies, whose activities are essential to the commercial functioning of ports and rivers, now require additional environmental consents from a unit within the Department for Environment, Food and Rural Affairs (DEFRA) which is properly concerned with ecological impacts but which, because of the inordinate time taken to issue consents, puts the viability of commercial dredging in doubt; and at a time when there is a growing emphasis on good pre-school childcare provision, private providers are being driven out of business by the time-consuming and bureaucratic criminal record checks required to satisfy the authorities that no one working with children is a known paedophile. In all of these cases, and many more, the issue is not about the principle of regulation – few would argue for a 'free for all' which provides no protection for the elderly and children from abuse, or rail travellers from reckless carelessness, or the ecosystem from predatory or careless operators – but it's bureaucratic, centralised and costly form, with little sense of proportionality or rational risk assessment and an apparent lack of awareness of possible unintended consequences.

Scepticism about the way regulation is being operated in the UK (and the EU) is reinforced by its sense of permanence and remorseless expansion, even in sectors where regulation might have been seen as temporary. Ofgem, the energy regulator, recently advertised for staff, offering 'a secure long-term career in an expanding business', although in some key respects — notably power generation and retailing – there is more competition and, thus, less need for regulation. The explanation for this sense of a permanent and growing regulatory culture is that regulation is becoming more complex and demanding, with regulators acquiring more responsibilities or firms being regulated by more regulators. Thus energy regulation no longer merely concerns access for competitors and price capping for monopolies, but involves issues of fuel poverty, 'security of supply' (which itself has several different dimensions) and environmental sustainability. Rail operators are subject – inter alia – to regulation in respect of price and performance (the rail regulator), investment plans (the SRA) and safety (three agencies). Water companies face traditional price controls via Ofwat and various social obligations (over disconnections), quality standards and environmental impacts via the Environment Agency.

Each step in the creation of this web of regulatory complexity may have its own logic, but the cumulative effect can be very negative. Complex and heavy regulation raises the cost of capital, which reduces investment and, in turn, undermines objectives such as security of supply (an issue with respect to both power generation and water). Companies are sent contradictory signals: water companies to promote water quality and high environmental standards, which raise prices, and also to meet consumer expectations by reducing them; rail companies to cater for growing volumes of passengers and consumer expectations of punctuality, cleanliness and comfort, while taking no risks (since a jail sentence awaits those who can be fingered as managerially responsible for a fatal accident), and making no long-term commitments (since franchises are kept short to sharpen performance).

Competitive private companies are, of course, used to operating in a complex environment, now being made more complex

147

by rapid technological change and globalisation. But complexity in firms is managed by having a clearly defined objective – to maximise shareholder value, subject to a series of constraints: safety and morale of employees, brand loyalty, corporate reputation etc. With regulation it is far from clear what the primary concerns are; this is, of course, a political question to which the technical nature of most regulation can provide no answers. Nor is the direct intervention of politicians necessarily a helpful one. By establishing the clear priority of the railways with passenger safety, they have re-created a risk-averse culture similar to that of the early nineteenth century, when men with red flags preceded trains at walking pace, thereby pushing passengers on to the roads where standards of safety are much lower. We have what Demos has called a 'regulatory mess'.

A wave of regulatory reform

The traditional calls for 'less red tape' (which Conservatives in particular have adopted as their mantra for modern governance) are understandable but do not take us very far unless it is clear which red tape is being cut. Business organisations rarely match the strength of their deregulatory rhetoric with a depth of specificity about which regulations they would remove. Liberal Democrats have tried to be specific, and wish to work with business (and other) organisations to produce longer and more radical lists of unnecessary regulation.

But something stronger is required: a wave of regulatory reform. There have been two such waves, post-war. The first, initiated by Harold Wilson under Clement Attlee, and continued by the Conservatives under Winston Churchill, dismantled many wartime controls over trade, production, prices – and consumer rationing. The second, initiated by Mrs Thatcher, dismantled exchange control, the lingering state restrictions on prices and incomes, and some labour market regulation; but it also spawned a new generation of regulators.

A new wave of regulatory reform has to take into account the fact that there is a long pipeline full of new regulation waiting to be enacted. There is impending legislation on age discrimination, partly prompted by the crisis in pensions, requiring workers to work longer to build up entitlements; legislation on worker consultation to prevent summary redundancies; and stronger consumer protection in respect of rogue traders and a variety of unscrupulous 'scams' at the expense of 'vulnerable' customers. All of these have a strong rationale in terms of market failure or wider social goals, and most politicians will be attracted to them in principle.

So how is a new wave of deregulation to compete with these pressures? Partly, the issue is a cultural one: forcing the regulatory state to undergo the same process of constant adaptation, with institutional death as well as birth, and with attention always to reducing compliance costs, as the companies it is regulating have to do. Mao Zedong may have been a tyrant, but his concept of 'permanent revolution' contained the crucial insight that state bureaucracies will always ossify and become self-serving without mechanisms to force self-criticism. In our gentler political climate radical, if less extreme, remedies are required both at a national and EU level.

First, all regulations and regulatory bodies should have a modest fixed life after which any continued mandate has to be legislated from scratch. The concept of 'sunset clauses' has been widely promoted but infrequently acted upon. Such clauses should be obligatory for all new legislation, with regulatory implications. But they should be systematically applied retrospectively. A timetable should be drawn up for the regular review of all existing regulators and important regulatory measures, the premise being that none should continue without a convincing justification, including an evaluation both by representatives of the regulated companies and by Parliament. The current review of the Financial Services Act and Authority has some of the flavour of what is required, but, more importantly, there should be a more searching review within a decade that calls into question the need for the Act and the FSA, at least in its present form.

Second, the highly prescriptive character of much British regulation should be replaced by broader, more flexible, obligations. A good model is the recent legislation to promote family-friendly flexible working. Employees can request flexible arrangements but employers can refuse if there are genuine business imperatives. If, however, an employer is acting 'unreasonably' he may find himself brought to a tribunal and faces the risk of compensation. There are tricky issues involved in getting a fair balance within tribunals to minimise trivial cases while not creating severe access barriers. Nonetheless, this approach is preferable to detailed regulation spelling out every contingency. This would also be an appropriate way to deal with worker consultation requirements (rather than prescribing a model of works councils as seems to be envisaged by the European Commission). Subtle and complex problems involved in legislation against age discrimination at work can only sensibly be dealt with in this way. Existing highly prescriptive and bureaucratic legislation like the British rules applying the Working Time Directive – with 80 pages of explanatory notes from the DTI and timesheet rosters required of firms – should be scrapped and replaced by more flexible arrangements, as above. There could be much more scope for local agreements between workers' representatives and individual firms on working time, with individuals free to use quasi-judicial procedures where, but only where, firms' behaviour is highly unreasonable. Similarly the entirely desirable aim of Health and Safety Executive (HSE) legislation, domestic and EU, to prevent industrial accidents is often frustrated in practice by intensely bureaucratic, prescriptive rules specifying precisely what technology and equipment can be used (and which are, then, not matched by enforcement action in case of breaches). The emphasis should be the other way round: allowing firms maximum flexibility as to how they are to meet specified objectives but with the certainty that negligence leading to serious injury will be properly investigated and penalised.

The approach has applications way beyond labour law. There is currently discussion of consumer protection legislation based on a 'general duty to trade fairly' that is opposed by the DTI, which insists that unfair trading practices have to be precisely specified, though they are numerous and constantly changing to reflect new technological possibilities. The 'general duty' approach favoured by consumer groups (and also the European Commission) inevitably lacks precision and certainty, but allows local regulators (trading standards officers) to adapt their priorities in line with market conditions.

A third and related point is that, whenever possible, 'command and control' regulation should be replaced by self-regulation reinforced by statute. The law does not regulate the behaviour of doctors, since the General Medical Council does so according to its own standards of training, competence and ethics. The system is not perfect – hence Dr Shipman – but certainly better than an unregulated anarchy which permits quacks or, on the other hand, a system in which medical standards are set and enforced by politicians and civil servants. The same approach could be applied elsewhere. Instead of the highly complex, box-ticking regime designed to prevent mis-selling by financial advisers (which has the effect of making independent financial advisers [IFAs] inaccessible to those who need them most), IFAs should be subject to the rules of a self-governing professional body which will set standards of qualifications and training (currently very low), and levels of indemnity insurance, including funding for victims of mis-selling. And in the ethical quagmire of the building industry – builders, electricians, plumbers, roofers – where 'cowboys' operate freely to the disadvantage of consumers and the cost of reputable firms, a similar approach could be applied through a statutory Federation of Master Builders. Those who choose to use an 'unofficial' financial adviser or builder then have no recourse; the principle of 'caveat emptor' would apply more meaningfully.

A fourth step is the use of markets rather than quantitative regulations, where this is possible (or, where quantitative limits are essential for safety or other reasons, to impose market disciplines, as with traded permits for pollution). Markets make the costs of regulation more transparent and enable firms and consumers to adapt their behaviour in line with changed costs. Thus, a levy on the first users of cars or bottles to finance their eventual recycling is a far more efficient environmental measure than arbitrary recycling targets. A carbon tax applied 'upstream' and percolating down to producers to switch fuels and consumers to conserve energy is superior to regulations that specify emission levels (unless emission permits can then be traded). After many years of theoretical, academic advocacy, congestion charging has reached the point of practicality to be used for dealing with the environmental externality of congestion – rather than the present inefficient system of quantitative rationing through queuing. Despite howls of protest from the telecommunications industry, the government was entirely correct to use an auction system to auction 3G telecoms licences and utilise a scarce environmental resource – the spectrum – to maximum efficiency. There are unutilised possibilities for adapting these mechanisms more widely – notably in the aviation sector, where the current system of regulation provides monopoly rents to producers who are allocated landing rights free of charge, pay subeconomic landing charges and no aviation tax, despite the environmental externalities involved. The value of market instruments goes much wider than environmental regulation. One of the great advantages of the minimum wage over forms of labour-market regulation such as the working time directive is that the first can be evaluated and calibrated according to the economic consequences; the latter has costs that are entirely hidden.

This leads to the fifth point: that there has to be a satisfactory and independent system for regulatory impact assessment, so as to ensure that regulatory action is proportionate to the size of the problem and the costs of regulation. The UK Government is beginning to apply such disciplines, though the assessments vary in quality from department to department and there is no consistent or independent methodology. Some departments do not even try to estimate the costs of their regulatory initiatives (notably the Home Office, whose recent record of indifference to practicality and cost is appalling and which now proposes to add the identity card to an extensive portfolio which it is currently unable to manage). That said, the British process is being taken seriously, is improving, and is much better than that of the European Commission.

It might be argued that regulating regulation is a bureaucratic rather than a liberal response, compounding the problem, not solving it. But the mere fact that civil servants and ministers are required to jump through the hoops of an assessment process – which should in future be both more rigorous and independent – will force them publicly to justify the costs they are imposing on the economy. One particular discipline that should emerge from such work is better risk assessment. The public assessment of risk is often totally at variance with any scientific assessment of risk, witness the different standards expected of road and rail safety. Some regulatory issues concern fundamental scientific uncertainty rather than risk (climate change; impacts of genetically modified [GM] foods; impacts of telecoms masts) but where risk can be qualified, it must.

Finally, there is a need for much higher levels of accountability. The question 'who regulates the regulators?' was less important when regulating was seen as both temporary and technical. But as it has become more entrenched and political, regulators have to be subject to more demanding levels of accountability. One model is provided by the Monetary Policy Committee of the Bank of England, where new members are required to be interviewed and evaluated by a parliamentary select committee, while the full committee is grilled at regular intervals and the MPC's decision-making and the reasoning behind it are fully published and transparent. The chairmen and chief executives of key regulators such as the Financial Services Authority, Ofgem, Oftel, Ofcom, Ofwat, the Civil Aviation Authority, the Environment Agency and the Rail Regulator should be subject to at least this degree of scrutiny as part of a constant process of requiring them to justify their existence.

Boundaries of the state: taxation, spending and public service delivery
Liberal principles
One of the defining characteristics of economic liberalism is a belief that a system with many individual consumers and competing providers will provide a more satisfactory outcome than one based on monopoly, either of the private sector or the state. But even the earliest economic liberals accepted that there were important exceptions. Adam Smith advocated compulsory, tax financed, state education as a public good, many decades before politicians rose to the challenge. He also foresaw, and justified, rising commitments to 'law and order' since (as he correctly foresaw) richer societies

are also greedier and in greater need of policing. Smith envisaged public borrowing to finance infrastructure, and, of course, national defence. Other collective goods have been added: transfer payments as part of a welfare state system (initiated by Liberal governments and the Liberal Sir William Beveridge); public libraries, a long-standing, popular and valued institution, even in the USA; and the NHS (though Victorian Britain long understood the importance of public heath through good public sanitation and controls over the spread of communicable diseases).

Choice and plurality in public services

A central issue for domestic policy, and a major challenge to economic liberals, is the question of how to achieve greater individual, consumer, choice and greater diversity and competition amongst producers in the field of public services, where the state provides a (near) universal service (usually) free at the point of use.

There are those, radical libertarians, who would argue that true public goods actually are far more limited and exclude many key public services – being, essentially, only defence, law and order, standard setting, (most) highways and sanitation. But a strong case can be made for including most education and health services for a mixture of economic considerations – the externalities arising from more educated and healthy populations – and social: the sense that citizenship carries with it basic educational and health entitlements regardless of ability to pay. Liberal Democrats subscribe to that view on grounds of social justice.

But reality does not comfortably fit the ideological stereotypes. As Table 1 describes, the key public services – health, education and policing – involve a complex mixed economy of private and public sector provision and consumption. The core services of the NHS and schools are provided by public servants, free at the point of use

---

Table 1 **The mixed economy in public services**

1A Health

Consumption/production	Public sector	Private sector
Public sector	NHS training NHS staff Screening services	Training doctors/ nurses Prescription drugs at market prices Regulation
Private sector	Agency staff Cleaning and catering PFI/PPP Consultants' contracts Care homes: council nominees NHS dentistry Drug supply	Chemists: non- prescription drugs BUPA/health insurance Care homes Hospices Dentistry Chiropody Opticians Complementary medicine Health & fitness centres

1B Education

Consumption/production	Public sector	Private sector
Public sector	State schools Teacher training Universities	Training teachers FE training courses Standards and testing
Private sector	Assisted places Nurseries PFI Management contracts Some special schools	Private schooling Tutoring/extra curricular education Much vocational training

1C Law & Order

Consumption/production	Public sector	Private sector
Public sector	Policing and public sector prisons	Policing commercial events
Private sector	DNA testing PFI (police/prisons) Security guards for hospitals etc Privately run prisons	Gated communities Security industry Private detectives Insurance Burglar alarms

and on a universal basis. But there is a strong, purely private sector in health, education and policing. Apart from private schools, there is a large amount of private tutoring and music teaching, and much post-sixteen vocational training is essentially market-based; the private sector operates in healthcare, from dentistry to care homes, chiropody, complementary medicine and community pharmacies; and many buy their own private security.

There are also public sector providers to the private sector (training of teachers and doctors; standard setting and inspection bodies; policing of commercial events) and – more substantially – private sector providers of public services (PFI; contracted out ancillary or front-line – nursing and teaching – services; places for council nominees in private nursery schools and care homes).

Individual choice

The issue, therefore, is rarely one of absolute ideological clarity, but of where the shifting boundaries are and should be. There are several principles that should apply. The first is providing as much individual choice as possible, albeit within the constraints of a universal service. In health, there is a constraint: that of medical knowledge. Doctors do invariably know better than we do what treatment is appropriate. That is their professional prerogative. A traditional view is that individual choice in public services does not matter: people are citizens, not consumers; they expect, and should be given, a basic, standard, public service by their local school or local hospital. An economic liberal would be both sceptical and repelled by the proposition that, particularly in a relatively affluent and educated country where there is a cornucopia of choice in most aspects of life, there should be general contentment with such an approach. There is evidence of growing 'leakage' into the private sector by those who can afford it; surveys which show that choice is now valued above extra tax-financed spending; and experience elsewhere that when there is choice (purchase of council houses; private transport) it will be seized avidly.

One solution advocated by US conservatives and British Conservatives is to create choice by simulating a market while preserving universality through vouchers of equal value issued to all: patient 'passports' and school vouchers. While the idea is intellectually elegant, it has encountered several fundamental problems in practice. First, it is very costly because of the 'deadweight' cost of providing free services, via vouchers, for those who currently pay. Second, it cannot ensure that meaningful choice is realised in conditions where there is shortage of capacity either in general (say, an overall shortage of radiotherapists) or a specific, local resource, like a heavily over-subscribed school or hospital which cannot accommodate all those seeking to use their vouchers. Third, and related to the last point, where there is scarce capacity, the well-off will 'top up' their vouchers with cash, making meaningless the promised equality of choice.

It is clear that this is not a useful way forward in mainstream education and health, but the concept would work better where there are fewer problems of capacity shortages and there are

Table 2 Personal choice in health and education

Health

Choice	Availability
Hospital	Limited (depends on referral and PCT contract)
Doctor	Possible to change, but limited
Alternative medicine	Private, subject to licensing practitioners
Drugs	Subject to prescription and/or cost and licensing
Screening and health checks	Limited. As prescribed
Inoculation	Prescribed inoculation only (MMR)
Place of birth	Limited (home birth)
Place of death	Limited: hospices; home carers
Hospital food/ accommodation	Limited unless paid
Dental service	Mainly private
Opticians	Mainly private

Education

Choice	Availability
School	Subject to admission procedure
Syllabus	Limited flexibility in later years
Religion	Yes. Choice of religious schools
Single-sex education	Limited. Depends on LEA

more complex choices involving individual preferences. Further education and vocational education are areas where vouchers might work better, though the experience of Individual Learning Accounts was not encouraging. A more successful model, and largely disregarded by commentators, are care payments for the disabled, which enable them to purchase a package of care which suits their individual needs.

There are many other ways in which choice can be exercised actually or potentially, and one of the key elements in a liberal system should be to maximise choice within the universal, free service as well as through the market. Table 2 sketches out one of the elements of personal choice that can be exercised in health and education. In some cases, choice is an 'extra' that can be bought – like a private room in a hospital or some extra lessons in music tuition. But in some cases, the universal service should try to accommodate it: like the availability of church schools or single-sex education, or a patient's preference for giving birth or dying at home or to be treated through 'alternative medicine'.

A plurality of providers
In some respects – choice of type of school, for example – individual consumer choice carries with it an expectation that there will be a variety of providers (e.g. church voluntary aided schools as well as the Local Educational Authority schools).

In fact, some services already involve very diverse suppliers. Residential care for the elderly now involves a mixture of council voluntary sector and mutuals (like Abbeyfield) and private homes (and the last range from single family businesses to large commercial chains). All provide for a mixture of private and (means-tested) public service. Standards are indeed variable. There have been scandals of poor care and exploitative labour relations in the private sector. But a system of regulation has been put in place to counter abuse (and, arguably, is excessively onerous at least in respect of design standards). The private sector also includes excellent examples of good practice.

Liberal Democrats should be instinctively drawn to arrangements that try to obtain the best synthesis of public service

ethics and the entrepreneurship, financial discipline and professional management of the private sector; we reject the dogma-
tists of right and left who oppose one or the other on ideological
grounds. As the party's Huhne Commission report *Quality, Innovation and Choice* makes clear, experience with the private sector
in outsourcing, PFI/PPP contracts and management contracts in
health, education and police and prison services is very mixed.
There are many examples of contractual relationships which are
overcomplicated (the London underground) or carelessly specified (cleaning contracts which disregard quality) or involve insufficient risk transfer to justify private contractors' risk premium.
But these experiences are arguments for getting better value for
taxpayers' money – as some Liberal Democrat councils have done,
impressively – rather than surrendering to the idea that a public
service involves a monopoly of public sector provision.

The vision should be one in which a mixture of public sector,
private and mutually owned enterprises compete to provide mainstream services. The private sector already provides nursery, special
needs and vocational education for LEAs or government. Voluntary organisations like churches are already substantial providers
of schooling. Provided the state performs its central function of
ensuring that there is a regime for standard-setting and testing,
and providing resources to pay for a quality service, there is no
overriding reason why the state itself should provide the service.

The one area where plurality of provision is being most strenu-
ously resisted is in the NHS, where the vast majority of hospitals
remain part of a centralised system of state managed institutions.
The government's foundation hospitals were an attempt to break
away from this model but are still far too tightly controlled to have
meaningful independence. Liberal Democrats have championed
mutuality in this sector, but it would need to be recognised that the
most successful mutuals (from BUPA to the Nationwide Building

Society to Linux computer systems) are disciplined commercial operations with a strong consumer service ethos backed by tight financial control and strong management; mutuality is not a soft option.

Decentralisation

Public services require a system of governance that is both democratic and decentralised. One of the most fundamental differences between the Liberal Democrat approach and that of the Government is the latter's insistence that decision-making should be driven centrally, at ministerial level, through operational targets. The target culture has arisen in part for good reasons; as a way of progressing beyond the idea that public services merely needed to be topped up with inputs of more resources, to a more challenging preoccupation with outputs. But the failings of a system managed through multiple, changing, and often contradictory targets far removed from the concerns of the local school, hospitals or police division are now amply documented.

A more satisfactory model is one in which the strategic framework for commissioning services is set by a democratically elected authority, as local as possible – the council in respect of schools and primary care/social services; a bigger, regional body, where it exists, for tertiary education, police services, health, emergency services – and the 'providers' (schools, universities, GP practices, hospitals) are independently managed at an operational level. An inevitable consequence of decentralisation is that there is likely to be more variety, including variety of standards and conditions of employment. Critics would say that there would be more of a 'postcode lottery' and there probably would be – though less of a postcode lottery than a postcode choice. Minimum standards could be established, but the hope would be that good practice and good example based on successful experiment would drive up standards. Democratic elections at a local level, under fair voting arrangements, provide a better source of legitimacy and community involvement than any amount of ministerial direction, or quangos stuffed with government appointees.

Prevention

In health (or law and order) a key, and often missing, dimension of public policy is the desirability of preventing disease (or crime) as opposed to dealing with the consequences. Preventative approaches are often institutionally disadvantaged since they do not contribute to higher output (as opposed to better outcomes). Where prevention works, there will be fewer NHS operations carried out or drugs consumed. Fewer crimes are solved because fewer are committed. Prevention is also less professionally challenging (routine check-ups arguably being less interesting than emergency intervention or surgery; attending to street lighting and street patrols being less glamorous than chasing villains). But prevention is important for two reasons: first, it may save resources on a large scale; second, it empowers individuals by enhancing physical well-being and personal security.

The broad point has been taken by the Government, which has developed health strategies for discouraging smoking, obesity and excessive drinking. But propaganda campaigns are of doubtful efficiency and teeter on the edge of 'nannying'. A more productive approach might be a greater emphasis on screening (which currently occurs systematically for breast and cervical cancer, and for diabetes) perhaps in the form of regular 'MOT tests' that screen for a range of conditions at different ages. More intensive testing has some problems, notably false positives that create anxiety, and false negatives that undermine the credibility of testing. For this reason, the frequency and type of tests would depend on clinical advice and health economics; partly also on the resources which primary care trusts put behind the initiative. There are important consequential issues: for example, should those who respond to medical and lifestyle advice generated through regular testing be given priority in waiting lists? How much effort should be put into identifying those who regularly miss tests? But a greater emphasis on preventative, proactive approaches to health is the direction in which to go.

The size of the public sector

A further issue is the choice to be made over the overall role of taxation and public spending in the economy. Although comparisons are difficult, there is a striking difference between Sweden, where the share of national tax to gross domestic product (GDP) is 54% and the USA where it is 30% (local taxation narrows the differential somewhat). The share of national tax in GDP in Scandinavian countries, with a long history of social democratic government, is in the range 45–50%; in Germany and Holland, with a long history of conservative (Christian Democrat) and Liberal rule, a little lower (35–40%) than it is in the UK (currently just under 40%). The USA (30%) has a tax take only a little less, however, than in neighbouring Canada (35%), which has long defended its distinct identity with a greater emphasis attached to collective services (and far more than in Mexico – 18% – in spite of almost a century of 'revolutionary' government there).

Some argue that a formal limit should be fixed to the share of GDP accounted for by tax and/or public spending. Without defined limits, there is potentially an inexhaustible call on public services to meet the needs of an ageing population (pensions; healthcare), a knowledge economy (education; public information) and expectations of a higher quality of life (parks and public open space; sports and cultural facilities open to all; clean streets; greater mobility through public infrastructure). Rates of tax would then have to rise inexorably to fund higher public spending, creating problems both in terms of incentives (to work, to take risks, to save) and public tolerance. Several European countries appear to have reached such limits: Sweden and Denmark, for example.

One issue to be considered is whether it would be sensible to establish in the UK, as an additional fiscal rule, the share of public spending and/or tax in GDP. There are some obvious problems with this approach. The share fluctuates over the economic cycle for reasons that have little to do with policy preferences. There are costly, unforeseen, natural emergencies and wars. Some distinction has to be made between current spending and public investment (as occurs within the 'golden rule'). Public preferences and tolerances vary over time: in 1997 and 2001 there was a clear collective willingness to pay more for 'underfunded' public services, and while the mood has changed (with growing concerns over tax fairness and 'value for money') there is no obvious clamour for a lower tax take in the aggregate.

Despite all of these problems, there is a strong case for such a fiscal rule using present levels as an appropriate base. Attention is thereby focused on two key issues: one being how to get greater value from the same level of financial input into public services; the other being the need to define priorities. As a first, modest step down this road, Liberal Democrats propose to couch their own expenditure proposals on the basis that any increased spending commitments should be met by cutting some other area of government spending.

Value for money and spending priorities
British political debate is increasingly focused on the issue of why apparently large increases in public expenditure have not produced commensurate improvements in services. Some resources have been swallowed up in public sector pay, which had hitherto lagged

behind comparators in the private sector. Some of the increase should eventually, after years of training, filter through into an increased supply of nurses, doctors and teachers, as new recruits are attracted to these professions. This will also reduce outlays for – less satisfactory – agency and other temporary staff. But, in the short run, there is little to show for the spending. Where there has already been improved recruitment – for the police, for example – officers may increasingly be deployed in ways that meet public anxieties (through beat policing; or anti-terrorist duties) but do not necessarily reduce crime or improve detection, the most obvious measures of 'productivity'. The railways are absorbing vast sums in public subsidy, much of it to allay public fears about safety rather than delivering tangible improvements in time keeping or comfort or competitive fares. So there may be good reasons for the alleged 'failure' of public spending. And where transfers are concerned – increased child benefit or state pensions – the issue is one of redistribution of income rather than the 'output' of public services.

Getting better 'value for money' from public services is not, therefore, a straightforward matter, and some superficially attractive ideas do not stand too close a scrutiny. The complaint that the public services are employing more 'bureaucrats' rather than 'operational' staff may in particular cases be justified; but it often makes sense to hire civilian staff (or retired police officers) to do routine tasks and free up uniformed officers for priority tasks; classroom assistants can enable teachers to concentrate on what they are qualified for; doctors and consultants should be relieved as much as possible of clerical responsibilities. Public services are often inefficient because they are under-, rather than over-, managed and because insufficient attention is paid to key support services like IT and cost accounting.

There are several areas where substantial economies could be made, though none is easy or painless. First, there is not the same pressure on 'head office overheads' as obtains in the private sector. This should change. The numbers of civil servants and other head office staff, together with management staff in semi-autonomous agencies (and regulators), should be drastically pruned to reflect cuts in central 'command and control' functions. Also, staff should be relocated from London to areas where office rents are much lower; there is a longstanding government relocation policy, but it is timid and lacks radicalism. It would set an excellent example if a key department, like the Treasury, were to be relocated to – say – Liverpool, excluding a small number of staff who have to interact constantly with ministers or other government departments. There is no reason also why many 'back office' functions – routine aspects of personnel management, accounting and travel – should not be contracted out to the private sector and, if necessary, overseas if this provides 'value for money'. The Gershon Report on public sector efficiency and the Lyons Report on relocation deal in detail with these issues.

Second, there is some evidence that while procurement prac- tices have become more professional, there is often a confusion of objectives. Purchasing of IT and systems to manage it; weapons for the armed forces; drugs for the NHS; all should be single-mindedly organised to provide quality and price and not, as is often the case at present, decided through a semi-political process or some kind of industry policy. The waste of resources in defence contracting as a result of trying to farm out work to favoured contractors is massive and scandalous, and ultimately detracts from the effective- ness of the armed forces. Nor is it the job of people who purchase drugs for the NHS to consider the interests of the pharmaceutical industry; if the right drugs can be obtained more cheaply from India, then so be it.

Third, there has been a concerted effort since Mrs Thatcher's

day to maximise revenue from asset sales. Much of the sentiment surrounding public ownership and 'family silver' has gone
and the issue is now largely a pragmatic one of deciding whether
greater value can be obtained by selling assets or realising income
from them. Classic privatisation has now largely run its course,
but there is one major candidate left: the Royal Mail, currently an
incongruous combination of the collection, sorting and delivering
system, and the Counters network of local post offices. The latter
should be retained as a public service, albeit operated through
private franchisees; the former could be privatised subject to
regulation and the maintenance of the Universal Service Obligation (USO) to deliver everywhere in the UK at the same price. If
an attractive price could be obtained (the privatised Dutch Post
Office has expressed interest) the realised value could then be used
to create a trust fund from which an income could finance the
USO, the Counters network until post offices generate new sources
of income, or other communications objectives like broadband
rollout. This would be a controversial idea for Liberal Democrats
to champion; but one worth pursuing. A portion of the proceeds
of any sale could also be used to grant shares to Royal Mail
employees.

Fourth, political decisions have to be made as to what areas
of government activity should be cut to give priority to others.
A prime candidate for cuts would be the DTI and its industrial
support functions, which should be scrapped with its more useful
functions – blue skies research funding; standards and metrication;
oversight of the trading standards network – placed elsewhere.
Agricultural support should go, too, to the extent that national
discretion is allowed within the CAP.

Fifth, there are some tricky issues around public sector pay.
One is the extent to which pay rates should be uniform regardless of local labour market conditions. To some degree, the idea of

regional variations in pay is accepted in practice through the system of London weighting – though the differentials do not remotely reflect differences in living costs. Also, the use of subcontracting introduces markets into pay. The issue, however, is whether, within a much more decentralised system of public administration, pay should vary. The logic of decentralisation is that it should.

Reforming the tax system

The issue of how to reconcile economic liberalisation with concerns about social justice comes into sharpest focus in relation to the tax system. From an economic liberal standpoint, a key issue is how much freedom individuals enjoy in spending their own money. Penal rates of tax destroy that freedom. There is no absolute standard by which to gauge what are 'excessive' rates of taxation; much depends on controls and past experience. But two rather simple guiding principles should apply. The first is that the state – national government – should not take more than, say, 40% of GDP in tax (currently the share is close to this level). The second is that marginal rates of direct tax should not exceed 50% at any point in the income range. This is – necessarily – an arbitrary threshold but broadly reflects current realities.

There should also be a matching concern with social justice. Richer people should, in principle, pay a high proportion of their income in tax to correct, in part, the often extreme inequalities thrown up by earnings from employment, financial assets, property or inheritance. Yet one of the most striking features of the UK tax system is that it is not even proportional, let alone progressive. The highest 20% of income earners pay a smaller proportion of their income in tax (35%) than the lowest 20% (40%). The regressivity of the tax system derives from two factors. One is the effect of some indirect taxes, notably cigarette duty, which are justifiable on preventative health grounds, but have probably now reached levels which are counterproductive since contraband has now become a major factor. The second is council tax, which operates not quite as regressively as the poll tax, but more so than other taxes. To address the overall structure of the tax system, the Liberal Democrats propose a local income tax to replace council tax; and believe that upper income earners should pay more whether through a higher rate of tax on earnings over £100,000, the current policy, or through a loss of a variety of tax reliefs and allowances, which often favour those on higher incomes.

Second, the tax system has, under Gordon Brown, become very complex, reversing tax reforming efforts (by Nigel Lawson notably). This is partly a result of very complicated arrangements governing some particular taxes: for example capital gains tax and the climate change levy. But it is also the result of numerous attempts to 'tweak' the system through tax breaks to favour particular industries (e.g. films) or regions (e.g. differential stamp duty) or attempts to change business behaviour (e.g. R&D tax credits). A key test of an alternative set of tax policies is how far they reduce the number of taxes and simplify the system. Scrapping many of the tax reliefs; scrapping capital gains tax (and taxing accrued income instead); replacing the climate change levy with a simple, upstream carbon tax: these could be first steps.

Third, significant disincentives are being built into the tax system. The growing use of means-tested benefits increases the marginal rate of income tax on low-income earners, while the low levels of savings 'disregard' imposes high marginal rates of tax on savings on pensioners. Almost all public debate on disincentives concentrates on the top – 40% – rate, and proposals to raise it, yet little consideration has been given to the impact on low- and middle-income earners. One of the aims of tax reform should be to pull those on very low incomes (and with small savings) out of – direct – tax altogether.

Finally, there are some structural factors at work that will, in the long term, affect the tax base. The growth of mobility and easier movement of goods will make it impossible to sustain big differences in indirect taxation (international comparison was one of the factors behind the – successful – protest against rising fuel duty). Internet purchases will make other indirect taxes difficult to collect. Big differences in company taxes will trigger relocation. The 'super rich', with multiple domiciles, are likely to evade many taxes, and this is one of the practical constraints for countries in relation to very high marginal rates of income tax, above 50%. There is no evidence so far that developed countries face a revenue crisis caused by these structural changes – but this could happen.

Amongst new revenue sources there is some attraction in the slogan 'tax pollution not people', but if pollution taxes work to reduce emissions (or congestion) they may fail as a dependable revenue source; conversely, if demand is highly inelastic, there is little environmental benefit, and the dependability of revenue has to be seen against the social impact – as was consistently overlooked with fuel taxation and its impact on rural areas.

The other potential source is land (with or without property; improved or unimproved) and there is a long Liberal history of enthusiasm for such taxes. However, we have seen that council tax is both highly regressive and politically very unpopular. National property taxation that does not have the regressivity of council tax would be welcome on both revenue and wider economic grounds.

Maintaining fiscal discipline
A market economy cannot work well without financial stability. Liberal Democrats were early advocates of an independent central bank and have supported the Labour Government's introduction of one, albeit with a few quibbles about the need for stronger

safeguards to ensure that members of the Monetary Policy Committee (MPC) are fully independent.

The formal adoption of fiscal rules is also welcome, and the public debt to GDP ratio, supported by the 'golden rule' for the budget balance over the economic cycle, is appropriate and has been applied seriously. There is, however, one major flaw: the lack of independence and expertise in the evaluation of fiscal policy. The National Audit Office can review budget assumptions, but only at the request of the government, and its analysis tends, inevitably, to be stronger on audit than economic analysis. This should change. There should be a fully independent Fiscal Policy Committee, like the MPC. But it should not set tax rates in the way that the MPC sets interest rates since tax setting is a fundamentally political role. Its job would be to evaluate budget assumptions and outcomes (and publish its evaluation in a fully transparent way). Its sanctions would lie in its authority and the impact of its judgement on Parliament, public opinion and bond markets.

One remaining issue is how far national fiscal rules should be subordinate to international disciplines. Since there is a degree of 'spill-over' from one country's fiscal policy to another (or at least from major economies), there is a strong case for mutual surveillance and peer review of policy and, in extreme situations, agreed policy coordination. The IMF exists to perform this role at a global level and its authority is sadly diminished.

It is EU fiscal policy that is more relevant, given the likelihood, and desirability, of the UK joining the euro zone at some stage. As currently designed, the EU Stability Pact has excessive authority at a European level. There is a legitimate concern that one country's macro-economic policy stance can destabilise others', as occurred with German reunification. And there is some merit in establishing a peer review process around agreed benchmarks for debt and deficits. But this has to be balanced against the need for policy flexibility, especially for countries within a monetary union, allowing flexibility over the economic cycle and to deal with exceptional circumstances ('asymmetric shocks', in the jargon). The Stability Pact did not incorporate such flexibility. The threat of large sanctions is simply implausible and, if ever invoked, would never be accepted in some member countries. The pact has collapsed, in any event, and that is not a matter for regret if it can be reconstructed along more sensible lines and if it is accepted that any individual country, which is irresponsible in its management of debt, will not be 'bailed out' but will face the disciplines of the international capital markets.

A better approach would be to concentrate on process rather than outcome, requiring member states to establish national, independent and transparent fiscal policy authorities that can evaluate government fiscal performance against national and European fiscal rules. The task of the commission then becomes a more modest one of reporting on the success or otherwise of national processes and identifying genuine, major, policy 'spill-overs', with a view to getting agreed, common action on a case-by-case basis. That approach would be consistent with the more decentralised approach to the European Union sketched out above in relation to regulation, and which will be even more important in the more tightly integrated market which will be created under EMU.

6 Harnessing the market to achieve environmental goals

Susan Kramer

Introduction

The preamble to the Liberal Democrat Constitution declares: 'We believe that each generation is responsible for the fate of our planet and, by safeguarding the balance of nature and the environment, for the long-term continuity of life in all its forms.' No party places the commitment to sustainable development more centrally in its policies, requiring that 'progress meets the needs of the present generations without compromising the ability of future generations to meet their own needs'. Yet conventional wisdom, even within our own party, often treats the environment and the market as if they were mutual enemies, rather than as allies. The purpose of this chapter is to explore and debunk that myth. The principle of choice, the creativity unleashed by competition, and the safeguards derived from transparency and accountability, offer an effective route to sustainable development. In this era, when we now understand the urgency of conserving resources and countering risks on the scale of climate change, Liberal Democrats should be harnessing the power of the market to the environmental cause.

Since, over recent years, regulation and taxation have been

the primary tools for managing policy towards the environment, this chapter will try to understand their advantages and limitations in promoting environmental goals. Clearly, neither has so far been sufficient for achieving our environmental goals, and the UK economy, like every other developed economy, is far from delivering the reforms necessary for long-term sustainability. This chapter will therefore consider how we can secure change more effectively, and with greater public acceptance, by harnessing market forces, including reviewing recent experiments with 'user charging' and 'depletion/pollution trading schemes'. The chapter argues for what are now seen as 'fringe' approaches to become a central feature of Liberal Democrat thinking, and calls for further work to expand the role which market forces can play in driving forward development that is sustainable and safeguards the future of our planet.

Regulation

Almost all governments, of every political persuasion, have turned to regulation as the traditional instrument for achieving environmental goals. It is not the purpose of this chapter to say that regulation has no place. Regulatory prohibitions or limits are most effective in dealing with specific hazards, especially extreme hazards that place the society immediately and clearly at risk. Regulation is essential, for example, in setting rules for the disposal of toxic waste or ensuring safe drinking water. There still may be gaps in the process, where regulation needs to be strengthened. It is Liberal Democrat policy, for example, to require all ships carrying oil in British waters to be double hulled, a policy that seems entirely sensible. Direct regulation is at its best when controlling a relatively small number of significant risks or setting minimum standards for a process or an industry. Monitoring needs to be unambiguous, and penalties must be clearly enforceable.

Regulation, however, becomes less effective the more diffuse the goal. As protecting the environment and achieving sustainable development impacts on more and more individuals and companies, and as the process becomes one of using industry itself to find ways of making those improvements, direct regulation can turn into a very blunt instrument. Cutting congestion is a good example, since the task involves changing a whole series of individual travel, and even lifestyle, decisions. Switching to renewable energy is equally difficult to achieve through regulation, since it requires the development of yet unknown technologies and industries. Regulation is a costly approach, both for the regulator and the regulated, demanding constant monitoring. And regulation also brings with it a bureaucracy that inevitably becomes self-perpetuating and gold plating. Ultimately, the regulation route threatens to become unmanageable.

Traditional taxation approaches

Frustrated by the limitations of regulation, governments in the 1990s increasingly turned to taxation to shift their economies towards delivering sustainability – in effect, providing an economic incentive to change an undesired environmental behaviour. In the UK, tax strategies have been used primarily in transport (fuel duties and vehicle excise duty [VED]) and landfill (the Landfill Tax). The logic is an appealing one. The tax translates the cost of environmental damage or resource depletion into a cost on the user or polluter – 'the polluter pays' principle. The tax system, in theory, creates an incentive to reduce the behaviour that Government seeks to discourage – it acts as a catalyst for change by encouraging different ways of delivering the same activity or with different resources, and provides businesses with greater flexibility on how to achieve those goals.

The effectiveness of such taxation, however, has historically been limited. While high fuel duties in the UK have played a role in dampening increases in car use, for example, say compared to the USA, car use has still grown steadily. None of the tax measures has stimulated much investment in either public transport alternatives or in cleaner cars and fuels. Indeed, the UK rail and bus networks have suffered from under-investment for decades. Even the switch from leaded to unleaded fuels has been little related to the duty differential and more to the fashion for buying newer cars. Amazingly, given our duty levels, the development of UK alternatives to petrol and diesel, such as liquid petroleum gas (LPG) and bio-diesel, is well behind the USA and continental Europe.

Fuel duty is also one of the most hated taxes in the country. Public antipathy to fuel duty increases, expressed through public demonstrations and refinery blockades, grew to such a level in 2000 that the Labour Government was forced to scrap the escalator attached to road fuel duty. Much of the popular resistance was spurred by the lack of travel alternatives, particularly in rural areas, and the public's cynicism about any genuine link between the tax and a vigorous environmental policy. Vehicle Excise Duty is similarly regarded as a money raiser, not as part of an environmental strategy. After recent reforms, VED is now differentiated by CO_2 emissions, but the maximum differential of £95 is pretty marginal compared to the price of a new car. In the eyes of the public, road fuel duties and VED, which together raise some £26 billion each year for the Treasury, are revenue-raising instruments for the Treasury, and any environmental justification is regarded as a fig leaf for the Chancellor.

Landfill taxes also seem to have been of limited effect. First introduced in 1996, the Landfill Tax has always been considered too low to do much to change behaviour, and is certainly inadequate to achieve changes that would meet EU targets. The UK still only recycles 12% of municipal solid waste. An escalator formula was attached to the Landfill Tax in 1999 but has yet to really bite. Ironically, the fall in total landfill volumes in recent years has been attributable to a drop in disposal of construction materials, which are taxed at the lowest rate. The landfill regime includes provisions for landfill tax credits to support approved environmental projects, but the scheme is widely criticised as contributing too little to recycling and not being well administered. Its ability to deliver alternatives has not been significant. The tax is levied on landfill operators rather than the producers of waste – in other words, not directly on the user – which may begin to explain why its impact has been so muted. The limited impact of the Landfill Tax raises interesting questions about where in the supply chain economic penalties and incentives need to be applied.

The effectiveness of the taxation system, as traditionally conceived, in delivering environmental goals is questionable. It has played some role in providing an economic incentive for change and innovation, but at the margins rather than creating major shifts in attitude and behaviour. The use of taxation creates a conflict for Government; it is supposed to be discouraging an activity whilst simultaneously building up a dependency upon the revenue it raises. The complexity of the tax system, a mire of paperwork and bureaucracy, all too easily reduces the effectiveness of the strategy. Most importantly of all, businesses and the public often resist the raising of taxes to levels where the impact might really bite.

Perhaps most importantly, as environmental protection and sustainability become stronger imperatives, driven by international, regional and national targets, the taxation system is often an inadequate tool because it cannot deliver guaranteed outcomes. The economic value of an environmental benefit is hard to determine, and appropriate tax levels are difficult to set. Even if assessed correctly, the cost of the tax is only one of many inputs into the price of an ultimate good or service. As we have seen in the UK with transport and landfill taxes, both individual and business decisions are influenced, but the extent of the change varies greatly and is exceedingly difficult to predict in advance.

Changes in the tax approach

In an attempt to make the economic incentive of taxation more effective, the Government has begun to shift the nature of its environmental taxes and levies. Rather than revenue-raising through road fuel duties and vehicle excise duty (VED), for example, the newer levies are typically revenue-neutral. Instead of taxing high up the supply chain, as in the Landfill Tax, the levies are more directly charged to users. In 2001, the UK Government introduced the Climate Change Levy, a tax on businesses based on their energy use, although not linked to the carbon content. Concessions were negotiated for energy-intensive industries in the form of an 80% discount for 44 industry sectors that agreed to specific energy-efficiency targets. To eliminate the conflict with revenue raising, the levy was offset by cuts in National Insurance (NI) – across the board, however – and a significant portion of revenue was earmarked for an Energy Efficiency Trust. Again, the verdict has been mixed. Surveys indicate that companies, particularly those with the 80% discount, are working to improve energy efficiency, but most efforts are modest. Small- and medium-size businesses seem poorly educated about the levy and just appear to be disgruntled by a new tax. Manufacturing as a whole complains that its competitiveness has been harmed by the levy and that the service sector, which by definition has no levy to pay, has benefited more from the cuts in NI than manufacturing. Virtually all agree that the levy is too small to fundamentally shift behaviour and is swamped by the volatility in energy prices, which have typically fallen in recent years. A similar levy, with similar offsetting cuts in NI, was introduced for aggregates in 2002, but it is as yet too early to identify any impact.

The poor record of taxation, to date, as a tool to shift businesses and consumers to more sustainable ways of working and living, is something of a blow to conventional Liberal Democrat thinking. We have, over the years, proposed cuts in taxes such as National Insurance (a tax on jobs), income tax, and cuts in VAT, shifting the burden to taxes on pollution and the use of scarce resources, in the expectation that this would change behaviour quite significantly. While some make the argument that environmental taxes simply have not been high enough to lead to changes in behaviour, others like me now conclude that tax approaches are simply too blunt and inflexible to do much more than raise money for the Treasury. Economic incentives and penalties need to be far more clearly designed to impact on decision-making. It therefore makes sense to focus on how choices are actually made and to use the market's ability to influence choice, as well as to develop creative solutions, to shift decisions by both individuals and businesses on to a more sustainable track.

Experiments with market forces

Sustainable development implies limiting the overall use of scarce resources, and then providing a means to allocate access to those resources, preferably in ways that encourage more efficient use and stimulate the development of non-depleting alternatives. Governments, at least in democracies, have always been particularly poor at setting economic constraints and managing resource allocation. Neither regulation nor taxation is a very helpful tool in determining the value of a resource, and neither has been particularly effective in optimising the way resources are used. Markets, by contrast, do these things rather well provided they operate within an appropriate framework. Programmes are now being tried, in different degrees in different parts of the world, to use market forces in this way. Two of the most promising are a) user-charging schemes and b) trading schemes, creating specific markets in scarce resources.

The Congestion Charge – an example of user charging

The potential application of more defined 'market-based' instruments to achieve environmental goals took a major step forward in 2003 with the introduction of the Congestion Charge in central London. The scheme prevents no one from driving a car into the city but acts as a powerful deterrent. The charge is not prohibitive, scarcely more than a public transport ticket for the equivalent journey, but it places on the 'user' a direct cost for the congestion damage caused by the decision to drive that particular journey into central London on a working day. After six months, the scheme had been acclaimed as a success, reducing car traffic in London by more than the targeted 15% and delivering over 30% improvements in key measures of bus services (excess waiting times). Over 50% of those no longer driving into the centre are now using public transport, while most of the rest have either diverted around London, changed their travel times, or found they can use a motorbike, bicycle or their own two feet. Relatively few, about 6%, have stopped making their journeys altogether. The only identified downside has been a drop in trade for some retailers (though this remains a mixed picture, with shops on the same street reporting very different experiences and the data complicated by factors such as the drop in American tourists after 9/11).

The characteristics of the Congestion Charge make it different from other levies like VED or the Climate Change Levy, and seem to clarify what is required for a charge-type economic incentive to be effective. First, the Congestion Charge tackled a clearly perceived problem. From the early stages of the London mayoral campaign in 2000 through to the implementation of the charge in February 2003, a very public discourse took place on the state of London's traffic. The public and business generally came to agree that gridlock was unacceptable and that 'something had to be done'. When the charge was introduced, the public campaign made sure that Londoners knew what it was about, with none of the ambiguity that seems to surround most other environmental levies. Crucially, the public transport alternative was improved and expanded ahead of introducing the charge. London already had a dense Underground and bus network, albeit lacking in investment for decades. One thousand new buses were added ahead of the charge, routes redesigned, driver training upgraded and security and policing increased, while traffic control measures were put in place outside the zone. The public transport network, for all its flaws, was in a position to deliver the required additional capacity. Unlike many other levies, the charge was intended to directly and swiftly change behaviour rather than eke out a gradual shift reliant on yet-to-be-developed technologies. The logic that users would find the charge acceptable if they could see immediate success proved accurate. The charge was set at a level designed to hurt enough to create immediate change while still seeming reasonable, and with a clear willingness by the Mayor and Transport for London to increase the charge if it was not sufficient to be effective. Interestingly, the Congestion Charge is not revenue-neutral. Londoners seem willing to pay more provided the revenue is hypothecated back into a service they want for themselves – in this case, improved transport.

On the back of the success of London's Congestion Charge, new enthusiasm is growing for road-use charges on a national scale. Austria, in January 2004, introduced a distance-based user charge on HGVs (lorries), which, even at this early stage, is reporting a shift in freight transport from road to rail; it is expected to become a blueprint for a wider EU scheme. The idea of charging for use of scarce road space fits well with the notion of 'polluter pays'. Unlike the blunt instrument of road fuel tax, such a charging scheme can be designed to set the charge at low rates for rural areas, where congestion is limited, and can be adjusted up or down according to traffic flows. The Commission for Integrated Transport has outlined a scheme that would place charges on 37% of vehicle miles travelled, leading to a 44% drop in congestion (although actual traffic would decline only by 5%). The average weekday charge would be 4.3 pence per mile (the motorway average would be only 3.5 pence per mile). Typically, people find the concept acceptable provided the revenue raised is offset by scrapping VED and lowering petrol duties. The London experience, however, demonstrates that if people are being asked to make a change in behaviour they want the alternatives to be immediately available. The state of our railways and much of the bus network has to come up to reasonable scratch before, not after, we charge people to change their travel. This requires a serious commitment to new investment, primarily from government, especially if the revenue-neutral assumption is kept.

Given the experience of the UK, it is reasonable to conclude that the user-charging strategy to achieve environmental goals is only effective in specific circumstances. First, the public and business must have 'bought in' to the problem, if not the programme. Secondly, the alternatives must pre-exist for the impact to be more than muted. Thirdly, the programme needs to be designed to deliver rapid, visible change. Lastly, the Government needs the will to set the penalties at a level where they bite sufficiently to change behaviour. Where environmental change is the goal, the Treasury has to eliminate the conflict with revenue-raising, and even then the proceeds are best hypothecated to improving the environmentally preferred behaviour.

Creating a market – trading schemes

While user charging is a promising approach to changing behaviour, especially when large numbers of consumers are involved, there are many circumstances where it is unlikely to be effective. Charging is too simplistic an approach, for example, when change requires the development of new technology or demands that businesses develop new ways of operating. Efforts to tap into market forces in order to stimulate creativity have led in some industries to the creation of an actual market for the right to pollute or deplete. These rights are typically allocated or auctioned to existing businesses, but can then be bought or sold. Such mechanisms have their own limitations, and our understanding of how to design them and how to best use them still has a long way to go. Changing and adapting schemes, however, as we move up the learning curve appears to be much easier and less controversial than changing either regulation or taxes.

In order to set up a trading scheme, the value of the 'good' which is being depleted or harmed must, in some way, be recognised and made measurable, and the right to deplete or harm must be shaped into a tradable instrument. This includes:

- → identification of the 'good' at risk (e.g. the economic, environmental and social benefits at risk from climate change);
- → quantification of the risk (e.g. assessment of the contribution to harmful climate change from global CO_2 levels);
- → creation of targets to limit causes of harm (e.g. the Kyoto protocol for CO_2 emission; country targets such as set in the UK; targets set by some US cities);
- → provision of an enforcement mechanism (e.g. allocating individual CO_2 emissions quotas which can be measured and monitored);

→ creation of a trading mechanism (including identifying potential buyers and sellers, creating pricing mechanisms, and ensuring the establishment of institutions to facilitate payments, provide financing, manage risk and provide oversight).

Unlike schemes based on tax incentives, the market sets the price for the right to deplete or harm. Businesses can make money from their ability to develop less depleting and harmful processes and operations. Governments can structure each scheme to achieve the specific targets it has agreed to by treaty or determined as part of policy, combining the strength of regulation with the flexibility of economic incentives.

No scheme is without its limitations. Allowing the market to set prices for the use of resources that have formerly been 'free' can conflict with goals such as social inclusion or protecting the poor. This is no different from non-progressive forms of taxation and can be similarly offset by exemptions or pricing thresholds or subsidies. Small firms particularly object to trading schemes, arguing that by definition they have less capability to administer the process of trading or to obtain financing or manage risk; recognition of their needs must be part of the scheme design. Schemes can also tend to 'grandfather' existing players unless credits are freely auctioned and traded.

In the UK, a CO_2 emissions trading scheme was launched in 2002 as a vital element in reaching the UK target of a 20% reduction from 1990 CO_2 emissions by 2010. The Government held an auction in which it 'bought bids' from companies committed to specific emissions targets, for a total of £215 million over five years. The 34 organisations in the scheme, which between them have committed to reducing emissions by more than four million tons over the five years, can now trade emissions among themselves.

The scheme links to the Climate Change Levy, since the 6,000 companies covered by agreements under the CCL can trade in the scheme. Other companies or organisations can trade without linking their activity to an emissions reduction target, providing liquidity to the scheme. In the first year, 150 trades were executed for one million tons of CO_2. The price has varied between £12.5 and £5 per tonne. The accounting profession now expects the cost of carbon, as much as 40% of market capitalisation for an energy-intensive industry, eventually to be considered in mergers, acquisitions and disposals. The scheme has its frustrations. Proper penalties are not yet in place for those who fail to meet their targets either by reductions or purchasing emissions reductions. Declines in output from weakening manufacturing are so far accounting for more of the reductions than is energy efficiency. In the UK, schemes for trading in landfill permits and other greenhouse gases are too early in the process to be assessed.

Outside the UK, the use of trading schemes across a broad range of activities gives a feel for the extent of the potential. In Australia, a seemingly insoluble problem of salinity in the Hunter River catchment area has been solved by allocating and permitting trading of salt discharge credits. Tradability gives the credit holders the flexibility to vary their discharge while capping the total amount of salt in the river. The system trades on-line. Twenty per cent of credits expire annually to allow for new auctions. Again in Australia, water trading has permitted the application of water to more profitable uses and enabled the development of the wine industry; as water taken from rivers needs to be reduced, the trading mechanism is becoming a key allocation instrument. In the USA, sulphur and nitrogen dioxide emissions are now traded, and industry claims to have reduced pollutant levels by developing and applying new technology at a lower cost than considered feasible under a tax regime. In California and in the Pacific North-West, trading mechanisms are being developed to conserve habitat for endangered species and to protect old wood forests.

In general, a trading scheme offers advantages in that it:

→ allows choice for the polluter or user on how to deliver the required goals, with flexibility to manage preferences and capabilities;
→ harnesses creativity and makes use of the 'expertise' of the polluter or user, who is often the expert, in providing more efficient and lower-cost solutions;
→ permits Government to move up the learning curve – a scheme can be put in place for a few years and then adjusted based on experience in a world where costs, benefits and behaviours are not well understood or measured;
→ allows the polluter or user time to adapt to a market approach – schemes can start small and expand, or begin with one instrument and move on to several;
→ tends to be seen as 'fair' by both the public and businesses, arguably bringing both 'with you rather than against you'. The business community, especially, puts far more faith in the fairness of prices set by the market rather than tax rates set by Government.

Accountability and transparency

Traditionally, full economic value has not been attached to the environment, and many of what are now being recategorised as environmental and ecosystem 'goods' have been regarded as free. Carbon storage, water purification, habitat, pollination (by insects) etc. would all cost billions if not provided by nature, yet are critical to sustaining life and the quality of life. The use of markets and trading mechanisms therefore offers a major benefit in the search to enhance environmental sustainability by starting to establish widely accepted values for environmental goods. The implications of this are significant. For many years, environmental activists have been frustrated by the unwillingness of businesses to report environmental accounts alongside their financial accounts. It is a resistance that disappears once the market sets a price. Accounting firms are now considering how to represent these values in formal statements. Since 1997, and under the auspices of the United Nations, an approach known as the Global Reporting Initiative has been in development, which would put environmental and social reporting alongside traditional financial reporting. Market values for greenhouse gas emissions or waste disposal, for example, would fit very neatly into this formal reporting. Under the old maxim of 'what you count, you manage', this shift in accounting should stimulate far greater environmental awareness among businesses. It is then logical to argue that if environmental costs can be measured at the level of an individual firm, they can be measured at the level of a national economy. By using the markets to make environmental values explicit, we gain an effective mechanism for measuring and monitoring the progress of our economy in terms far broader than just financial benchmarks like GDP. Such explicit measures can change attitudes, leading the public to demand that governments shift policy towards sustainable development. The same mechanisms also provide many of the tools to achieve such goals.

Policy and direction

Harnessing market forces is an attempt to bring the business and the environmental communities together to reframe the traditional 'either/or' view of sustainability and development. This creates an instrument that motivates business to take account of the environment. Government sets the framework. Market mechanisms over time then lead to full cost pricing and force producers to take responsibility. The expectation, for example, both that companies report environmental accounts and that actual market values in an acquisition or disposal will adjust to reflect factors like carbon use, shows how far thinking has changed. Just as the UK scheme for CO_2 trading will merge into a broader EU scheme in 2007, markets will expand beyond national boundaries. The Government, in time, will have to explicitly measure and explain its environmental performance to the people and to other nations.

All of this fits ideally with Liberal Democrat thinking. We believe fundamentally in sustainable development but we have always valued choice, flexibility and creativity in the search to achieve our goals. We prefer market-driven solutions to central government direction. Our challenge now is to expand our thinking into these new ways of harnessing market forces. Regulation will always have a place in managing the environment, especially where health and safety issues are key. Taxation incentives are likely to play at least a bridging role as we find better approaches. But we need to explore the potential for user charging as a substitute for fuel taxes to manage the demand for road space. Charges for household waste collection should probably shift to a user basis, accompanied by conservation and recycling schemes to enable households to virtually eliminate their waste and their costs. Trading schemes for the emission of greenhouse gases and other pollutants could be expanded much more rapidly to accelerate our response to climate change. Similar schemes might well be used to encourage developers to prefer brownfield over greenfield sites, or to give farmers an incentive to protect biodiversity. The opportunity to trade airport landing slots may play a part in weaning the airline industry off its addiction to ever-expanding airports. We face a steep learning curve, but as we recognise the importance of sustainable development, market mechanisms offer the most promising tools to get us to efficient, effective and widely accepted solutions. The Liberal Democrats, with our commitment to sustainability and our preference for markets over government control, are uniquely placed to take this thinking forward.

7 UK health services: a Liberal agenda for reform and renewal

David Laws

Introduction

All political parties in Britain seem presently to be agreed that the National Health Service (NHS), in spite of its many and continuing successes, is failing to deliver a standard of health service which lives up to the aspirations of today's generation of British citizens.

There is, of course, significant disagreement between, and within, political parties about the right solution to this problem.

The purpose of this short chapter is to seek to understand the present failings of the NHS, and then to sketch out a Liberal alternative for the future.

The traditional ('economic liberal') liberal commitment to the principles of choice, competition and decentralisation, as well as to the value of the private and voluntary sectors, should provide a good starting point for the Liberal Democrats to think constructively and radically about a reform agenda. Such an agenda should surely seek to exploit the power of choice and competition, in terms of delivering better services, in an efficient manner.

The economic liberal heritage of our party should mean that we are better placed than the Labour Party to rethink whether the current, cumbersome, centrally directed public sector monopoly that is the NHS is really the best way to deliver health services in the 21st century.

But, in addition to this, the Liberal Democrats' strong and long-standing commitment to 'social liberalism' – including equality of access to essential services regardless of ability to pay – makes us well placed to consider such reforms without compromising the basic principles on which the NHS was founded.

This means that Liberal Democrats should have the ability to make proposals for reform with greater boldness and confidence than the Conservative Party, which is hampered by the public perception that for the Conservative Party, 'reform' means only better services for the affluent minority.

The challenge

The present performance of the National Health Service is open to criticism in a variety of different ways.

Firstly, and most fundamentally, health outcomes in the UK are generally poor compared with other major developed economies. The Government's own Wanless Report[1] accepted this critique – citing shorter female life expectancy, high infant mortality and poor survival rates for cancer as just a few of the examples of poor health outcomes in the UK.

Secondly, long waiting times for diagnostic tests, consultant-to-consultant referrals, and inpatient and outpatient appointments are endemic in the NHS. Many people wait months, or even years, for important operations and diagnostic tests, and it is far from unheard-of to wait up to two years for a consultant appointment.

Long waiting times are undesirable not only because they increase anxiety for patients – they also add to pain, inflate the NHS drugs budget and social care budgets, increase risks to health, reduce people's quality of life and employment prospects, and damage the chances of full recovery after treatment. Long waiting times are unhealthy, cruel and costly.

Even though waiting times for inpatient and outpatient appointments have recently fallen, there are still some 413,000 people waiting over thirteen weeks for an outpatient appointment, and some 330,000 people waiting over three months for an inpatient operation (as at the end of March 2004).

As for diagnostic waiting times and consultant-to-consultant referrals, nobody even knows how many people are waiting and for how long – as the Government presently neither centrally collects nor therefore reports these figures.

Some of the longest waiting times in the NHS are for these diagnostic tests and consultant referrals, yet all the political pressure is for reductions in the inpatient and outpatient waiting times – as the other waiting times lack measurement and targets.

Long waiting times add to the unfairness of the NHS, as only those with access to private sources of finance can afford to escape the waiting lists by seeking treatment in the private sector. This private sector treatment is often with the same consultant it would take six months or a year to see on the NHS.

A third problem is that patients often have a poor 'customer' experience within the NHS. As well as enduring long waits for treatment and consultation, patients are offered little choice over treatment locations or appointment times and dates. Operations are often cancelled at short notice due to capacity constraints.

Patients are frequently treated in poor-quality buildings, many of which date back to before the founding of the NHS. Hospital wards often include an excessive number of beds for an age when patients aspire to higher standards of privacy and care.

Indeed, NHS patients are too often cared for by staff who are under intense time pressure due to capacity and staff constraints, and who therefore do not give enough attention to basic care and communication with patients and families. In too many hospitals, standards of food, hygiene and care are below what many people would expect.

In short, NHS patients are all too often treated not as 'customers' whose needs must be attended to, but as the passive recipients of a second-rate state monopoly service.

Fourthly, the NHS is so stretched financially that it is often unable to provide the full range of health services that would be regarded as 'standard' in other countries. New technology can take many years to 'roll out' within the NHS.

Another striking example is access to NHS dentistry. In some parts of the country, it is necessary to travel long distances to find an NHS dentist who will treat new adult patients. This has reduced access to dentistry for many people – particularly those on lower incomes who cannot afford private care or travel costs.

The problem has been exacerbated by the system of remuneration in NHS dentistry, which is regarded by dentists not only as insufficiently generous, but also irrational – traditionally rewarding dentists for filling teeth, instead of for preventing decay.

Dentists have, unsurprisingly, left the NHS and gone increasingly into private practice – something to which successive governments have turned a blind eye. The patient lists of NHS dentists are often twice the size of private practice lists. As a consequence, the lack of time for treatment, the low level of remuneration, and the bizarre incentive structure for remuneration, must all raise questions about the quality of some NHS dental care.

Finally, perhaps because of these pressures on the NHS, the NHS has remained fundamentally a sickness service – not a health service. There is very little priority given to prevention instead of cure.

Road vehicles have a regular 'MOT' to anticipate problems

before they arise, but in the NHS customers are unlikely to be seen by the service until they get sick.

In the NHS, it is possible to be registered with a GP for twenty or thirty years, but he or she may never see the patient for that entire period of time unless the patient gets ill and approaches the GP. The NHS seems to think that its preventative role is an optional extra, not a core requirement.

Who loses?

Who suffers from this poor quality of service provided by the NHS?

One set of 'losers' are the staff, of course, who often have to work under intense pressure, in some cases for modest pay. More fundamentally, of course, all those who use the NHS suffer in one way or another – but those on low incomes may well suffer most.

People on low incomes are least likely to have private medical insurance, are least likely to be able to purchase private sector treatments when NHS waiting lists are excessive, and are least likely to be able to afford private dentistry when NHS dentistry is unavailable. Lower income groups may well also be higher users of NHS services, as many health problems seem, in part, to be related to income deprivation and its side effects.

Those on low incomes are therefore more likely to need NHS services, are often less vocal in having their complaints heard and attended to, and are much less likely to be able to opt out of the NHS service where this is failing to deliver.

The underlying problems

Why does the NHS perform so badly in so many key areas?

There appear to be a number of problems. The first is financing, and therefore resources. The NHS has consistently received lower levels of funding than most other health services in developed economies.

According to the Wanless Report, the cumulative underspend on the NHS, compared with the European Union, is £267bn over the period of 26 years from 1972 to 1998 (on an income-weighted basis).

The NHS has to compete with other areas of public spending for money, and has gone through successive periods of 'boom' and 'bust' funding, based on the state of the economy and the political party in office. As a consequence, it has fewer doctors and nurses per head of population than other developed economies, relies on older buildings, has a shortage of equipment (for example, for diagnostic testing), and has under-invested in information and communications technology.

The second problem is linked to the first problem – and it is the fundamental lack of capacity. The NHS, as a large monopoly employer keen to keep down costs, has been successful – too successful – in reducing beds and in holding down pay. As a consequence, there are endemic staff and bed shortages. 'Winter flu' crises frequently lead to cancelled operations and rocketing waiting times due to lack of capacity.

Here is an area where 'efficiency', defined as low wages and high bed usage, actually contributes to severe delivery problems.

The third weakness of the current NHS model is the lack of choice and competition. Without these, there is little momentum to drive up standards. In what service would it be possible to offer a two-year waiting time, if there were competition? The customer is too often treated as the captive recipient of a second-rate state monopoly service, because that is precisely what he or she often is.

In place of choice and competition, the Government has introduced NHS targets. But these cannot cover all aspects of NHS care, and too often they end up merely distorting priorities.

NHS complaint procedures are often ineffective or counter-productive ('we don't want to upset the consultant'), and in practice there is usually only one alternative – paying 100% of the cost by going private. This is an 'alternative' that is available to few people. The consequence of lack of choice and competition is, therefore, poor customer service standards and acceptance of intolerable delays and waiting.

The lack of choice and competition is not just a problem because of the NHS's monopolistic position. The problem is worse because of the lack of incentives within the NHS for hospitals to compete to attract patients.

Money does not usually move with patients, therefore hospitals often have little incentive to attract new patients. Indeed, a hospital which is struggling to deliver Government waiting-time targets may decline to take patients from another, failing, local hospital because this would result in missed targets rather than more cash!

The fourth problem of the NHS is inefficiency. In truth, we know all too little about how efficient or inefficient the NHS is. Some recent evidence does suggest that private sector providers are more efficient than the NHS, though reliable comparisons are always difficult to obtain. Cost comparisons need to take into account fixed costs; non-clinical standards of care; and the effects of economies of scale.

The NHS has little competitive pressure on it, for the reasons set out above. However, it is also quite successful, perhaps 'too successful', in holding down staff pay (two-thirds of costs) and in maximising the use of its capacity (bed utilisation rates are phenomenally high).

The NHS might be imagined to have the problems of inefficiency that would result from any state monopoly provision of a good or service. For example, imagine if cars were considered to be a basic necessity, and that the state decided to become the monopoly provider of cars to 'keep costs down and reduce the social stigma of automative inequality'. Taxes would be raised to provide a standard, low specification car for every household. Households not wanting the state car would have to buy privately at the full cost.

What might be expected? The state car would probably be low-cost, due to the low specification and mass production. But what would its quality be like, and its reliability? Would the state invest the resources to improve the car and introduce new technology?

The state car might be low-cost, but not necessarily very good quality or reliable – and low cost might be a poor proxy for 'efficiency'. A private company might be able to provide the low-quality product at even lower cost, or at least might be found to be more efficient on a 'quality adjusted' basis.

The point is that 'low-cost' and 'efficiency' are not the same. Recent research suggests that the NHS may be relatively low-cost, but inefficient.

The fifth problem is political interference, which can lead to expensive changes in policy, time-consuming reporting requirements, and distorted priorities. The Secretary of State for Health has been responsible for running a service which employs one of the largest numbers of people in the world – around 1.3 million at the latest count. There must be serious doubt about how effectively a huge political bureaucracy, with its rapid changes of direction and focus, can really run a national healthcare system.

The vision

So, what is our Liberal Democrat vision for the future of health services in Britain?

Obviously, at a minimum, our vision must be of a health service that addresses the weaknesses identified above. More specifically, most Liberals would be likely to agree on a vision based on these core criteria and principles.

1. *Increased resources to match increased demands.* Any new health scheme must bring in additional cash to improve health services, and to meet the needs of an ageing population, more expensive medical technology, and higher consumer aspirations. This suggests the need for a closer connection between the money we pay in to the Exchequer for health services, and the levels of spending on health services.

2. *Access for all.* There must be access for everyone in the population to the standard – high quality – health service package of clinical services, regardless of ability to pay. The success of any new system of health provision must be judged as much by how it provides for those on low incomes as by how it caters for the needs of the better-off.

3. *Fairness.* Financial contributions to our health services should be clearly related to ability to pay, and unrelated to risk characteristics such as age, disability, health problems, etc.

4. *Choice.* Consumers must be offered choices, so that they have a good chance of securing the standard of service they want – punishing poor performance and rewarding good performance. Choice could also mean looking at the scope for variations in non-clinical services, where people are willing to pay for such variations. Efficient allocation of consumer incomes means maximising people's ability to spend their money as they think fit. If people would rather spend their own money on enhancing access to non-clinical services, rather than on a foreign holiday, they should be allowed to do so.

5. *Timely treatment.* People must be seen quickly. Long waits must become a distant bad memory.

6. *Competition.* Competition must help to keep costs under control, as well as to widen choice and reduce waiting times. This means more competition within the NHS, and more provision from the private and not-for-profit sectors, where this delivers quality treatment and is good value for money. The state must fund health services on behalf of its citizens, but it need not provide them itself.

7. *Cost control.* Some healthcare systems are notoriously poor at controlling costs. The NHS, however, is often seen as being 'too successful' at cost control. Cost control is an important issue given the international trends in health costs.

8. *Patients, not politicians, in control.* The service must respond to patient needs, not to unstable, short-term, political imperatives.

The alternatives

There seem to be four basic alternative models, in terms of the future organisation of UK health services. This section sets out these alternatives and looks at how they might deliver on the above eight core principles.

1 *A better-funded status quo*

There are people within the Labour Party and within the trade unions who argue that all that is needed to improve the NHS is a better-funded status quo. These individuals are actively opposed to more choice and competition in the NHS because they believe that such 'market mechanisms' cannot be consistent with delivering the aspiration of high-quality treatment available to all on the basis of need, as opposed to ability to pay.

There seems little reason to doubt the commitment of these people to delivering more resources for the NHS, paid for fairly out of general taxation. The fairness test is therefore passed, but is the test of 'more resources to meet increased demand' necessarily passed?

The answer must surely be 'no'. The test is not whether a few people in the trade unions or the Labour Party are committed to better funding of the NHS, but whether the favoured system is likely to secure these extra resources over time.

The problem is that it is precisely the existing system of funding the NHS that has failed to deliver the necessary finance for most of the past sixty years. The existing period of sustained increases in NHS funding looks more like the exception than the rule, and (without significant improvements in service delivery) there is good reason to believe that the public will call a halt to the rapid increases in overall public spending.

To the extent that the funding test isn't passed, the access test is also potentially compromised – for the reasons set out above. Nobody can doubt the commitment of those who favour this model of delivery to the principle of access for all – but we have already seen how this principle has been compromised because of inadequate funding. Any robust system of funding our health services cannot be reliant on one part of one political party holding power over the entire period of any comparison with alternative health systems.

If the 'better-funded status quo' potentially fails on the funding test, it certainly fails on most of the other tests – choice, patient control, competition and timely treatment. Only on 'cost control' are there reasons for believing the present system may be a success, but this very control has led to other problems within the NHS – with staffing, technology and capacity.

So this potential solution scores well only on fairness and cost control; poorly on choice, competition, timely treatment, and patient control; and unimpressively on funding and access.

2 *Investment and reform*

'Investment and reform' is shorthand for the policies of the present Government – according to the present Government! These policies have changed over recent years, not least in relation to the earlier obsession with central targets.

At present, Government health policy can be understood to mean: rapid rises in real health spending out of general taxation; a modest loosening of central government control over some hospitals; greater use of the private sector to deliver more capacity and value for money; and an emphasis on greater choice, delivered through primary care trusts.

These policies continue to score well in relation to 'cost control' and 'fairness', but they are open to the same criticisms on the funding test as the 'better-funded status quo' option.

Essentially, the argument set out in the Wanless Report was that the current NHS funding system is the best system in the developed world, which just happens to have delivered some of the worst health and funding outcomes in the developed world!

The Chancellor does not appear to have seen the inconsistency. How can a particular funding mechanism be regarded as a success when it has delivered a £267bn funding gap over just 26 years, compared with the rest of the EU?

The reservations over the issue of funding mean that we must also qualify the 'access' and 'timely treatment' conclusions.

On 'competition', the initial indications are that the Government is willing to allow some competition within the NHS funding structure, but there will be no competitive alternative to the NHS itself. In other words, the hope is that there will be 'intra-monopoly' competition.

The Government wants the NHS to use the private, not-for-profit and overseas sectors to increase its capacity and to keep down costs, and there will be greater incentives for hospitals to 'win business' from non-catchment Primary Care Trusts (PCTs).

But there will be no alternative to the NHS, no competition on price, and a reliance on PCTs to introduce this competition. Where PCTs opt not to proceed with competitive alternatives, there is no obvious 'sanction' they face.

There is, as yet, little evidence that PCTs are successfully taking over as purchasing champions for the consumer, as opposed to organisers and coordinators of local NHS primary care services. Patient control and patient choice are therefore limited. Patients are reliant on PCTs to deliver choice; they cannot choose for themselves; they cannot opt for another state-funded provider other than the NHS; they cannot choose to join another PCT; and they cannot exercise choice in relation to non-clinical services.

The suspicion must be that the Secretary of State (who will continue to decide how much autonomy can be granted to different institutions) and the NHS bureaucracy (of varying quality and ideological orientation) will continue to call the shots, rather than the patients themselves.

So 'investment and reform' scores well on fairness and cost control; better than the 'status quo' on competition and therefore on timely treatment; scores unimpressively on funding and access; and is very weak on patient choice and patient control.

3 A passport to the private sector

This section deals with the private sector alternative to NHS provision.

There are a number of potential private sector alternatives. One option is increased incentives for more private medical insurance cover.

Private medical insurance incentives generally have high 'deadweight costs', with the cost to the taxpayer of the tax relief being higher than the cost savings from people not using the state health services. These deadweight costs would then potentially reduce the funding available for the 'majority' state-funded service.

An alternative would be to require people to take out private medical insurance, with access to a state-funded service only for those people on low incomes – such as the unemployed and those on benefits.

Such a system might well have the same strengths and weaknesses as the US healthcare system. The US health system scores well on funding, with one of the highest shares of gross domestic product (GDP) in the world being spent on health services. Patient choice will generally be high, competition will be maximised, and political control reduced. Waiting times for operations are generally low. However, access is potentially severely compromised for those on low incomes, and fairness also scores badly. The US health system also has a severe problem with cost control.

Overall, US healthcare outcomes suggest that a significant minority of the population experience poor health outcomes in spite of the very high level of national spending on healthcare. The US healthcare system therefore represents a costly way of delivering high-quality medical care for a part of the population, while many people on lower incomes have to make do with second- or third-class medical care and cover.

In the UK, the Conservative Party has recently proposed an alternative, more modest, private sector solution. This is the 'patient passport', which appears to be designed as a way of escaping from some of the perceived problems with systems that rely on private medical insurance.

Under the patient passport scheme, the NHS apparently remains much as it is, but patients experiencing long waits or unsatisfactory treatment would be able to take a portion of the cost of their treatment as a 'voucher' or 'passport' to use in the private sector.

The patient passport is therefore a passport out of the state sector and into the private sector.

The scheme will clearly assist some people who do not wish to wait for an operation in the NHS but who could not otherwise afford to access private treatment. However, the scheme also has some obvious and serious deficiencies.

→ There are likely to be significant deadweight costs if people can access the passport quickly. Many people who would have paid for private treatment anyway will now receive a 'windfall gain'. The only way of reducing the deadweight costs is to make the passport accessible only after a long wait – but this reduces its significance as a policy and cuts the number of people who can benefit.

→ In a cash-limited system, with significant staffing and resource restraints, some people taking their 'passport' (and hence NHS cash) to 'go private' may well mean other people waiting longer for their treatment. In other words, the patient passport could well prove to lift some people up the waiting list escalator – but only by pushing others down a step or two.

→ By its very nature, many people who need faster treatment may still not be able to access it because they will not be able to afford the top-up to the patient passport.

→ The policy will therefore do nothing to address the wider problems of long waits within the NHS, and will do relatively little to increase competition, patient choice and control, and resourcing.

→ Finally, the policy could deter people from taking out private medical insurance, by offering bigger state subsidies for those who buy private treatments instead of paying for insurance.

It is therefore difficult to disagree with the conclusion of David

Green, the Director of the think-tank Civitas, who wrote in *The Times* (6 June 2003) that:

> ... the Conservative policymakers have adopted the rhetoric of choice but failed to see that their 'patient passports' retain the worst elements of collectivism – central direction and public sector monopoly – while increasing officially sanctioned shortcuts for those who can afford them. The NHS does not need more escape routes for people with ready cash, it needs a radical transformation to make freedom of choice and pluralistic provision a reality for everyone.

Mr Green goes on to describe the policy as ' ... little more than an electoral ploy to persuade middle-income voters captured by Labour that the Tories will provide them with new ways of circumventing the NHS rationing that the majority have to put up with'.

Even the *Wall Street Journal*, in a leader article (26 February 2004), commented that ' ... the Conservatives' approach to healthcare reform merely tinkers with the existing system ... '

Neither the 'patient passport' nor additional private medical insurance therefore seem to offer a way ahead which meets the basic principles set out above.

The only plausible role the 'patient passport' concept could play would be to act as a backstop guarantee of basic waiting time commitments within the NHS. However, in order to ensure equality of treatment between people on very different incomes, the 'passport' would need to be for 100% of the cost.

This would mean, for example, that someone waiting one year for an operation under the NHS would be able to 'go private' after one year, with the entire cost paid by the NHS. This could act as a useful 'discipline' on NHS delivery, with a heavy penalty for failure to provide an adequate service. But there would still need to be care taken to avoid establishing ambiguous incentives for NHS consultants working both privately and for the NHS.

4 A national health insurance scheme

I have called the fourth alternative a 'national health insurance scheme', borrowing the name itself from Deepak Lal.[2] The proposal is essentially for a far-reaching reform, which can be regarded as being similar to a system of competing social insurance schemes, with the existing NHS service representing one of the competing options (as well as the default option). In other words, the proposal is about potentially radical change, but delivered in an evolutionary manner.

The proposed system would be broadly similar to some of the social insurance systems in use in continental Europe, but it would seek to avoid some of the problems associated with particular schemes. In addition, the proposed system would be designed to grow out of, and alongside, the existing NHS provision.

The proposed national health insurance scheme would have the following basic characteristics.

→ Every citizen would be a member of the National Health Insurance Scheme (NHIS) – either within the NHS itself or an alternative insurance provider. The alternative providers could be private, not-for-profit or voluntary sector, including unions, employer groups or mutuals. The insurers could either provide their own services or buy these in.
→ Insurers would have to accept any applicant, regardless of health risk characteristics. All citizens would have a smart NHIS entitlement card, with medical record details contained on this.
→ Every citizen would be entitled to change scheme at the end of each full year.

→ Every scheme would levy the same maximum annual charge for membership, for a standard range of all mainstream clinical services. Additional charges could be paid by those people willing to pay for higher quality non-clinical services, such as private rooms. Such 'enhancement' charges would be set by each health insurance provider.

→ The state would pay the annual charge for each citizen for the full range of clinical services. Over time, this might well need to rise to accommodate higher expectations and the rising costs and potential of medical technology.

→ The state would pay for these annual charges by levying an NHIS tax on income, so people would also contribute to the scheme on a progressive basis. The NHIS tax would replace a portion of income tax/national insurance contributions. The scheme would not include any increase in existing employer contributions.

→ The Secretary of State for Health and his department and agencies would only be responsible for the overall regulation of health services; for licensing the social insurance (NHIS) providers; and for setting the nature and terms of the full package of clinical services. The Government would cease to manage the NHS on a daily basis.

→ Members of the NHIS who stayed with the NHS itself would be members of a local NHS scheme, based on health authority boundaries or on (larger) primary care trusts. People would be entitled to switch between different NHS provider schemes.

→ The annual NHIS maximum charge would be set by an independent office of the NHIS, which would be responsible for calculating the charge needed to deliver the full health service specification of clinical services. There would be a separate, independent, NHIS inspectorate – which would publish information on insurer standards and performance.

Such a scheme would directly address the key principles set out above; there would be significant choice as well as competition; an absence of political interference; access for all; better funding; fairness; a clearer link between funding and the service provided; timely treatment; and stronger incentives for cost control.

Naturally, the transition from the existing state monopoly service to the system described above would take time, and involve transitional costs – but the rewards would be very significant.

This proposal builds upon existing Liberal Democrat policy in relation to the NHS – including our proposals to decentralise delivery of NHS services; fund the NHS through a hypothecated NHS tax; increase choice for patients; and involve non-state providers, including the not-for-profit sector, the private sector and mutuals.

Conclusion

The NHS is failing to deliver a health service that meets the needs and expectations of today's population. A 'better-funded status quo' or the modest 'investment and reform' agenda of the present government will both fail to address the key problems facing the NHS.

The Conservative proposals on patient passports are poorly designed, leave most of the NHS unreformed, and would benefit only an affluent minority of the population.

This country should be looking at some of the experiences of those European nations who succeed in delivering health services with greater choice and competition than our own, but also with better health outcomes and fairer access for lower income groups. There is no justification at all for associating additional choice and competition with greater inequalities in service provision.

The Liberal Democrats have an opportunity to marry the prin-ciples of our economic liberalism with our commitment to social liberalism. The Labour Party has failed to embrace economic liberalism. The Conservatives have refused to accept social liberalism. The Liberal Democrats should champion and help to fashion a new 'national health insurance scheme', which could deliver a better quality health service for our country without compromising our aspiration to improve access and quality for every single citizen.

Indeed, only such a radical reform of the funding and organisation of our health services is likely to deliver a high quality of service for those on lower incomes – who are presently those who pay the highest price for NHS failure.

Notes

1. Derek Wanless, *Securing our Future Health: Taking a Long-Term View, Interim Report*, November 2001.
2. Sheila Lawlor, Greg Baum, Jean-Louis Beaud de Brive and Deepak Lal, 'A National Health Insurance Scheme', in *Systems for Success: Models for Healthcare Reform*, Politeia, 2004.

8 Tough liberalism: a liberal approach to cutting crime

Mark Oaten

The central tenet of Liberal Democrat philosophy is liberalism. For all the disagreements about what is and is not 'liberal', liberalism embraces one key concept – that people should be free from unnecessary burdens, including those from the state. This principle also applies to how 'free' citizens feel in the conduct of their day-to-day lives in other contexts. How free is someone if he fears walking down his own road late at night? How free is someone who is loath to go to the local shopping mall because of the menace of local thugs? How free is someone who knows that his attacker will be out of prison and roaming the streets, and no less likely to reoffend – as most prisoners do? These anxieties are common sentiments. And let us be clear how far our prisons make the country safer: of 18- to 21-year-olds in prison, 71% will come out and commit a new crime. That's bad value for the taxpayer, poor safety for the victim, and an endless merry-go-round of crime and punishment for the criminal.

Liberal Democrats aim to maximise freedom, and this applies to the perpetrator and victim alike. It is the responsibility of government to ensure that its citizens are free from fear of crime, which profoundly affects people's quality of life. It is also the job of government to remove, then rehabilitate, that element in society that is restricting other people's liberty – the criminals.

This seems simple enough, but in a cynically populist attempt to win favour with more hard-line parts of the press, New Labour has capitulated and 'got tough on crime' – which translates into longer sentences, overcrowded prisons and prisoners doing less. These prisoners, at present, spend most of their time sitting in their cells all day, and leave prison no less likely to reoffend.

The problem is, whether we like it or not, prison invokes highly emotive images to the electorate of punishment and retribution, with which people can easily associate as fairness or justice for crimes committed. The task for Liberal Democrats is to explain that tough prison sentences are those that actually cut reoffending. Since politics is ultimately about selling ideas, it is my vision to develop new, innovative policies that are liberal but not perceived as soft: 'tough liberalism'.

If we are to improve the quality of life of our citizens, then we need to improve the way our prisons are run: if we can turn offenders' lives around then clearly they are less likely to reoffend and less likely to restrict the liberty of the majority of law-abiding citizens by committing more crime. The key to maximising the liberty of citizens is, put simply, to have less crime and fear of crime: this means constructing a prison system that succeeds in steering offenders away from crime, not one that just churns out more criminals. The entire British prison system is based on the dubious premise that prison works – it doesn't. My vision for a major overhaul of the prison system has at its heart the system's resuscitation.

The British prison system is caught between the two mutually reinforcing problems of overcrowding and reoffending. A vicious cycle has been created in which overcrowding reduces the chances of offender rehabilitation. Consequently, reoffending rates have been increasing, a problem which has led to higher numbers of prisoner incarcerations, thus worsening the problem of over-crowding. This situation is spiralling out of control: the capacity of Britain's prisons is currently 66,671 prisoners – but it is predicted that by 2009 there will be over 109,000 prisoners in the prison system. Swift and effective action must be taken to prevent the prison system from sinking even further into chaos.

It is clear that despite the Government's 'tough on crime' rhetoric, the state of the British prison system continues to deteri-orate rapidly. It is my belief that this situation has been caused by a failure to properly identify – and to formulate – innovative responses to the problems facing Britain's prisons. This chapter will therefore outline a new blueprint for Britain's prisons, inspired by European prison successes and informed by consultation with both prisoners and staff, through the proper identification of the problem and an examination of my proposed solution to it. This solution consists of five key elements: Justice – for the victims of crime, both individuals and communities; Assessment – a compre-hensive, electronic assessment procedure to identify offenders' needs; Learning – a focus on education, particularly numeracy and literacy; Exit – a multi-agency approach to prisoners' release for smooth settlement, and Employment – the culmination of the aforementioned procedures. Only by reforming 'jail' to JALE[1] can we succeed in cutting reoffending and overcrowding, and create a prison service fit for the 21st century.

The problem

Over twelve years after the publication of Lord Justice Woolf's report on the Strangeways riot, British prisons are more over-crowded than ever. Despite this landmark document, it appears the lessons of Strangeways have still not been learned. The UK now has the highest imprisonment rate in the European Union – with our prison population currently at its highest ever recorded level. That population has grown by 71% in the past twelve years, despite evidence showing that both overall crime and the number of prosecutions have fallen over the same period.

The current prison population stands at 74,055.[2] However, as noted earlier, the total capacity of British prisons is 66,671.[3] This causes a myriad of problems for the prison system as it struggles to accommodate all prisoners by moving them around to different parts of the prison estate and different parts of the country, in order to use up every inch of available space. This process, frequently occurring now that the prison system has exceeded its total capacity, is known as the 'churn effect', and it has an incalculable effect on prison life.

What has become a merry-go-round of transferred prisoners is not only wasting the time and resources of the prison system, but is also hugely disruptive for the prisoners themselves: educational and drug rehabilitation courses are stopped midway through and prisoners are sent hundreds of miles from their families and homes. Often moved with only hours' notice, it is not surprising that prisoners often feel more unsettlted than when they entered the prison system.

The churn effect has undoubtedly contributed to the increasing failure of the prison service to meet nine of its fifteen Key Performance Indicators (KPIs) – which monitor such things as time spent in purposeful activity and the incidence of assaults.

Understandably, the pursuit of pre-release focus is diminished in such a situation – simply coping in these circumstances becomes a prison's overriding priority. Unfortunately, the net effect of imprisonment on prisoners becomes negative, and incarceration for rehabilitation becomes a self-defeating act.

Instead of tackling these problems, the current government

is merely postponing the action needed by expanding capacity through prison building. Last year, the Home Office announced an extra £275m to help expand the prison estate and deliver an extra 2,320 prison places across Britain. This policy, however, is no panacea; it is at best a medium-term solution since capacity is filled as quickly as it is created.[4] Moreover, current projections of prison population suggest that this policy is not sustainable: although the prison capacity is expected to rise to 78,700 by 2006, current projections suggest there could be 91,000 inmates by then.

Given our knowledge of the relationship between reoffending and overcrowding, the future for the prison service under the present government's penal policies looks grim. Policies that merely tackle the symptoms of the problem and fail to target the causes of reoffending, and therefore overcrowding, are doomed to fail, and empirical evidence demonstrates that they have done: between 1993 and 2000, the rates of reconviction within two years had increased from 53% to 58%. This problem is particularly virulent among young offenders with short sentences, of whom a staggering 92% will be reconvicted within two years. Most worryingly, this statistic only reflects those reconvicted; it is estimated that only one in five offences results in a conviction. Considering the magnitude of the problem of reoffending – released prisoners are responsible for at least one million crimes per year – the Government's target for cutting reoffending rates seems woefully inadequate: it aims for a reduction of only 5%.

The solutions
Justice
Victims of crime invariably feel an immense sense of injustice. In many cases, prison is clearly the most appropriate way to deal with this injustice: not only is it punitive but it provides communities with freedom from the individuals who have menaced them.

215

Understandably, however, victims of crime and local communities increasingly feel that justice is not being served. Where is the justice for victims when a repeat offender emerges after only a six-month sentence more likely than ever to reoffend? Without rehabilitation – which requires longer sentences – there is no justice. The statistics support this observation: short-term prisoners make up only 17% of the prison population and yet comprise 65% of prisoners discharged from the prison system each year.

The short, sharp shock approach in prisoner sentencing is not working. Most prisoners leave with no form of post-custodial assistance, to find that they have little chance of employment or a stable home – a situation more disruptive than their prison sentence itself. The only effective solution for this situation – providing for the needs of both the local communities and the prisoners themselves – is a policy of sentencing focused on rehabilitation and constructive preparation for the future once offenders are eventually released. Additionally, there is a good case for replacing *some* custodial sentences with community-based sentences – particularly if they are applied to first-time offenders, leaving jail for the persistent and dangerous criminals.

Assessment

Arguably the most important part of the new system is prisoner assessment, since it will be central to our efforts to provide constructive and need-focused sentences. An effective assessment system needs to provide targeted and personalised programmes for prisoners. The consequences of a poor assessment procedure can be stark: for example, in 1997, 27% of suicides occurred within the prisoner's first week in custody. The most recent policy venture aimed at improving the assessment systems in the prison service is named OASys – the Offender Assessment System. OASys is purported to be a core assessment tool for logging the key information on offenders, a tool to be used from the pre-sentence report stage onwards until a prisoner's final release into the community. It is, however, riddled with failings that make it both an inadequate and incomplete tool for assessment.

Firstly, and most crucially, offenders with sentences of less than twelve months are not assessed. These are often the most prolific offenders and, as such, are undoubtedly the most in need of a comprehensive assessment and sentence plan. OASys will never resolve the problems of reoffending and overcrowding as long as it fails to provide for these key offenders.

Secondly, OASys does not cover all the educational needs and history of prisoners – despite the fact that 95% of all prisoners need help with basic literacy. As long as we continue to set our targets for education too low – both in numbers of prisoners in education and level of education provided – prisoners will grow even more disillusioned. Yet we cannot provide targeted education unless each prisoner is properly and comprehensively assessed.

Thirdly, OASys is not being used to its full potential. Prison staff are key to the success of the assessment procedure and yet the system is discouraging its use by these very people because of the practical difficulty of completing the OASys form. Our already overburdened prison officers are being asked to spend over five and a quarter hours filling in each form – it is clear that we need to make OASys more user-friendly so that this potentially successful tool does not become neglected and abandoned.

Fourthly, OASys needs to be accessible to all the relevant agencies – the police, the prisons and the probation service. It needs regular input from all these agencies so that an up-to-date picture of the offender can be maintained.

Lastly, the information from OASys must be properly dissem-inated and implemented in the form of an overarching sentence plan. At the moment, 55% of sentence plans do not even refer to tackling offending, or do so poorly: a refocusing of objectives is drastically needed here since the sentence plan is the key vehicle in our efforts to tackle reoffending. However, it is not merely the content of the sentence plans that needs to be carefully reconsidered, but also the actors involved. The success of the Dutch system is testimony to this: Holland is committed to the multi-agency approach. In Holland, all the relevant participants – employers, teachers, housing associations, local government, health services and the probation services – work together to formulate the sentence plan and to cater for prisoner needs. This is referred to as a 'chain partnership', the end result of which is a successful, holistic approach: each agency signs a contract with the prisoner, committing itself to delivering its part of the bargain; prisoners are given the support they need to rehabilitate from the moment of incarceration; and everyone involved is accountable, instead of the buck-passing that continues to plague our own system.

Considering these serious flaws in the OASys system, it is no wonder that the pilot scheme of OASys three years ago was considered a failure. Only when these problems are tackled will our prison service have an effective, comprehensive and overarching assessment scheme – and only when we have such a scheme will we successfully reduce the dual problems of reoffending and over-crowding.

Learning

Education is the key to the successful rehabilitation of prisoners and must be the cornerstone of prisoners' sentence plans. This may not fit with the current Government's conception of 'tough on crime' and its accompanying policies. However, upon closer inspection, it soon becomes obvious that, in their current form, 'tough on crime' policies are merely resulting in overcrowded, disillusioned, innumerate and illiterate prisoners – and hence reoffending.

These policies are failing victims, society and the prisoners themselves. It is paramount that we adopt a hard-hitting approach that focuses on reducing reoffending: education, when properly harnessed, can be a powerful tool in tackling this problem. Unfortunately, prison education has been de-prioritised and now the system, suffering a paucity of focus and financial backing, is incapable of deploying effective, targeted programmes for prisoners.

The situation is damning: 95% of prisoners need help with basic literacy.[5] Half of all prisoners are at, or below, the level expected of an eleven-year-old in reading, 66% in numeracy, and 80% in writing. And yet these basic skills are required in 96% of all jobs.[6] When it comes to young offenders, the statistics are even worse – with over a quarter having numeracy and literacy levels equivalent to or below those of the average seven-year-old.

How is this situation currently being addressed? In 2000, the average time spent on education in prisons was under five hours a week in local prisons, and a little over eight hours in open prisons. Eighty-two per cent of prisoners do not even have access to this education. Despite the vital role education plays in reducing the likelihood of reoffending, prisoners are subjected to what amounts to a postcode lottery for prison education funding: the Government has ring-fenced education spending based not on prisoner needs but on historic levels of funding. Consequently, the Labour Government's 'tough on crime' rhetoric amounts to little more than locking up more offenders and denying them the vocational training and basic literacy skills that are often needed for rehabilitation: many leave prison unable to fill out documents as simple as a job application form.

'Locking them up and throwing away the key' may sound like a policy that is tough on crime but its failure to tackle reoffending illustrates how short-sighted that approach truly is. Prisons are no longer solely punitive institutions – their purpose is also to prepare offenders for release. If that means working eight hours a day to improve basic reading and writing skills, then so be it. If it means gaining difficult vocational qualifications, then that is what prisoners should be required to do. Prisoners must not be given an easy ride – they will need to work hard from the very start of their rehabilitation.

A new ethos that puts a premium on education must be created. The idea that education is the soft option has to be laid to rest – among society at large but particularly among prison staff, who are the key to the success of education schemes and whose participation will be decisive. The vehicle to do this is a new approach that places education at the centre of prison life and reinforces the compulsory obligation to undertake it.

We need to embrace the notion of 'enforced education'. Clearly, where offenders lack key skills in literacy and numeracy, it is necessary for parole boards to insist upon courses in these areas. In the long term, this will improve the confidence of offenders and will prepare them for release and their eventual entry into the job market. Integral to the enforced education approach, there will need to be some scope for allowing prisoners to choose the courses they take. By transferring a sense of responsibility and choice on to the prisoner, prisoners will take on a more mature attitude towards learning and will leave prisons endowed with a set of transferable skills for the real world.

As with many programmes within the prison service, the group most in need of an adequate education regime – reoffenders serving short sentences – are those denied the programmes because their sentences 'are not long enough' for the training. The sentences for these prisoners are often not even long enough for their identification and assessment procedures to be completed.[7] A new prison education system is needed – and one that will provide for the educational needs of all the prisoners.

The practical manifestation of this new education system within prisons will be fourfold.

First, basic numeracy and literacy lessons must be provided for every prisoner who does not possess these skills. Prisoners are often too embarrassed to admit and confront these problems, despite the occupational and social difficulties they pose. Every prisoner should have the ability and confidence to fill out a job application form or read a prison food menu. This ability and confidence is only borne out of encouragement and assistance from the prison service and from the prisoners themselves. Indeed, there are schemes in action whereby prisoners act as reading guides for their illiterate peers. Unfortunately, this type of practice is limited and faces opposition from prison staff who are sceptical about prisoners' motives.

Secondly, there needs to be vocational training. Many businesses are suffering a labour shortage – particularly in the construction trades. Already, pilots of such vocational training schemes are scattered around the country: prisoners are given theory and practical training to develop the skills needed for their chosen area of work. The results are impressive: this year not a single trainee on the Transco project, which trains prisoners to lay gas pipes, reoffended. These results did not come at a cost to the prison service – they were entirely funded by the employing company. Although they were required to work extremely hard to be successful (Transco considered the work worth £14,000 per annum per prisoner), these prisoners could finally feel that they had accomplished something – many for the first time in their lives. Unfortunately, despite the dramatic success of these types of project, the Government has been all too slow to take advantage of such opportunities to cut reoffending.

Thirdly, 'education' – in its traditional conception – must be offered to prisoners at all levels. This approach to education is proven to seriously reduce reoffending rates. A twenty-year study in Canada[8] provided such courses to inmates and the results were compelling. Over this period, university liberal arts courses were offered to prisoners. Each programme attempted to foster a demo-cratic, participatory community by establishing student councils and encouraging student participation in the administration of the programme. This was a conscious attempt to shift the balance of allegiance of the student from his engagement with the criminal world towards the realm of the university and its community. So in each prison an 'academic community' was created. Fifty-eight per cent of the prisoners were expected to reoffend, but only 25% did.[9] The most encouraging result was the success of the most prolific reoffenders, those aged 16 to 21 years old, whose reoffending rates dropped to just 25% – that is, 46% below their predicted rate.[10]

The prisoners with the least to lose, it seems, were the ones who gained most; the very people who are neglected most in our prison system seemed to thrive most in this environment.[11] Educa-tion is by no means a panacea, but these successful schemes and programmes give a clear indication that this type of measure yields positive results in efforts to reduce reoffending.

Lastly, a successful prison education system must aim to continue the educational and occupational development of offenders after their release – and must ensure that an environment conducive to this continued learning is created. A recent study has suggested that as few as 6% of prisoners have an education or training place to go to on release, and that poor links between training inside and outside prison can undo any good work achieved in prison. Understandably, education and training may not be at the top of prisoners' priorities when faced with the need to find housing, get an income and tackle other personal problems. Clearly, therefore, a holistic approach with seamless interaction between agencies is needed to prevent difficulties such as homelessness, unemployment or simply bureaucratic red tape from reducing prisoners' access to further education once they are released.

In the face of a plethora of successful schemes and programmes demonstrating the effectiveness of education at reducing reoffending, policy-makers in the UK continue to resist improving the provision of education in prisons. Information of best practice needs to be effectively disseminated so the prison community can move forward together in combating crime. For example, it would be a tragedy if the successful elements of the Canadian scheme detailed above were banished to the annals of history. Unfortunately, until there is a new ethos embracing education in prisons, even schemes purportedly inspired by the Canadian model are doomed to fail to cut reoffending. Why? Because they lack the holistic vision – the present Government's 'thinking skills' programme, for example, focuses on exam preparation and fails to set up the academic and social community within the prison that is needed for success:[12] prisoners only spend a few hours a week on a course and are immediately sent back to their cells – while staff are ill-motivated and do not respond to the prisoners' needs, and the programmes aim to meet targets rather than to educate.

A Dutch prison officer once explained the simple principle behind an extremely successful prison education project that was running: 'If you give a prisoner something simple and stupid to do, he will react stupidly. But if you give him something meaningful to do, you get a meaningful response.'[13] Education is that meaningful response that will lead to personal progression and hard work. Moreover, it is often the only way to reach the most hardened people in society who, given the opportunity, could lead crime-free lives. The choice facing the prison service is therefore stark: either we provide a system of education that endows prisoners with the skills to gain employment and lead fulfilling lives, or we leave them without prospects upon their release – sending them straight back to a life of crime. This choice represents the difference between communities ravaged by the virulence of recidivism or the prospect of communities free to enjoy life without the threat of crime hanging over them. It is clear that education *is* the new 'tough on crime'.

Exit

Exit from prison *should be* the culmination of a process involving a multiplicity of agencies throughout the duration of the prisoner's sentence. So, on leaving the prison gates, the ex-offender is properly prepared for life and resettlement on the outside. For many prisoners, though, the very notion of 'resettlement' itself is misleading – many prisoners have never been settled. The prison service has to grasp this nettle – it has the opportunity to steer these people's lives and contribute positively to their settlement in society.

The process of settlement in the world outside prison can often be fraught with difficulty. Having just left a world offering very little scope for choice, making even the most inconsequential of decisions – such as choosing a variety of bread – can be an extremely difficult and stressful process.[14] The current Government's narrow aim of being 'tough on crime' completely overlooks the importance of a settlement after a prisoner's release and, consequently, prisoners are totally under-prepared for the life-change that awaits them. The false assumption that 'prison works' has led to the neglect of some of the most important needs of prisoners – rehabilitation, pre-release activities and settlement. As a result, the 'tough on crime' rhetoric has proven itself decidedly weak in substance.

A prisoner's release is the pivotal time for the prison system – it can either consolidate the work that has been done, or all that work can go to waste. Consistency, familiarity and preparation are paramount. Agencies responsible for a smooth transition have to be accountable and proactive, and need to work together in a joined-up rather than piecemeal fashion, to provide effective post-release support for every offender. Worryingly, those most in need of such assistance are currently those most often denied it. Those adults most likely to reoffend – the short-term prisoners – are not currently supervised by the probation service and are released in a completely unmanaged fashion.[15]

With such a paucity of post-release supervision, the development of a comprehensive and fully-coordinated multi-agency approach is desperately needed. The scope of different partnerships that need to be established to work effectively means that prisons have to work with a plethora of different organisations with often conflicting cultures. This demands very tolerant, imaginative and flexible handling – not something for which the prison service is known. As the situation currently stands, 19% of prisons have no links with outside agencies and only 43% of those that do enter into partnerships for resettlement purposes.

This situation seriously hinders effective resettlement for many types of prisoner. For example, prisoners on a drugs rehabilitation programme will still need this ongoing support after prison. Indeed, the need for assistance will often be greater than it was when they were in prison. There needs to be a multi-agency approach, with each contributor taking responsibility for its share of input, wherever the offender is. As mentioned earlier, in the Netherlands this approach is known as chain-partnership. All agencies are accountable and work together to contribute their expertise in assisting the prisoner. Knowledge is pooled so that after release prisoners can access the help they need; and financial assistance is provided when needed to ensure stability for the prisoner. Compare this to the British system where, as standard, there is no joined-up approach or pooling of knowledge and where prisoners are discouraged from submitting claims for benefits early enough to ensure stability.[16]

Some simple changes to the benefit system, making sure that prisoners can get by in those key weeks after release, could make huge differences to reoffending rates. Equally, why not have a Citizen's Advice Bureau opened in every prison to help prisoners access the knowledge and assistance they will need after release? One has been opened at Wormwood Scrubs and, since 1994, 22,500 prisoners have made use of it, with short-term prisoners particular beneficiaries.[17] The majority of advice covers housing problems, legal matters and benefits. Other areas include relationship issues, tax, employment, utilities, education, health, immigration and nationality. If this were private enterprise, these market-leading ideas would rapidly be replicated and copied. But there is a tangible inertia in the prison service, and innovative ideas like this remain the exception rather than the rule. Despite the existence of these simple and effective ways of preparing prisoners for release, very little action has been taken on this front.

Given the barriers in accessing employment, benefits, housing and other services that ex-prisoners will face when they are first released, prisoners will need more than advice and financial assistance as they near the end of the their sentences. Prisoners need to develop the life skills that will help them remove these barriers for themselves – and they can often develop these skills through day-release schemes. The development of the 'Release On Temporary Licence' (ROTL) policy goes some way to combating the institutionalisation that prisoners suffer by allowing them to be released during the day to undertake work and make contact with housing, benefits and employment agencies. Though ROTL helps to establish a smoother custody–community transition, many prisoners do not have the benefit of it because its provision is very patchy nationwide. The current Government's neglect of the importance of resettlement in its penal policies is undoubtedly to blame.

Another difficulty being caused by the Government's neglect of prisoner resettlement is the lack of regionalism built into the prison system. Prisons tend to be monolithic, centralised organisations lacking community roots. Out of 73,000 or so prisoners, 27,500[18] are held over 50 miles away from their home and 12,500[19] over 100 miles away. As a result, 43% of prisoners have lost contact with their families since entering prison. When family contact is often a key stabilising factor, especially among young offenders, the distancing of prisoners from their families has a particularly pernicious impact upon prisoner stability. Besides family contact, many prisoners have little contact with their local probation officer. Of those serving sentences of more than four years, 20% say that they have not had any contact with their local probation officer during their time in prison. Perversely, these prisoners serving longer sentences are far more likely than the persistent reoffenders – who arguably need such post-release supervision more – to have seen their local probation officer. By locating prisons nearer to local communities, the strong links that are necessary for success in this field can be developed between prisoner, probation officer and the local community.

The Dutch are trail-blazers in the community prison system approach: their entire prison estate is geared towards serving the local community and its offenders. Their multi-agency approach is implemented at the regional level, where the prisons liaise with agencies that are local and have a direct impact on prison life. The regional orientation of the Dutch system makes it far more efficient than its British counterpart – imagine the relative simplicity for Winchester City Council of finding housing, employment and assistance for a prisoner to be released from Winchester Prison compared to the needless complications of trying to do the same from Manchester. The regionalisation of the prison estate would help cement the links between prisons and their local communities, and this is invaluable to the post-release experience. Unfortunately, the Government's failure to see the importance of resettlement means that the example set by Holland has not been followed.

Currently, the resettlement assistance that is offered to ex-offenders comes from a mix of government-run and charitable services. The proliferation of voluntary organisations, however, is as much a reaction to the paucity of government provision as it is a gesture of goodwill. Clearly there is an abundance of goodwill and passion, but without adequate financing there is only so much that dedicated individuals can do. The question must be asked: what incentive is there for the prison or probation services to provide this finance and improve their settlement function?

The Dutch criminal justice system has answered this question: enough money is saved through reduced reoffending rates that it can be reinvested back into probation projects.[20] Rather than wasting money by building more prisons without stemming the flow of prisoners coming into the system, the Dutch proactively tackle reoffending by developing good settlement structures, which becomes self-funding. The accepted wisdom of penal policy – an orthodoxy that has proven itself incapable of dealing with the ever-deteriorating problems of overcrowding and reoffending – must be confronted and challenged if we are to tackle these problems.

Employment

An important facet of prisoner settlement is employment. Research shows that employment reduces the risk of reoffending by between a third and a half.[21] Yet only one in 30 offenders leaves prison with a job or interview to go to, and short-term offenders fare even worse. Unemployment clearly makes it harder to maintain stable accommodation or to earn money legitimately. There is an obvious premium, therefore, in channelling offenders' energies into employment-related activities so that on release they either have a job to go to or the skills to attain and retain one.[22]

Vocational training is crucial to achieving post-release employment. Unfortunately, whereas traditional education – though inadequate – has earmarked funding, vocational training has no such allocated funding and is therefore de-prioritised in relation to other demands for finance. The same problem exists regarding time allocated – because no targets have been set for hours spent on vocational training, it loses out against other activities that do have such targets to meet. As a result of these two problems, there is increasingly poor provision of vocational training in prisons.

Consider, for example, construction training: the construction industry could undoubtedly be a key employer of prisoners leaving custody and yet the provision of construction training has been reduced by 50% in the past seven years.[23] The absence of a joined-up approach is worsening the prospects of prisoners after release by failing to prepare them for the employment they so desperately need to gain in order to be reintegrated into society. This situation is particularly frustrating because there are hugely successful pilot schemes in Britain that are testimony to the importance of vocational training and employment in prisoner settlement.

One successful model, as mentioned earlier, is run and fully financed by Transco. As part of the programme, Transco offers prisoners training in pipe-laying and fork-lift truck driving, in addition to all the theoretical training prisoners need to take up employment with Transco once they are released. The programme is not limited simply to vocational training – any requisite numeracy and literacy is also provided. This is all aimed at young offenders – for whom the reoffending rate is 78% – and has proven extremely successful, with not a single person this year reoffending. With these stunning results, it is a tragedy that only three of the 134 prisons in England and Wales run these schemes. The Government, moreover, cannot plead ignorance because Transco and other companies are lobbying both the Government and the construction industry – which could alleviate the industry's severe labour shortages by developing similar projects.

All prisoners should be able, and indeed encouraged, to access these employment schemes. Whether through face-to-face contact, video-conferencing or via the internet, there needs to be a forum where prison governors and companies can communicate and share information. Programmes like the one run by Transco could be operating nationwide if only the infrastructure and resources were there and the value of such schemes publicised.

Alongside an extended ROTL scheme ensuring prisoners can access job centres pre-release, vocational training programmes will vastly increase the chances of prisoners being successfully reintegrated into society once released and can do so at little cost or inconvenience to the prison system.

Instead of the gradual erosion of existing work skills and the lowering of prisoners' self-esteem through mundane prison work, the prison system should be ensuring that prisoners are not released without job prospects by offering them the education, vocational training and access to potential employers that they need. Only through earning their own living, instead of becoming dependent on government assistance, can prisoners truly be settled after release and the problems of overcrowding and reoffending ameliorated.

Conclusion

This is the blueprint for a prison service in the 21st century: a progressive, holistic and multi-agency approach. To complement this new reformed system, however, perhaps we need a reformed approach to sentencing as well. We must think 'outside the box' and consider the possibility that prison is not where all offenders are best placed. For those criminals who are not believed to be dangerous to themselves or to society, prison ought to be a last resort – used when other attempts at helping the offender fail. A suitable alternative might be a regional system of national service camps where a new ethos founded on discipline, training, education and working in the community is cultivated. Though the prisoners would find the national service camps hard, they would also find that the system is working hard to help them – with local agencies coming together to help prisoners find accommodation, work and continued training after release. National service camps may eventually provide a feasible alternative to prison for non-dangerous criminals; in the meantime, however, the prison service is in desperate need of serious reforms if it is ever to overcome the problems of overcrowding and reoffending and become a prison service fit for the 21st century.

Britain's prisons are failing: they are failing victims, local communities and the prisoners themselves. The key problems the prison service faces are overcrowding and ever-increasing reoffending rates – two problems that current penal policies, like prison expansion, do not resolve. Simply incarcerating ever-increasing numbers of prisoners is not working: we need to ensure that there is justice for communities; that sentences are long enough to rehabilitate rather than make things worse; that prisoners are properly assessed and their sentence plans focused on helping the individual prepare for a crime-free life upon release; that improved education – including vocational training – is provided within and outside of prisons; and that proper exit and employment strategies are drawn up to give prisoners the best possible chance of being resettled and reintegrated into local communities.

This blueprint for Britain's prisons is based on a multi-agency approach geared towards education, rehabilitation and resettlement. Such radical reform will be a long-term project, but government ministers must see that with time and investment the prison service will reap the benefits in the form of reduced criminality.

In any event, the prison service cannot go on as it has – the 'tough on crime' policies have proven themselves to be totally inadequate in dealing with crime and, in fact, seem to have compounded the problem by providing such a poor environment for prisoners that reoffending rates have only increased further. From now on, a successful prison sentence should be defined by participation in education and vocational courses, by the opportunities these give the offender, and, ultimately, by reduced offending after release. The current crime 'merry-go-round' cannot be tolerated – this commitment to rehabilitation in prison must be the *new* 'tough on crime'.

Notes
1. A particularly appropriate acronym for the approach outlined above.
2. Home Office figures as of November 2003.
3. Uncrowded capacity as opposed to the total operational capacity, which is slightly higher because prisoners are moved around the prison system to fill any spare capacity elsewhere.
4. Nine of the new prisons built in the past ten years are already seriously overcrowded.
5. Chief Inspector of Prisons' Report, 1999.
6. Meeting with David Ramsbottom, August 2003.
7. Social Exclusion Unit (SEU).
8. Stephen Duguid, Prison Education Research Project: Canada, May 1998.
9. Success was defined as a three-year period after release without reoffending.
10. 52% were predicted not to reoffend, whereas 75% succeeded in not reoffending. Incredibly, violent offenders were even more successful,

with 89% not reoffending, and for those taking courses of longer than one year the figure was 94%.

11. One explanation lies in what is known as the 'improver hypothesis'. The offenders who outstripped their own expectations, or whose grade constantly improved, often fared the best when compared with those who found the courses too easy.

12. This raises the relevance of Therapeutic Communities (TCs). TCs are the epitome of the holistic prison approach in which a democratic community is fostered and prisoners (often with mental illnesses) address one another's problems – each prisoner being answerable to both his fellow prisoners and prison staff. This approach encourages prisoners to take an active role in the running of the prison, in doing so creating a far less dictatorial environment. I saw a transitional project of this type under way at a prison in Winchester, and there was a discernible atmosphere that was conducive towards personal progression and hard work. All aspects of prisoners' needs are addressed in these Therapeutic Communities – instead of piecemeal and irregular help which is the norm in Britain's prisons.

13. Meeting with prison governors in Westligne Prison, October 2003.

14. I heard a story by an ex-offender who, having been given one type of bread during his three years in prison, went into a supermarket and found eleven different types of bread to choose from. He spent ten minutes trying to choose and became so stressed that he left without anything. For many ex-offenders it's true what they say – the sentence begins the day they get out.

15. Before 1991, only young offenders and those on parole were subject to statutory post-release supervision. All others were on 'voluntary aftercare'. In 1991, statutory post-release supervision was introduced for those sentenced to over twelve months, but made no statutory provision for adult prisoners sentenced to less than twelve months, a group that includes some of those most likely to reoffend. Adults (over 21) are eligible to apply for voluntary supervision but, unsurprisingly, increasingly few do.

16. According to SEU consultations. Prisoners can submit claims up to three months before release but are encouraged not to because their circumstances may change prior to release. Consequently, prisoners often do not have enough money in their first few weeks after release, drastically increasing the danger of reoffending. Some simple

changes to the benefit system, making sure that prisoners can get by in those key weeks after release, could make huge differences to reoffending rates.

17. Sixty prisoners, including those on remand and serving short sentences, are seen each week.
18. October 2002.
19. Including 700 children in the prison system.
20. E.g. 'Exodus': a church-run organisation.
21. SEU.
22. This is particularly pertinent given that 66% of prisoners enter prison unemployed – thirteen times the national average.
23. SEU.

9 Children, the family and the state: a liberal agenda

Steve Webb and Jo Holland

A person may cause evil to others not only by his actions but by his inaction, and in either case he is justly accountable to them for the injury.

John Stuart Mill, *On Liberty*, 1859

Introduction – Liberals and family policy

By instinct, Liberals are suspicious of the power of the state. Liberals believe that individuals should be free to lead their lives in the manner they themselves see fit, provided that the exercise of that freedom does not restrict the freedom of others. In few areas is this wariness of state interference more acute than in our approach to what might loosely be described as 'family policy'. The unhappy experience of the Major Government's 'back to basics' campaign has reinforced the view of most Liberals that governments should not be judgemental about people's private lives or seek to stigmatise people whose families are structured in non-traditional ways. Where families break down completely and children are suffering abuse or neglect, we have always been prepared to intervene, but

235

beyond this our approach to what happens inside families has been *laissez-faire* in the extreme.

In this chapter, however, we will argue that this hands-off approach is actually a betrayal of what Liberalism should be about. Whilst we say we believe in enabling each individual to make the most of his potential, the evidence is that large numbers of children are not doing so. Parents are responsible for the way that they raise their children, and they need to recognise that their children's well-being is not simply a private matter but impacts on the whole of society. In turn, parenthood is a role that society needs and values, and citizens who have chosen to become parents therefore have a right to expect support in this role. We will argue that our failure to support and encourage parents in their relationships with their children and each other, and in meeting their responsibilities, has a seriously detrimental effect on the welfare of children and parents alike. Furthermore, if some children 'go off the rails' as a consequence, any resultant anti-social behaviour is clearly an infringement of someone else's liberty.

Standing idly by whilst pressures on families are causing real problems for children and parents alike is not a liberal response. It is an irresponsible response. We certainly want to be sure that any state intervention is proportionate and effective, but this chapter will make the case that a series of government policy changes could give children and parents new choices and new opportunities, to the benefit of all.

Symptoms – all is not well with the nation's children

Every generation has its moral panic. Plato famously bemoaned the condition of the 'youth of today' almost 2,500 years ago. Therefore we must keep our sense of alarm in perspective. However, there is plenty of evidence to suggest that many young people are not getting the start in life that most of us would want for our own children. Surveys, statistics and anecdotal evidence all point to worrying levels of unhappiness and ill-adjustment among many young people.

It is widely accepted that the early years of a child's life are critical in forming the adult he or she will become. Yet there are growing indications that many children are not getting the attention and security they need from their parents in those vital early years.

David Bell, head of Ofsted, said recently that: 'youngsters appear less well prepared for school than they have ever been before. For many young people, school is the most stable part of what can be quite disrupted and dishevelled lives.'[1] This view was echoed by the Welsh Basic Skills Agency, which found that half of all five-year-olds now start school lacking the basic talking and listening skills essential for an effective start to learning. Two-thirds of teachers questioned in the same survey believed that standards have declined in the past five years.[2]

In many cases, the children described in these surveys are suffering from a 'low-level' lack of parental attention. In other cases, the problems are more severe. Four out of ten children on the child protection register are under five years old, and 'neglect' as a cause of registration has increased from 27% of cases in 1994 to 39% in 2002.[3]

It is not only very young children who are suffering. The Audit Commission estimates that one in ten school-age children needs professional help with mental health problems, a dramatic increase over the past 50 years.[4] The charity ChildLine reports that 1,500 suicidal children phone its helpline every year, often citing problems of abuse, neglect and low self-esteem that have built up throughout childhood.

Department of Health evidence suggests that young people are also increasingly turning to alcohol. Between 1990 and 2003, the amount of alcohol consumed by 11- to 15-year-olds 'in the last seven days' doubled from 5.3 units to 10.5 units.[5] Survey evidence also suggests that one in four 15-year-olds has used illegal drugs in the past year.[6]

Of course, many of these are extreme examples: many children have secure and loving childhoods, grow up to be well balanced and form stable family relationships of their own. However, the shocking statistics above suggest that there is an issue to be addressed. Why are so many young people's lives so 'disrupted and dishevelled' even by the time they reach school age? What pressures do they face?

The importance of the early years

There is overwhelming evidence to demonstrate that the strongest influence on children, especially young children, is their home background. This is vital to their educational achievements, relationships and employability in later life. Therefore, if things are going wrong with children, we must look first in the home.

One of the most startling pieces of research on the difference that parents can make has been undertaken at the London School of Economics, where researchers examined the key factors determining how well children perform at school. They find that the single most important determinant of a child's performance is the amount of interest that parents take in the educational development of their children, particularly in the early years. This is more significant than a child's social class, family size, or parental education levels.[7]

The researchers also conclude that: 'very early parent-child interactions ... are much more important in the determination of ability than school-age experiences.' Despite the subsequent work in a child's life at primary and secondary school, differences at 42 months strongly predict final educational qualifications. In short, family background plays an important role in determining the continued development of children's ability.

These findings are backed up by a separate study funded by the Department for Education and Skills. This found that young children aged three to five whose parents are involved in their learning have better language skills and better numeracy than those whose parents are not involved.[8]

As well as improving educational performance, Audit Commission research has found that a stable and supportive home life and involved parents improve the mental health of children. Children with mental health problems are, in turn, more likely to be responsible for juvenile crime, to be abusing alcohol or drugs, to be suffering from eating disorders and to have attempted self-harm.[9]

An insecure start to life can also have long-term consequences that last well beyond childhood. Almost one in three prisoners was formerly in local authority care; almost all had a record of emotional or behavioural difficulties in childhood; and just over half had no formal educational qualifications.[10]

This is a just a small sample of numerous research studies and reports that tell the same story. An insecure home life and lack of parental involvement in a child's development in the early years lay the groundwork for real problems throughout school and beyond. And yet the vast majority of parents want to give their children the best possible start in life. So what generates this gap between aspiration and reality?

Problems in the early years
Parental time with children at a premium
Growth in lone parenthood

In the introduction to this chapter, we said that we are not in the business of stigmatising families, and we restate that position here. But the inescapable truth is that the vast majority of people do not set out to bring up a child on their own. Most people who conceive children do so within a loving relationship, and expect to bring that child up with someone else. But with relationship breakdown on the increase, more children are being raised by only one parent, which inevitably makes life more difficult for parents and children alike.

Two decades ago, the number of children in lone parent families was 1.5 million. In 2001/02, the figure had more than doubled to 3.2 million. The trends among young children are even more striking: in 1979 just 300,000 under-fives were being brought up by one parent. Today that number has trebled to 900,000.[11] Given everything that we found in the previous section about the critical importance of the early years, that is an alarming trend. The majority of lone parents will, of course, do everything they can to give their children the best possible start, and many will be outstanding and committed parents. But the emotional disruption associated with stressful relations between a child's parents and the economic implications of coping on one income – or on benefits – are bound to take their toll on children.

Lone parents are also under considerable pressure from government to move off benefits and into paid employment, giving them still less time for their children. The Government has a target to get 70% of lone parents into paid employment by 2010, and it is making progress towards that target. In 1979, just 100,000 children under the age of five were being brought up by a working lone parent, but now that figure has trebled to 300,000. The number of school-age children being brought up by working lone parents has also increased.

It is not, of course, essentially a bad thing for a lone parent to be in paid work. There is evidence that the greater income and the greater self-esteem that a good job brings can benefit both parent and children. But the pressures that any parent faces in spending enough time with a child are magnified when you are the only parent in the family home and you are also out at work for part or all of the week.

Furthermore, it seems highly unlikely that the free and informed choices of lone parents about the balance they want to achieve between employment and time with their children will magically add up to the Government's arbitrary 70% employment target. As the National Council of One Parent Families (NCOPF) itself says:

> Many lone parents make the decision that, for now, it is more
> appropriate for them to be at home to care for their children,
> either because their children are still young or because they
> are in need of parental care at a difficult time, for example,
> soon after their parents have separated or divorced. These
> judgements about what is best for their children should not
> be brushed aside carelessly on the grounds that work is always
> best.[12]

Growth in two-earner households

Two decades ago, a little under half of children under five were being brought up by two parents, with one in full time work and one not in paid employment. Today, that proportion has fallen to a quarter. Over the same period, the proportion of young children being brought up by two parents who are *both* in full-time employment has trebled, from 3% to 9%.[13] These changing patterns of work must inevitably have implications for the amount of time that parents are able to spend with very young children.

Growth in 'atypical' working

It is not just the fact that parents are working longer hours or having to struggle on their own that has changed in recent decades.

241

The sorts of jobs that parents are doing have also changed considerably. What was once regarded as 'atypical' working – regularly working evenings or weekends – is now so common that the label 'atypical' scarcely fits.

Research carried out for the Joseph Rowntree Foundation by Ivana la Valle, a leading authority on this subject, has found that 'atypical' working patterns are widespread among parents. Her research has shown that half of all mothers and four-fifths of fathers frequently work outside the regular 8.30am – 5.30pm day. This means that parents are having to work at times of day when the children are home from school, including evenings and weekends; with a quarter of mothers and a third of fathers regularly working one or more Sundays a month. Parents are also working long hours, with almost a third of fathers and 6% of mothers regularly working over 48 hours a week. 'Family unfriendly' working patterns of this sort are becoming increasingly normal.[14] And yet there is evidence that many parents are unwilling participants in this high-pressure existence.

Parents – the unwilling workforce?
The same research that documented the long and 'atypical' parental working hours also discovered a very clear link between the number of hours that the parents worked and disruption to family activities, and identified high levels of parental dissatisfaction. In particular, 'long working hours and Sunday work seemed to cause the greatest disruption to family life'. Parents in lower socio-economic groups were more likely than those in professional jobs to feel they had no option but to work atypical hours. In most cases, working Sundays was a job requirement. One-third of mothers and nearly half of fathers with frequent atypical hours said that their work limited the time they could spend reading, playing and helping children with homework *every* week.

A particular pressure point for parents is immediately after the birth of a child. A survey by *Mother & Baby* magazine in 2003, which spoke to 2,000 women, found that only a handful of mothers would freely choose to return to work full-time after childbirth. But of those mothers who did, in fact, return to work, the vast majority cited 'financial pressures' as their main reason.[15]

Parents also recognise that if they take a career break or work only part-time, they are likely to undermine their career prospects. The charity One Parent Families, commenting on the Government's employment targets for lone parents, wrote: 'All kinds of parents – men and women – are less likely to be promoted if they have a large family or their children are young. Part-timers and employees not working overtime are also more prone to be overlooked for promotion.'[16]

Parents are also spending less 'quality time' with their children. A recent *Good Housekeeping* survey found that half of working mothers would leave their jobs tomorrow if they had the choice financially, because their home lives are suffering. Two-fifths said they were too tired to enjoy being with their children.[17]

We must also consider a wider social context. Just as paid child-minding is a relatively low-status and low-paid occupation, staying at home to bring up a child is also frequently looked down upon. A survey by the National Family and Parenting Institute (NFPI) found that many parents feel under pressure not to stay at home, and believe they have little choice about when and how to return to work and organise their working lives.[18]

Indeed, even the Government's own 'Minister for Women', Patricia Hewitt, has admitted that government rhetoric has devalued the importance of time away from paid work, bringing up children. She said:

If I look back over the last six years I do think that we have

> given the impression that we think all mothers should be
> out to work, preferably full time as soon as their children
> are a few months old … We have got to move to a position
> where as a society and as a Government we recognise and
> we value the unpaid work that people do within their
> families.[19]

The National Family and Parenting Institute – set up by the
Government – believes that a combination of the prevailing
culture and Government policies

> … places huge burdens on parents struggling to juggle work
> and family commitments …The drive to get parents back
> to work continues; indeed it is one of the major planks of
> government attempts to reduce poverty. However, it would be
> wrong to ignore the signs of strain and stress that this policy
> appears to be creating amongst families.[20]

In response, the Government has stressed the need for 'family-
friendly employment' and 'work–life balance'. It has extended
unpaid maternity and paternity leave, and introduced new rights
for parents of young children to request more flexible working
arrangements from their employer.

But the evidence is that these measures have achieved little so
far. The Chartered Institute of Personnel and Development has
concluded that 'the Government's campaign on work–life balance
has had little or no effect to date', whilst rights to unpaid maternity
leave are of little value to those who cannot afford to be without
pay in the first place.[21]

In short, modern parents are increasingly finding themselves
under social and economic pressure to work longer and longer
hours, frequently at times that are disruptive to family life, and it

is hard to believe that this is not having an adverse effect on the quality of family relationships and the welfare of children.

Can childcare substitute for parental involvement?

The implications for children of growing levels of paid work among parents are hotly debated. The effect on young children of non-parental childcare clearly depends on the age of the child and the nature of the childcare.

A Bristol University study suggests that there are negative effects of parental employment only for the 'relatively unusual' group of children whose mothers return to work before they are eighteen months old.[22] Recent research by the Institute for Education found that children gained intellectual and social benefits from being in nurseries from the age of three and above, but that 'high levels of group care before the age of three (and particularly before the age of two) were associated with higher levels of anti-social behaviour at age three'. The study emphasised that 'one-to-one care for babies is essential'.[23]

The main issue seems to be whether the child feels loved, supported and wanted by his or her parents, rather than simply whether or not the parents use paid childcare. The child is more likely to feel secure if his or her parents are both there when they are wanted, and are not too stressed by work to give the child enough attention and love. The child psychotherapist Asha Phillips sums it up by saying: 'What matters for children is the idea of having a space in somebody else's mind.'[24]

Domestic instability on the increase

In addition to experiencing long working hours by their parents, increasing numbers of children are also experiencing the trauma associated with the breakdown of the relationship between their parents. Among children born to married parents, roughly four in ten are likely to see their parents divorce by the time they are 16.[25] Break-up rates among cohabiting parents are higher still: Office for National Statistics research has found that, by the time their child is five years old, 43% of cohabiting parents will have separated, compared with just 8% of married parents.[26]

Of course, it is not only when a relationship ends that the welfare of a child can suffer. There is clear evidence that children can fail to prosper when their home life is full of parental discord. Children seem to attach more importance to the quality of the relationship between their parents than many parents do themselves. Nearly three-quarters of teenagers in a survey by the National Family and Parenting Institute considered that their parents getting on well together was one of the most important factors in raising happy children, whilst only a third of parents agreed.[27] Roughly one in four calls to ChildLine in 1998 were from children concerned about their parents' relationship.[28]

In some cases, the roots of worsening parental relationships can be found in the labour market trends described above. Joseph Rowntree Foundation research has found that more than one in four mothers living with a partner have adopted 'shift parenting' where each parent works times of day that don't overlap with the other, in order to share childcare, with the consequence that parents spend less time together. Roughly 40% of couples where both partners frequently worked atypical hours were dissatisfied with their time spent together as a couple, compared with only 17% where neither partner regularly worked such hours.[29]

Evidence increasingly demonstrates that when relationships between parents deteriorate, so does the quality of their parenting. Research by One Plus One indicates that conflict between parents 'can prevent parents providing the warm, secure, care-giving environment that is so crucial to the development of an emotionally healthy child'. Parents become depressed when they are struggling financially or stressed at work. This can create or exacerbate marital conflict, which in turn influences the child, and the researchers conclude that 'partners find it difficult to parent well when they are distracted by stress at home and discord in their relationship'.[30] Family 'processes', such as conflict, explain children's psychological health better than family 'structure'. Although other factors are involved, evidence suggests that parental discord is one of the primary triggers for the emergence and persistence of behavioural problems.

Study after study tells the same story: children are more disturbed and more likely to suffer mental illness or commit crime or underachieve at school if they are unhappy and stressed at home.

The Audit Commission found that 80% of children with mental health problems had difficulties in their family life and relationships.[31] The charity Young Minds states:

> There has been an increase in childhood mental problems
> over the last 50 years. Family breakdown involves conflict and
> the frequent subsequent loss of a positive relationship with
> one parent (and support to the other parent). Changes in the
> labour market have added to the strain on babies' attachments
> to their primary care-givers.[32]

The Social Exclusion Unit found that children suffering from higher levels of family stress are more likely to be excluded from school, and that these levels have worsened in recent years.[33]

Two-thirds of young homeless people questioned in a survey gave family problems as reasons for leaving home, especially if their parents had divorced or separated before they were six years old.[34]

Department for Work and Pensions (DWP) research into

247

outcomes for children in poverty found that 'growing up in a non-intact family has negative consequences for children's well-being across the entire range of outcomes under study.'[35]

According to young people's charity Young Voice, older children notice their parents' stress and may want to avoid burdening them with their own problems. Around two-fifths of teenagers admit to worrying about their mothers' stress levels as they watch them juggle work and parenting – they are tired, tense and preoccupied and their children keep their problems to themselves to avoid burdening them further. But the teenagers' problems do not simply disappear, and instead their stresses may manifest themselves in a range of anti-social behaviour.[36]

Parents ultimately bear responsibility for the way that they raise their children. But many struggle to parent effectively. The charity Parentline Plus points out that: 'Parenting is probably the most important task any of us will undertake, yet it comes with no instructions or training.'[37] People do not simply inherit or absorb the attitudes and methods that will enable them to be good parents. Children need a great deal of love, care and attention, in order to develop into emotionally healthy individuals, yet anecdotal evidence suggests that many parents have no support with bringing up their children. One head-teacher said of the children in her primary school: 'It is not just verbal skills; they seem to have no notion of danger or idea how to sit still. Many can't fasten buttons or use a knife or fork … Some children have never sat at a table because their parents let them eat their tea sitting on the floor in front of the television.'[38] Recent research by the Early Learning Centre found that nearly 60% of children under six years old have a television in their bedrooms, and watch it on average for 2.1 hours a day.[39]

Some studies suggest that it is not merely the presence of two parents but the level of commitment implied by marriage that is particularly beneficial to children. For example, a recent Office for

National Statistics publication states: 'there is accruing evidence ... that children born to cohabiting parents ... have less advantaged lives than their contemporaries who are born to married parents.'[40] This research found that 21% of children with cohabiting parents are in the lowest part of the household income distribution, compared with less than 8% of married parents. New DWP research also concludes that 'cohabitation itself may be associated with disadvantage'.[41] As liberals, we would be understandably nervous of using the power of the state to encourage particular family forms, but if the welfare of children is often enhanced where such family structures are adopted, we should not rule out such an approach.

The trends we have cited above – the growth in lone parenthood, atypical working hours and domestic instability – may all contribute to weaker parental role models for young parents. The fragmentation of local communities and extended families has also cut away traditional support networks, and it is no wonder that so many are struggling.

Policy responses

We have argued that a *laissez-faire* approach by the state to how children are raised has contributed to a situation in which too many children are failing to thrive, in some cases quite seriously. We have identified the critical importance of parental involvement in a child's early years and the need for a stable and secure family background within which a child will prosper. We have also highlighted how trends in relationship breakdown, fewer role models, and atypical working patterns mean that many children lack the start in life that we would wish for our own children. Below we provide some indications of how the public, private and voluntary sectors can intervene positively to improve this situation. Our proposals cover two broad strands of intervention:

→ *Supporting stable and secure families.* Huge sums of money are spent by governments on dealing with the consequences of problems, and tiny sums on preventing them from arising in the first place. In few areas is this truer than in the case of relationship breakdown. Some have put the cost to the Exchequer of handling the consequences of broken relationships at perhaps £15 billion a year.[42] In comparison, the amount spent on supporting relationships is a pittance. The voluntary sector runs much of the family support available in communities, but is pitifully underfunded, whereas the state has traditionally largely kept out of this area. We will consider some of the ways to redress this balance.

→ *Enabling parents to spend more time with their children.* The Government could initiate a number of interventions to give people real choices about the hours that they spend working or with their children. For too many parents, working long or 'atypical' hours, or while children are very young, is an unwelcome financial necessity rather than a free expression of personal preference. Again, as Liberals, we should be enthusiastic supporters not of telling people how to run their own lives, but of giving parents genuine choices for ordering their time according to the best interests of the whole family.

At the same time, it does no good to ensure that parents have more time to spend with their children if they lack the knowledge and skills to enable them to parent their children effectively. We believe that the Government needs to focus on prevention ahead of remedial policies, to provide families with tools to nurture healthy relationships just as they are taught to look after their physical health.

These interventions fall into a range of categories, which we consider below:

Voluntary Sector

The voluntary sector provides vital support and advice to families in their local communities. Many projects and organisations aim to tip the balance away from spending all their money on addressing existing problems by trying to prevent relationship breakdown and tackle the challenges faced by young people before they get out of hand. The following are a few examples of effective local projects that equip people with valuable relationship skills. They offer just a flavour of the extent of the latent potential in the voluntary sector, which we believe should be built upon and supported.

→ In Bath, the register office and local churches have teamed up to form a Community Family Trust (CFT). Their starting point is the observation that everyone choosing to get married does so in the hope and expectation that it will work out. The trust aims to help couples achieve that goal. It offers engaged and newly married couples an opportunity to learn how to relate to one another in order to build a strong relationship. A computer-based programme provides an inventory of questions to help couples understand how their partner thinks, to identify potential points of conflict in the relationship, and to equip them with the communication skills to deal with problems that might arise.

Since it is a legal requirement to register all births, the office also accesses every single family with a new baby, including those where the parents cohabit and have therefore not come into contact with them before. This suggests that register offices are ideally suited to act as advice and education points for new families – even if they do not offer all the services 'in-house' themselves.

There are currently seventeen CFT groups running in towns

across the country. Their philosophy is to educate people across the community in the essentials of lasting relationships. The programme is delivered in schools, health centres, churches, register offices and workplaces so that adults and children are given the opportunity to learn relationship skills at all key life stages. CFTs have only been running for a couple of years so it is too early to judge results. However, the front-line professionals in Bath are extremely positive about this new approach and have received encouraging feedback from couples taking part in the programme.

→ Home-Start UK is a well-established initiative that is run in 330 communities across Britain. It trains parent volunteers to visit families who are finding it difficult to cope with the stresses of raising small children. This parent-to-parent approach provides a stigma-free personal friendship, and emotional and practical support. Parents can share their concerns and problems, and regain confidence in their own abilities to care for their children, which in turn enables the children to flourish. Evidence suggests that this type of support from fellow parents in the local community can prevent situations becoming more stressful and can even help to avoid family breakdown or child abuse.

Last year Home-Start helped more than 60,000 children, and according to its 2003 annual report, 612 children receiving support were taken off the child protection register. Eighty-four per cent of families reported a significant improvement in the physical and emotional well-being of their children during Home-Start support, and a similar number of parents saw a significant improvement in their own well-being and self-esteem.[43]

→ The children of teenage parents suffer multiple disadvantages, and the Teens & Toddlers project aims to prevent teenage pregnancy by challenging young people's perceptions about the nature of parenthood.

The project in Tower Hamlets, East London, is based in the nursery of a primary school. Eight teenagers thought to be 'at risk' by their schools of becoming teenage parents spend one afternoon a week with the three- to five-year-olds in the nursery. They are each paired with a child and spend time playing together, so that they learn to appreciate the amount of energy and attention that small children need. The teenagers also have classroom time, where they learn about parenting skills, sexuality and relationships. Counselling is offered to those considered most at risk.

Formal evaluation of the UK schemes is yet to be completed, but evidence from the USA is encouraging. From a project set in a high school in California, national statistics suggest that there should have been seven pregnancies in the first calendar year. However, over the four years of its operation, there was not a single reported pregnancy among students at the school.[44]

→ The National Childbirth Trust (NCT) runs post-natal classes, where new mothers have a chance to meet others and discuss issues such as the difference between the expectation and reality of motherhood, returning to work, and balancing time. The NCT group offers to 'spend time with you, listening to your feelings and concerns and helping you adjust to motherhood'.[45] Groups run drop-in classes and longer courses. They also give advice on adjusting to a changing relationship between partners when the baby is born, which can be a key stress point in any relationship.

These projects all focus on equipping parents, partners and young people with the knowledge, skills and support to enable them to deal with stress points in their current or potential relationships. They are a few examples of the vital work carried out by the voluntary support sector; successful because they offer local, personal services that meet people's needs. Aside from their evidence, there is good reason to believe that most parents themselves recognise the vital importance of a healthy relationship beween a couple for the well-being of their children and would appreciate support in building that relationship. A 'listening to parents' survey undertaken in 2001 by the National Family and Parenting Institute (NFPI) found that 'there is a clear message from parents that a good relationship is vital'. It concluded that 'focusing on the parents' own relationship and making sure that help is available if it runs into difficulties is important for the health of the whole family. Yet relationship support services are thin on the ground.'

Much more could be done to go with the grain of what parents themselves want and to help to nip problems in the bud.

We must also look at how the state is involved in assisting the voluntary sector. Many projects and organisations run on a shoe-string budget, dependent on donations, and there are various government funds that provide money to assist their work, such as the Children's Fund, the Family Support Grant and the Parenting Fund. The Children's Fund aims to prevent poverty and social exclusion among children and young people by supporting them and their families. Local partnerships divide up the money available in their communities. The Family Support Grant funds organisations such as the NFPI, Parentline Plus, and Home-Start UK, and offers three-year funding for 'activities to support parents in their parenting role'. It is worth up to £6.3m, and last year was oversubscribed tenfold.[46] The Parenting Fund is a new fund, worth £25m over three years, which will provide funding to support parenting for families 'facing a range of difficulties'.

These funds are welcome, but they are very limited in scale. Grants are time-limited and highly conditional, and organisations have to reapply every three years, jumping through various hoops to secure funding. Whilst it is important to have safeguards in place to ensure responsible spending of government money, there is a very real danger that voluntary organisations can find themselves spending more time chasing their next source of funding than actually concentrating on their core activities. We should encourage diversity and creativity to flourish, instead of stifling them with too rigid funding criteria.

The issue of funding raises the question of priorities. Government has a limited amount of money to spend across its whole range of policies. However, in our view, there is a very strong case for allocating a respectable amount to investing in relationship support. All the evidence points to the fact that enduring, committed parental relationships and effective parenting are better for children, and we must therefore seriously consider the long-term consequences of supporting partners and parents.

It seems clear that government should aim to provide core funding to projects that have proved themselves successful and invaluable in their local communities. It should perhaps also consider funding innovative pilot projects, to discover what initiatives work well in which areas. When a group could demonstrate that their venture was successful, a more secure stream of public funding could then provide long-term stability to ensure that it did not throw all its efforts into finding money for the next three years. The state should employ a light touch, freeing up volunteers to be creative, flexible and responsive to local needs, whilst still maintaining necessary safeguards, as well as offering security to allow innovation without the fear of losing funding.

Government interventions

It is not just in the voluntary sector that action is being taken to support families. The Government is piloting a number of interventions. The flagship Sure Start programme focuses high levels of resources on children and families in the most disadvantaged communities in the country. The philosophy behind the initiative, which has been widely welcomed, is to integrate services and to break down traditional barriers between different professional groups and sectors. Families and children need to be seen as a whole, and not as separate consumers of social services, health services, etc.

Sure Start West Bermondsey has been running for a relatively short time, but already the Director, Karen Coffey, has commissioned eighteen partners across Southwark – including speech therapists, health visitors, advice workers and a safety equipment company – to enhance the services available to families across the borough. The service providers meet each month to identify gaps in current provision, build confidence among the partners and to look at how to contact the hardest-to-reach groups in the community. As part of the initiative, health visitors and midwives now issue a pack to all parents of new babies in the target area, listing all the services that are available to them, such as health advice and local nurseries. When children reach eighteen months and three years old, their health visitors issue book packs containing more information.

The Sure Start initiative has so far only been applied to the most deprived fifth of the community, but it is clear that the long-term effectiveness of such programmes depends on being perceived as mainstream provision for 'normal' families, rather than as rescue services for 'problem' families. Indeed, the perception that using such services will be seen as a sign of failure can itself be a barrier to their effectiveness. Research for the Institute for Public Policy Research (IPPR) has found that:

> ... most parents are crying out for more support but dare not voice their concerns for fear of being labelled as failing. This strengthens the case for universally available services, rather than the target approach on 'problem' families that the Government has pursued to date.[47]

We would like to take the idea of good universal provision further, by finding imaginative ways to ensure that those who most need preventative and effective support are encouraged to access it without feeling stigmatised. An obvious way of doing this would be to work through existing professional networks. The research group One Plus One has found that the health visitor or midwife is the most trusted person with whom many mothers with young children come into contact. All health visitors are qualified nurses or midwives, and have also been trained in child health, and health education. Every family with a child under five has access to a named health visitor who can advise them and help to support the whole family. There is no stigma attached to a mother talking to a health visitor about her child's well-being, and openness can provide an avenue to raise other issues such as relationship pressures, provided that the health visitors themselves feel confident and competent to respond appropriately.

The Government is making positive noises about developing the 'untapped potential' of these professionals, encouraging them to develop a 'family-centred public health role' looking after people's mental and emotional health as well as their physical health.[48] Voluntary groups also recognise the potential of this network: Home-Start UK reports that health visitors refer 60% of the families that it supports.[49] One Plus One has also undertaken training of health visitors and midwives to enable them to support new parents on a wider range of issues than their own professional specialism. They are taught to recognise early signs of relationship distress, build up the confidence to talk through the issues with the parents, and direct them to other services that may be able to support them through specific difficulties. The results of this training have been highly encouraging and have created much stronger bonds of support between the parents – fathers as well as mothers – and the health visitor in such circumstances.

An expansion of the system would obviously require some serious investment and training, but in our view this is a vital link in the chain. If these are the people to whom women turn when they are under pressure at key crisis points, then it must be worth making the effort to enable this sector to flourish.

These examples all make the case for expanding preventative services – both universal and targeted. But there are also many things that can be done to help minimise the harm when things have gone wrong in a relationship or in a young person's life. For example:

Parenting Orders

The Youth Justice Board applies Parenting Orders to parents of persistent youth offenders, requiring them to attend parenting classes. This programme partly reflects the results of the Board's own research into the attitudes of young offenders, which found that young people 'continue to say that the views of their parents are the most significant deterrent to their offending'. It concluded: 'this indicates that positive parenting remains a powerful influence over young people ... A difficult relationship between a young person and their parents is one of the major risk factors in young people's lives.' [50]

The early experience of parenting orders has been remarkably positive, despite their compulsory nature. Parents felt that they had built better relationships with children and were better able to cope with parenting. Nearly all said that the programme was helpful, and more than nine out of ten would recommend it to other parents. Strikingly, there was a 50% reduction in recorded offences by their children in the year after the programme. The Government has recently extended this scheme to parents of persistent truants, which is a significant step as many children found outside school without permission are with their parents.[51] There certainly seems to be a case for building further upon this type of intervention.

Reducing the trauma of divorce

Research by the University of East Anglia in 2002 found that resort to the law and the adversarial process during divorce made matters worse for children at an already difficult time. But alternative approaches have been found to diminish this problem.

In the 1980s, the state of Florida instituted a 'therapeutic justice' system, under which virtually all divorce cases are now resolved long before they reach court. The couple are required to take part in mediation and parenting classes, not to teach them how to be good parents but to 'refocus their attention on the needs of the child and the different challenges that come with a restructured family'. The aim of this approach is to try to take some of the vindictiveness out of the courts process.

In New Zealand, early intervention and mediation have reduced contested cases to one-tenth of their previous level. The philosophy is that separating couples are taught to realise that 'while they may live apart, for the sake of the children the family has to continue'.[52]

This section has looked at areas where the state has a role in setting up its own initiatives, and policies where it should take a lead in funding, promoting and encouraging projects. Other interventions can be made through existing structures run by the Government, such as the tax and benefits systems, employment law, education and childcare policies. Many of them can be applied to enable parents to make real choices about spending more time with their children.

Tax/benefits system

One controversial issue is the extent to which the tax and benefit system acts to encourage or discourage particular family structures. Based on the arguments we have advanced so far in this chapter, there would be a case for designing a tax/benefit system to make it more likely that children would be brought up in secure and stable homes, by both parents wherever possible. At the very least, we would want to ensure that the existing system did not discourage the formation of such households.

For example, if parents report that financial necessity drives them back to work sooner and more fully than they would wish, realistic levels of financial support for non-working parents, especially those with young children, could address this. Finland, Norway and France all have a simplified maternal allowance that enables mothers of pre-school children to choose between day-care and family care. In the UK, one approach would be through enhanced tax credits for young children. This targeted approach would be of most value to lower income families where financial necessity would otherwise be most likely to force them back into work. It would be much more focused than a system of transferable tax allowances, which could easily benefit high earning couples the most.

There is, however, a strand of thought that believes the existing benefits system discourages the formation of stable couple-based households.

The welfare state as enemy of the traditional family

It is sometimes argued – usually on the political right – that a welfare state offering decent levels of support to lone parents must be 'anti-marriage', and the phased abolition of the married couples' tax allowance has reinforced this impression.

One of the most trenchant advocates of this position is Patricia Morgan of the Institute for Economic Affairs, who writes:

> The combination of the destabilisation of male earnings with expanded welfare programmes has been destructive of marriage, particularly among the poor. A woman may be no worse off, or even better off, without the father of her children.[53]

She argues that generous lone parent benefits lead to the creation of lone parent households because the financial implications of unplanned conceptions among single women are greatly reduced. She also believes that good levels of support for lone mothers make men into an economic luxury: low-paid men bring no net financial advantage, whilst those in insecure employment offer less financial certainty than state benefits. We examine each argument in turn.

Does more generous social security for lone parents lead to more lone parents?

The relative generosity of social security support for lone parents has increased considerably over recent decades, as has the total number of lone parents. What is less clear is whether, or to what extent, the one is the cause of the other.

We should first note that the majority of lone parents were once married to the father of their children. Given the upheaval associated with divorce and separation, it is hard to believe that the prospect of a life on benefits acts as a strong incentive to separation. It seems more likely that more liberal divorce laws, and the reduced social stigma associated with divorce, explain the growth in this category of lone parent households.

The fastest growing group of lone parents, however, is never-married single mothers. In the past, such women might have lived at home with their parents. Today, they are more likely to obtain local authority accommodation, although the standard of this accommodation varies considerably. They are also entitled to benefits of around £5,300 per year.[54] To put this in perspective, the current 'poverty line' for a lone parent with a baby is £5,800 per year.[55]

In short, therefore, single parenthood has become more economically viable than in the past, although it is probably not a very comfortable existence. Patricia Morgan observes that few young women probably seek to become lone parents by design, but they may be less careful about trying to avoid getting pregnant. This seems credible, although there is little hard evidence on the subject.

However, even if supporting lone parents has some marginal impact on the growth in lone parenthood, it is far from clear that Government could or should address this. If we were concerned about the welfare of all children, we would not want to withdraw support for such families. Indeed, since the welfare of children is seriously adversely affected by growing up in poverty, it seems perverse to suggest across-the-board cuts in lone parent support simply because we suspect that a small number of lone parent households are being formed due to welfare state incentives. This should certainly be monitored, but we believe it is easy to exaggerate the scale of the problem.

Does more generous social security for lone parents discourage marriage or cohabitation?

A second argument about the incentive effects of the welfare state suggests that the benefits system may discourage a lone mother from living with the father of her children.

If both partners are working, this is probably not a major issue. Provided that their combined income lifts them clear of means-tested benefits, they will probably be better off with their joint income and one household to run, rather than two.

The issue is less clear-cut for low-income households. For a lone mother on income support, the addition of an unemployed male will increase her benefit entitlement.[56] The additional mouth to feed will, however, probably offset any net gain in benefit. If the new partner is in low-paid work, his earnings are deducted pound-for-pound from the mother's benefit entitlement. Instead of the two partners enjoying the mother's social security income and the father's earnings in full when they were living separately, the couple now simply have the mother's benefit income, slightly enhanced by an extra sum for an additional adult, and by a small 'disregarded' amount of the father's earnings. Whether or not they are better or worse off overall will depend on how much money the father saves by no longer having to run a separate household.

It is hard to believe that the benefit system discourages many lone parents from living with the father of their children. Where the father has a good job, his addition to the household will probably benefit the family financially. Even if he is unemployed or low-waged, the couple are unlikely to be significantly out of pocket when he moves in, and there will be non-financial benefits to the couple from their new arrangement. At present, therefore, we are not convinced that the welfare state is having a seriously detrimental effect on the willingness of mothers and fathers to live under the same roof.

Are there any financial advantages to marriage?
Whilst debating the alleged 'bias' of the welfare state against

marriage, it is worth mentioning that there are still several financial reasons why women in particular may do better financially by marrying their partner, rather than just cohabiting. Members of cohabiting couples have very few legal rights in the event of separation or death of one partner. The main financial advantages to marriage are as follows:

→ Many pension schemes provide benefits for widows (or widowers) only in the case of legal marriage. In most pension schemes, including the state pension, surviving partners get no pension at all, although this is gradually changing.
→ When one member of a couple dies, the surviving partner is exempt from inheritance tax on the family home if he or she is the spouse of the deceased, but not if they were only cohabiting.
→ Transfers between spouses are exempt from capital gains tax, but transfers between partners are liable.
→ Where a relationship breaks down, a married partner may be able to claim financial support from his or her ex-spouse, whereas cohabiting couples take away only what they bring into the relationship. A cohabiting woman who sacrifices many years of earnings and pension rights bringing up children can find herself in a very poor financial position if the relationship should end.

Conclusions

We reject the view that a welfare state that is more generous to lone parents is, of itself, undermining marriage. We note that there are some financial advantages to marriage compared with cohabitation (or not living together at all), particularly for those on higher incomes. For those on lower incomes, incentive issues may make younger single women less concerned about becoming pregnant, but we stress that the standard of living afforded to a lone parent wholly dependent on state support is far from generous and not one to which most people would aspire.

We are sceptical of the argument that mothers are, in significant numbers, declining to live with the father of their children because of the financial effects of the benefit system. Furthermore, to the extent that incentives of this sort do exist at the margins of the system, we regard the most likely 'cure' – namely a reduction in the level of support for children in lone parent families – as far worse in terms of its impact on the welfare of children than the 'problem' it is seeking to solve.

Employment law/working culture

If we are serious about giving parents choices, and enabling them to spend more time with their children, we desperately need to tackle the 'long hours' and 'atypical hours' working cultures, and to consider the inflexibility of some of the current policies. A range of strategies might be examined:

→ *Right to flexible working hours.* A survey by the National Family and Parenting Institute found that the most popular policy proposed to make Britain more family-friendly was to give parents a right to flexible working, rather than just a right to *ask employers* for it.[57]

→ *Right to paid parental leave for mothers and fathers.* One Parent Families found that 'unless it is paid, parental leave for most lone parents amounts to a right on paper only'.[58] Most lone parents simply cannot afford to take unpaid leave. In Sweden and Norway, fathers are given a 'daddy quota' of parental leave, with a 'use it or lose it' condition for fathers. In Sweden, a couple can take up to thirteen months off work between them, with the state paying 80% of lost wages (up to a ceiling).

The take-up rate for fathers is around 77%, and about 85% in Norway.[59]

→ *Scrapping employment targets for lone parents.* Arbitrary targets contribute nothing to the well-being of parents or children. If we believe that parents should be given real choices, it cannot be right to expect the sum of those individual choices to add up to a pre-determined target. Government has a legitimate role in explaining to lone parents the potential benefits of paid employment, and setting out the financial support that would be available in work, but there should be no attempt to coerce people to choose a particular course of action simply to meet a government target – especially where much of the work available can itself be low-paid and of low status.

Education

Britain has the highest rates of teenage pregnancy in Europe. The Government has been taking action, but 90,000 teenagers still become pregnant every year.[60] Teenage mothers are less likely to finish their education or find a good job than older mothers, and are more likely to be single parents and bringing up their children in poverty. Their children are also at greater risk of becoming teenage parents themselves. Why do we have such a high rate of teenage pregnancy? The Social Exclusion Unit suggests that one of the main reasons is ignorance: 'Young people lack accurate knowledge about contraception, STIs [sexually transmitted infections], what to expect in relationships and what it means to be a parent.'[61]

The role of sex education in schools is controversial, and a whole chapter could be written about this issue alone. There are two prevailing schools of thought. The first is that too much information is given to children when they are too young, without setting it in an appropriate context – which will only encourage them to experiment before they are mentally and emotionally ready. The other view is that young people will experiment anyway, and are far less likely to end up pregnant or contracting an STI if they are given all the facts, set out clearly and openly within a framework of responsibility and relationship, at an appropriate age. The Social Exclusion Unit believes that teenagers receive mixed messages from the world around them, suggesting, as one young person said to them, that 'sex is compulsory but contraception is illegal'. Teenagers are bombarded with sexually explicit messages whilst the adults in their lives are embarrassed to talk about it.

There is not room here to rehearse the pros and cons of both these arguments. However, it is clear that, aside from the issue of when and how it is taught, sex education in schools should not simply be about biology but about setting a sexual relationship within a committed, loving relationship. Young people need to understand the responsibilities that they will be taking on, both when they commence a sexual relationship and when they have a child.

Schools need to focus on 'relationships education' rather than 'sex education', which could also include sessions on how to look after children and how to treat a partner in a relationship. This is obviously a controversial area for discussion, but it would certainly help to prepare young people for the stresses and realities of couple and parenting relationships. These sessions could be taught as part of the new citizenship classes, which became part of the national curriculum in 2002, and which aim to teach young people about 'socially and morally responsible behaviour', including the role of young adults as family members.[62] These aims have been criticised by a recent Ofsted report as 'ambiguous',[63] and so an overhaul of this subject's objectives would be an ideal opportunity to rethink the way in which relationships education is taught, including the responsibilities of becoming a partner and a parent.

Research also indicates that poverty – of income and aspiration – is also an important risk factor in teenage pregnancy. Young women who feel that they have good employment and education prospects are less likely to become pregnant. Professor David Paton, of the University of Nottingham, says that: 'The biggest reason that youngsters do not get pregnant is because they do not want to.'[64] This suggests that tackling poverty and encouraging teenagers to believe that they have a bright future are also important factors to be considered in the context of relationship education and government interventions.

Childcare

As Liberals, we want to give people genuine choices to enable them to raise their children to the best of their abilities. Parents may want to spend more time at home with their children, and have this care recognised and valued; or they may opt to combine raising their children with paid employment, in which case they want to be confident that their children are being well looked after. Many mothers say that they find it hard to trust others to care for their children, and it is vital that the childcare provided is of the highest quality, and that it is available and affordable for anyone who wants to use it.

The research cited earlier demonstrated that very young children, in particular, need intensive adult supervision, and it should be stressed that ensuring a supply of high-quality, affordable childcare does not come cheap. Yet existing subsidies for childcare are often inadequate and may mean that working parents cannot afford childcare of the quality that their child needs. Making childcare more affordable, even at existing levels of charges, could be expensive, but combining this with overdue moves to increase the status and pay of those who provide childcare would increase the cost of such a policy considerably.

The various projects and schemes described in this section are primarily focused on preventing families and children from getting into difficulty in the first place, rather than picking up the pieces when things have gone wrong. There is a huge agenda here for interventions that help people to make the most of their own relationships, both as partners and as parents, and it is one with which Liberals should feel entirely comfortable.

Many of these policies would have an up-front cost. But most would yield a huge long-term return by preventing negative outcomes and building up the welfare of children and their families.

Conclusions

Liberals have long accepted that the state needs to intervene in family life to prevent harm to children – to alleviate income poverty, and for child protection. Yet the harm that children today are suffering goes much wider than this. Too many children are suffering the consequences of a disrupted and insecure home life. Too many parents find themselves unable to give their children the time and attention they need, even in the vital early years of their life. And too many people are finding it difficult to build and maintain strong relationships with their partners and their children. Doing nothing about this harm is not a neutral act – it is to deny children themselves their freedom to grow to their full potential. This is deeply illiberal.

A secure and loving family environment is the key. Virtually everyone who has a child wants the best for that child. And citizens who have chosen to have children take on responsibility for the well-being of their children. Yet the whole of society has a stake in the welfare of the next generation, and parents therefore have a right to expect help and support from society to protect and build their relationships, both with each other and with their children.

269

They also need to be freed from some of the pressures they face as parents so that they can make their own free choices about how best to raise their own children.

In this chapter we have given a brief flavour of some things that could be done. Many projects already exist, especially in the voluntary sector, which have great potential to support families and children and to prevent things from going wrong in the first place. But all too often they are hopelessly underfunded. Billions of pounds are spent on picking up the pieces of young people's 'disrupted and dishevelled lives', whilst the costs of positive interventions such as community family trusts and the parenting fund are a drop in the ocean in comparison. Our proposals include:

Supporting stable and secure families

→ *Supporting relationships.* Relationship breakdown is not inevitable. Nobody enters a relationship hoping that it will end miserably, and the evidence shows that children thrive best in families where the parents care for each other and for them. We propose greater emphasis on equipping people with opportunities to learn skills that will enable them to handle and manage their relationships as partners, as parents, and as children, to the best of their ability. These services need to be repackaged as mainstream support for normal families rather than rescue remedies for 'problem' families. The voluntary sector should be encouraged in its role, as should government schemes such as parenting orders.

→ *Equipping professionals.* Health visitors and midwives come into contact with every young family. They can be specifically trained to be able to recognise relationship problems, act as trusted advisers and signpost families to other services if appropriate. Similarly, registrars access every new parent and, along with local churches, every marrying couple. They can also act as a mine of information and advice to assist people at these key stages in their relationships. There is vast untapped potential in these professional groups, and we strongly advocate harnessing it to strengthen family support in the community.

→ *Reaching young people.* Teenagers are bombarded daily with conflicting messages from the media, the adults around them, their peers and their own hormones. They vitally need 'preventative' support at this crucial time in their lives, as they begin to think about entering into relationships and starting families. Teachers need to be supported in providing balanced and age-appropriate relationship education in schools, ideally as part of students' citizenship classes, and assisted by voluntary sector projects such as 'Teens and Toddlers' that reach the most 'at risk' teenagers.

→ *Supporting families in the community.* We support the extension of Sure Start-style children's centres to every community, not just the most deprived areas. Families should be able to access help and advice in their own localities, where they can meet and support other parents at similar life stages.

Enabling parents to spend more time with their families

→ *Tackling employment law.* We desperately need to tackle the 'long hours' and 'atypical hours' cultures. Government should lead the way by offering parents the right to flexible working hours and providing more paid parental leave along Scandinavian lines.

→ *Reassessing tax and benefits.* We need to consider measures that do not drive parents back to work against their will. We would scrap targets that aim to get 70% of lone parents into work, regardless of their family situations. We are also attracted by the Scandinavian-style 'maternal allowance'

271

which enables mothers to choose between day-care and family
care. Alternatively, enhanced tax credits for young children
would benefit lower-income families more than a system of
transferable tax allowances. Tackling child poverty through
the benefits system continues to be a top priority.
→ *Investing in childcare.* A secure and stable environment
in the early years lays the vital groundwork for children's
development. Where parents are balancing caring for their
children with going out to work, we must therefore ensure
that they have access to affordable childcare of the highest
possible quality, which will nurture and support children
during the hours that they are away from their parents.
We must also tackle the prevailing attitude that mothers
(or fathers) who choose to stay at home to look after their
children have a less important role than those who go back to
work.

These are just a few aspects of public policy which could be
changed to enable parents to spend more time with their children
and each other, and to give them back real choices about their own
lives. We believe that Liberals should embrace this agenda enthusi-
astically, and that parents and children would be the winners.

Notes
1. Interviewed in the *Sunday Telegraph*, 31 August 2003.
2. *Young Children's Skills on Entry to Education*, Welsh Basic Skills
   Agency, 2003.
3. *Factfile 2000*, NCH Action for Children, 2000; *Summary of Child
   Protection Register Statistics*, NSPCC, 2002.
4. *Children in Mind*, Audit Commission, 1999.
5. Department of Health Statistical Bulletin – 'Statistics on Alcohol:
   England, 2003'.

6. Figures quoted in *Listening to Parents*, National Family and Parenting Institute, 2001.

7. Leon Feinstein, *Pre-school Educational Inequality? British Children in the 1970 Cohort*, LSE, 1998; L. Feinstein and J. Symons, *Attainment in Secondary School*, LSE, 1997.

8. Sure Start press release – 'Kids Benefit from Parental Involvement in Learning', 20 October 2003.

9. *Children in Mind*, Audit Commission, 1999.

10. Written Parliamentary answer to Paul Burstow MP, 24 April 2002, col. 324W; McCann et al., *British Medical Journal* 313, 1996; Department of Health Statistical Bulletin, 'Educational Qualifications of Care Leavers, year ending March 2002: England', November 2002.

11. Written Parliamentary answer to Steve Webb MP, 10 November 2003, col. 150-151W.

12. *Working to Target: Can Policies Deliver Paid Work for Seven in Ten Lone Parents?*, NCOPF, 2003.

13. Written Parliamentary answer to Steve Webb MP, 10 November 2003, col. 150-151W.

14. Ivana La Valle et al., *The Influence of Atypical Working Hours on Family Life*, Joseph Rowntree Foundation, 2002.

15. Quoted in *The Times*, 'Price is too high for new mothers returning to work', 15 October 2003.

16. *Working to Target: Can Policies Deliver Paid Work for Seven in Ten Lone Parents?*, NCOPF, 2003.

17. *Good Housekeeping*, October 2003.

18. *Is Britain Family Friendly?*, NFPI, 2000.

19. Quoted in the *Telegraph*, October 2003.

20. *Making Britain Family Friendly*, NFPI, 2003.

21. 'Women prefer motherhood to going to work' – *The Times*, 16 May 2002, based on a survey by *Pregnancy and Birth* magazine.

22. Paul Gregg and Liz Washbrook, *The Effects of Early Maternal Employment on Child Development in the UK*, University of Bristol, 2003.

23. 'The Effective Provision of Pre-School Education (EPPE)', Technical Paper 8b, Institute of Education, 2003.

24. Quoted in 'Stop feeling guilty', *The Times*, 18 August 2003.

25. *Looking to the Future of Children and Families*, Childcare Commission, 2001.

26. Kathleen Kiernan, 'Childbearing Outside Marriage in Western Europe', *Population Trends 98*, ONS, 1999.
27. *Teenagers' Attitudes to Parenting*, National Family and Parenting Institute, 2000.
28. *Unhappy Families, Unhappy Children*, ChildLine, 1998.
29. Shirley Dex, *Families and Work in the 21st Century*, JRF, 2003.
30. *Not in Front of the Children? How Conflict Between Parents Affects Children*, One Plus One, 2001.
31. *Children in Mind*, Audit Commission, 1999.
32. *Risk and Mental Health in Children*, Young Minds, 2003.
33. *Truancy and Social Exclusion Report*, SEU, 1998.
34. *Counting the Cost: The Consequences of Family Breakdown*, CARE, 1999.
35. *Outcomes for Children of Poverty*, Research Report 158, DWP, 2001.
36. Adrienne Katz, *Stress: Tackling it with Teenagers*, Young Voice, 2003.
37. http://www.parentlineplus.org.uk/downloads/who-we-are.pdf
38. Quoted in the *Sunday Telegraph*, 31 August 2003.
39. Cited by BBC News Online, 3 September 2003.
40. Kathleen Kiernan, 'Unmarried Parenthood: New Insights from the Millennium Cohort Study', *Population Trends 114*, ONS, 2003.
41. Alan Marsh and Jane Perry, *Family Change 1999 to 2001*, Research Report 180, DWP, 2003.
42. *The Cost of Family Breakdown*, Family Matters Institute, 2000.
43. Home-Start Annual Review, 2003.
44. *Teens and Toddlers in Southwark*, a report by Children: Our Ultimate Investment, 2003.
45. http://www.nctpregnancyandbabycare.com/
46. Family Support Grant 2004/05 guidance for applicants, Family Policy Unit, 2003.
47. Liz Kendall and Lisa Harker, *Improving Support during Pregnancy and the First 12 Months*, IPPR, 2003, quoted in the *Guardian*, 'Parents need help', 4 June 2003.
48. *Making a Difference*, White Paper, Department of Health, 1999.
49. Home-Start Annual Review, 2003.
50. *Gaining Ground in the Community*, Youth Justice Board Annual Review, 2002/03.
51. See 'Fixed penalty truancy fines begin', BBC News Online, 27 February 2004.

52. Quoted in the *Independent on Sunday*, 14 September 2003 – 'Listen to Bob, patron saint of divorced dads'.
53. Patricia Morgan, *Farewell to the Family?*, IEA, 1999, p.76.
54. 2004/5 figures based on a lone parent, aged under 25, with one child.
55. 2004/5 figures extrapolated from Households Below Average Income 1994/5–2000/1, based on a poverty line of income after housing costs of 60% of the national median.
56. The Income Support rate for a couple is higher than the rate for a single adult; leaving aside the amounts payable in respect of children.
57. *Making Britain Family Friendly*, NFPI, 2003.
58. *Working to Target: Can Policies Deliver Paid Work for Seven in Ten Lone Parents?*, NCOPF, 2003.
59. Quoted in the *Guardian*, 'Care and share alike', 24 October 2003.
60. *Teenage Pregnancy*, Social Exclusion Unit, 1999.
61. Ibid.
62. www.dfes.gov.uk/citizenship
63. *National Curriculum Citizenship: Planning and Implementation 2002/03*, Ofsted 2003.
64. Quoted in 'The puzzle of teenagers and sex', BBC News Online, 12 March 2004.

10 Pension reform: a new settlement for a new century

Paul Marshall

Introduction

Britain's system of state pension provision is under immense strain. There are a number of reasons for this, but one overwhelming one – the failure of the body politic to face up to the financial implications of rising life expectancies and to devise a new strategic 'settlement' which can cater for both present and future generations.

Rising life expectancies and an increasing dependency ratio have left the 'pay-as-you-go' contributory system designed by Sir William Beveridge increasingly unable to cope with the scale of intergenerational transfers required to make it work. This has already led to a series of 'defaults' on pensioner entitlements and, most recently, to the introduction of a new 'Brownian' settlement, which, behind all the complexity, essentially marks a return to the pre-Beveridge world of means-testing.

A Liberal strategy for pensions should be both honest about the scale of the financial challenge and liberal in its proposed solution. It should combine realistic 'supply-side' reforms (including an increase in the pension age) with a recasting of the pensions architecture that draws on Beveridge's founding ideals (notably the contributory principle) but recognises the different demographic circumstances of the 21st century.

The essential enhancement to Beveridge proposed here is to create a second pillar of state pension provision in the form of a 'universal funded pension' that would supplement the existing 'pay-as-you-go' basic pension. Such a proposal marries the principles of Beveridge with the advantages of asset-based welfare (an approach to welfare which is likely to gain increasing political ground in the 21st century).

The creation of a second pillar based on a compulsory funded pension would pave the way for a reform of the private pension provision (effectively the third pillar). Private pension provision would no longer have the role of ensuring that people do not retire into poverty, but rather that of allowing people to top up retirement income above the basic level that would hopefully be assured by the first two pillars. With the introduction of a new pillar based on compulsory savings, there would be less basis for some of the tax reliefs currently used to encourage voluntary savings. Their reform should be considered.

The Liberal heritage

Liberals have a strong heritage in pension reform. It was a Liberal Government, in 1908, which introduced the first basic state pension of five shillings a week. The Lloyd George pension was non-contributory, means-tested and, perhaps most strikingly, only available to those over 70 years of age. Given that the average life expectancy in 1908 was only 49, this limited the scope and the cost of the reform. It was none the less a radical step.

And it was another Liberal, William Beveridge, who was the architect of the old-age pension legislation at the heart of the post-war welfare state in 1948. Beveridge made the state pension part of a system of compulsory social insurance, based on the principle of universal flat-rate contributions and benefits.

It is important to understand the defining principles of the Beveridge 'settlement', first, because these principles have stood the test of time for so many years and, secondly, because Beveridge's contributory principle now provides a clear contrast to the Brownian world of state-dependency and means-testing:

→ *The contributory principle.* 'Benefit in return for contributions, rather than free allowances from the State, is what the people of Britain desire.' Beveridge's justification of the contributory principle was a Liberal one. 'Management of one's income is an essential element of a citizen's freedom.' The notions of responsibility and empowerment implicit in Beveridge's reference to citizenship are even more relevant in the 21st century than they were in 1948.

→ *Compulsion.* Integral to the contributory principle, but none the less distinct, was the principle of compulsion. People could after all have been invited to make their contributions voluntarily, but Beveridge understood that a voluntary system would not attract enough participation, and certainly not the participation necessary to achieve his aim of the 'abolition of want'. For Beveridge, compulsory social insurance was the central method of pension provision, 'with national assistance and voluntary insurance as subsidiary methods'.[1]

→ *Universalism.* Beveridge believed that the system of social insurance should be all-inclusive and that everyone should contribute and receive benefit at the same flat rate.[2] He believed that means-testing discouraged saving and took away from people the dignity of making provision for their own needs. 'This objection (to means-testing) springs ... from resentment at a provision which appears to penalise what people have come to regard as the duty and pleasure of thrift, of putting monies away for a rainy day.'[3]

→ *Adequacy of benefit.* Beveridge intended the rate of benefit to be 'sufficient without further resources to provide the minimum income needed for subsistence in all normal cases.'[4] Beveridge recognised that the definition of 'reasonable human subsistence' was a matter of judgement, but when implemented by the Attlee Government it was intended that the basic state pension would be worth more than means-tested national assistance (which it remained until 1967).

A fifth principle, which was certainly not explicit in Beveridge's programme, but which can be seen with hindsight to have been a key ingredient in its success, was simplicity.

The flaw in Beveridge

The Beveridge settlement survived at least two generations of pensioners. However, the system is now coming under almost overwhelming pressure because of one major flaw, namely the failure of a 'pay-as-you-go' system to cope with the rising levels of life expectancy.

When Beveridge produced his blueprint for pension reform in 1942, the average life expectancy was around 65 for males and 70 for females. With pension benefit entitlements only available at 65 for men and 60 for women, pension expenditure was not a pressing burden on the Exchequer. Total pension outgoings in 1948/9, the first year post-reform, were only £4,217 million in 2002/3 prices, compared with today's outlay of circa £40 billion p.a. (the latter figure only covers basic state pension and SERPS and so excludes the substantial means-tested benefits now required to top up the basic pension).

Because the sums involved in 1948 were not too big, Beveridge could get away with a pay-as-you-go system. The generation in work would support the generation in retirement. No doubt, if life expectancy had remained static, this system of 'minor' inter-generational transfers would have prevailed for many years and the Beveridge architecture would still be very much intact. It is not clear how much debate there was at the time about the likely evolution of life expectancies, but, in any event, the planning assumption seems to have been a continuance of the status quo.[5]

Life expectancies have, of course, risen inexorably since 1942 and the average life expectancy is now 75.7 years for men and 80.4 for women. As the numbers in retirement have risen, the Beveridge settlement has come increasingly under strain, and the result has been a steady erosion of pension entitlements.

The most infamous such erosion was the decision by the Thatcher Government in 1980 to switch the indexation of the basic pension from average earnings to price inflation (you might call this 'the great default'). There have also been cutbacks to entitlements under SERPS in 1986 and 1995.

As a result of the Thatcher reform, the basic state pension has fallen from 26% of average earnings in 1979 to 16.2% today. It is forecast to fall further to around 11% by 2040.[6] And so, because of the erroneous planning assumptions behind the 1948 settlement, and the failure of the political establishment to face up to the issues of affordability and funding, Beveridge's most dearly held objective – the adequacy of benefit – has been lost. The universal state pension has now fallen hopelessly below the basic subsistence level (£77.45 for a single pensioner compared to the minimum income guarantee of £102.50), and more than half of all pensioners are now eligible for means-tested benefits. Recent research by the DSS suggests that 47% of pensioners have an annual income of less than the poverty threshold (currently defined as £5,200 p.a.).[7]

The return of means-testing and the end of Beveridge

Rather than attempt to reverse the steady erosion of the basic state pension, Gordon Brown has embraced the trend as it enables him to better target (i.e. means-test) his scarce resources. The Labour Government has introduced the Pension Credit, a means-tested top-up to the basic pension designed to take the recipient's income up to subsistence level (minimum income guarantee). Means-tested benefits will increasingly take up the slack as the universal state pension continues its decline. According to official statistics,[8] the proportion of pensioners on means-tested benefits is set to rise from 50% in 2003 to 82% by 2050.

This reversion to means-tested provision effectively signals the end of the Beveridge settlement; we are leaving behind (or massively de-emphasising) the principle of 'benefit in return for contributions' and the reliance on compulsory insurance and entering a paternalistic Brownian world where provision for pensioners is almost entirely dependent on the Chancellor's willingness to divert other taxpayers' money. National insurance contributions will continue, and presumably the national insurance fund will continue to balance its books, but the contributory system will play an ever-diminishing role in overall pension provision.

The dismantling of Beveridge has taken place with a whimper rather than a bang. Yet the Brownian settlement, which is being cobbled together in its place, is almost a case study in how not to build a sustainable pensions system. The dilution of the contributory principle removes the notion of personal responsibility ('benefits in return for contributions'). The reversion to means-testing increases the disincentive to save. And the failure to guarantee adequate universal benefit will almost certainly exacerbate pensioner poverty.

The Brownian settlement has no architecture, no unifying principles, and will not last. Yet paradoxically, Brown may have done us one favour. The mess we are in today may create the groundswell needed in favour of more considered reform.

Today's planning assumptions

As the history of pension provision shows, any attempt at reform has to begin with an extremely hard-headed look at the numbers.

And the bottom line is that the demographics are going to get a lot worse. Average male life expectancy is forecast to rise from 75.7 years in 2001 to 79.9 years by 2050, female life expectancy from 80.4 to 84.1 years.[9] Based on the same assumptions, the retirement population is expected to rise from 10.9 million in 2002 to 15.3 million by 2040.[10]

At the same time, Britain's dependency ratio (the ratio of those in retirement to the working population) is forecast to rise from 24.1% in 2000 to around 40% in 2040 and 47.3% by 2050.[11] The dependency ratio will rise particularly sharply from 2020 as baby-boomers reach retirement age.

These problems are obviously not unique to the UK. Indeed, in some European countries (e.g. Italy, Spain) the expected rise in the dependency ratio is much more extreme.

The consequences of this demographic shift for Britain's pension system are stark, but it is emblematic of the body politic's short-term orientation that in-depth analysis of the 'demographic deficit' – one of the most serious strategic issues facing Government today – is hard to come by.

The National Insurance Fund's most recent Quinquennial Review[12] forecasts direct spending on contributory pension entitlements to rise (in 2000 prices) from £39.6 billion in 2000/1 to £68.1 billion by 2040/1. These numbers take account of demographic change, but of course they understate the real expenditure on pensioners because they ignore the increasing requirement for

Figure 1 **Old-age dependency ratio, %**

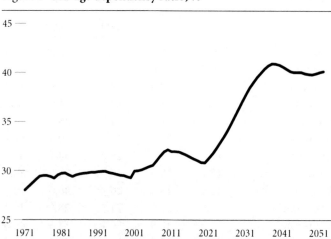

Source: *HM Treasury Long-term Public Finance Report: An Analysis of Fiscal Sustainability,* November 2002

means-tested benefits as more and more pensioners fall below the Government's definition of poverty.

A proper assessment of the level of pensioner provision should therefore include the means-tested benefits that will form a growing component of the Brownian settlement. A back-of-the-envelope calculation using the Government's own figures and assuming all pensioners receive the equivalent of today's minimum income guarantee (but no more) suggests annual outgoings to pensioners by 2040 (in today's prices) of £79.5 billion.

This effective doubling of state spending on pensioners is at its most worrying when set against the backdrop of a rising dependency ratio. Due to the increase in the female pension age from 60 to 65, the number of people of working age is forecast to remain broadly stable or even to rise marginally from the current 36.5 million to 37.5 million by 2040.[13] However, this will not stop the

283

Table 3 **Old-age dependency ratios in developed countries**

	1950	1975	2000	2025	2050
Austria	15.5	24.0	22.9	37.9	62.5
Belgium	16.2	21.8	25.9	38.0	51.2
Denmark	14.1	20.9	22.5	35.8	43.8
Finland	10.5	15.8	22.3	41.8	48.8
France	17.3	21.5	24.5	36.2	46.7
Germany	14.5	23.3	24.1	39.0	54.7
Greece	10.5	19.1	26.0	38.1	64.6
Ireland	17.7	19.0	16.9	24.5	37.2
Italy	12.6	18.9	26.7	40.6	68.1
Luxembourg	13.9	20.0	21.5	28.5	31.4
Netherlands	12.3	16.9	20.1	34.3	45.0
Portugal	11.0	15.9	23.1	31.7	53.5
Spain	11.1	16.1	24.8	36.1	73.8
Sweden	15.5	23.5	27.1	41.5	54.5
UK	16.0	22.2	24.1	34.8	47.3
Weighted average of EU member states	14.3	20.7	24.5	37.1	54.7
Australia	12.4	13.6	18.2	29.2	37.5
Canada	12.2	12.9	18.5	32.6	40.9
Japan	8.3	11.6	25.2	49.0	71.3
New Zealand	14.5	14.2	17.9	28.9	38.5
USA	12.8	16.3	18.6	29.3	34.9

dependency ratio from almost doubling, and therefore the tax-take per active employee required simply to pay for pensioner provision will almost double, to over £2,100 per annum by 2040.

The problem of intergenerational transfers did not take up too much of Beveridge's time because the numbers were not big enough. Today, the numbers are overwhelming. It is no longer realistic to expect the level of intergenerational solidarity required to make a pure pay-as-you-go system viable. A programme of reform is required that incorporates both supply-side measures (i.e. measures to limit the 'supply' of retirees) and a fundamental review of the pensions architecture.

Supply-side reforms

Britain has not raised the male pension age since 1948, despite the fact that male life expectancy has risen from 63 to 75. The female pension age is scheduled to rise gradually from 60 to 65 between 2010 and 2020. Political opposition to this change has been notice-able by its absence.

Under current plans, all major OECD countries will have seen retirement ages rise to 65 by 2030. Ironically, the one country so far planning to raise the pension age beyond 65 is one of the only countries which does not need to (see Table 3 above), namely the USA. Perhaps the USA is one of the few OECD countries that retains a work ethic. A German government commission has also recently recommended that the German pension age should be raised to 67. Britain should, in the first instance, consider joining the US in raising the pension age to 67 by 2030, and should also review the feasibility of gradually raising it further, in line with rising life expectancies.

Britain (in common with the OECD in general) has another problem, which is that increasingly large numbers of the popula-tion between 55 and 65 are retiring early. In 2000, only 59.8% of older male workers (55–64) were still in employment, down from 62.6% in 1980.[14] Clearly, people should have the freedom to retire before their pensionable age. Indeed, one of Keynes's great aspira-tions was that as society got richer and more productive we would have more time for leisure. Hopefully, this is an aspiration that can be realised, and particularly for the elderly. However, what is clearly inappropriate is that many employees are obliged to retire before the pension age by company-specific mandatory retirement schemes. Early retirement schemes of this nature should be made illegal.

Other legislation should be introduced to encourage more flexible (including later) retirement, and to counter the age discrimination which bedevils the workplace. It is already Liberal Democrat policy to scrap the Inland Revenue rule that prevents an employee from continuing to work for a firm from which he or she is drawing a company pension (if the employee moves to a different firm, the rule no longer applies). Employment tribunals should also be required to hear all cases of unfair dismissal, regardless of age (currently, tribunals do not hear cases when an employee is over the age of 65).

There is also a strong argument for reviewing some of the privileges enjoyed by public sector workers, where they are allowed to retire excessively early. For example, some policemen are in a position to retire at the age of 48, if they have been in the service long enough, and many police retire at the age of 50. In addition, many public sector workers retire at the ages of 55 or 60. It is not clear why the public sector should enjoy different treatment from the private sector, and consideration should be given to aligning practices between the two.

The Government's proposal to 'reward' people for working beyond pension age through a one-off lump sum is a positive step. But it has to be borne in mind that people already get a reward for deferring their state pension (each year you defer, you get a higher rate for the rest of your life) – and those increments are already due to rise. The benefit of a lump sum instead of five years' worth of pension is fairly marginal. In essence, all the Government is doing is giving you the equivalent of what you would get if you took the money yourself and invested it in a decent interest-bearing account for five years.

Principles of reform – Beveridge plus?

Beveridge's contributory principle should be at the heart of any Liberal approach to pension, and indeed welfare, reform. It sets personal responsibility and empowerment at the heart of the pension system. And it is in sharp contrast to the Fabian/Brownian approach, which is essentially paternalistic, relying on the state to dispense welfare to its dependents.

Compulsion is less obviously a Liberal principle, but it was advocated by Beveridge because it is the only way a contributory system will work without engendering the 'moral hazard' that discourages people from saving in the knowledge that they will receive 'means-tested' benefits whether they save or not (see 'Objections to a universal funded scheme', below).

The problem with the Beveridge model, as set out above, was the collision of a 'pay-as-you-go' system with demographic change – thereby undermining its affordability.

The way to address the issue of affordability and to restore the spirit of Beveridge is to introduce a new pillar into Britain's pension provision in the form of a universal funded pension. Such a scheme would combine the contributory principle with compulsion. And it could clearly be made compatible with the other Beveridge principles of 'universalism' and 'adequacy of benefit'. It would also have the immense advantage (particularly compared to what is currently on offer) of simplicity.

This enhancement to Beveridge ('Beveridge plus') also sits very happily under the increasingly popular banner of asset-based welfare.

Asset-based welfare and the case for a universal funded pension scheme

At the heart of asset-based welfare lies a belief in the need to shift from 'subsistence welfare' to 'development welfare'.[15] Welfare states have traditionally been based upon a system of income support (i.e. the transfer of money across society through payments via the state), designed to supplement the incomes of those who need assistance. But income transfers do nothing to foster people's self-reliance or dignity (rather the contrary), whereas giving people responsibility for their own assets would do much to further individual self-respect and instil a sense of citizenship. Asset-based welfare is a Liberal idea.

This asset-based approach to welfare has already produced a number of policy initiatives in the USA, notably the introduction of Individual Development Accounts (IDAs). In Britain, we have recently seen the introduction of child trust funds (or 'baby bonds' as they have come to be known), whereby all children born in Britain will receive a token lump sum from the Government as a sort of pre-emptive welfare package. This dalliance with asset-based welfare is tokenistic, paternalistic, and almost certainly a waste of taxpayers' money. It will do nothing to foster a sense of self-reliance or citizenship – rather, the contrary.

A much more obvious and urgent application of asset-based welfare is to pensions. Funded state pension schemes already exist in Singapore, Hong Kong, Chile and most other Latin American countries, and have recently been introduced in Australia (1992) and Poland (1999). They are likely to see a much more widespread introduction over the next ten years. The case for a funded pension scheme in Britain is compelling, for the following reasons:

→ Fairness. A funded scheme avoids the need for intergenerational transfers.

→ Trust. A funded scheme could restore trust in state pension provision by making entitlements something akin to property rights.

→ Hypothecation. A separate funded scheme could allow contributions and entitlements to be hypothecated, a thoroughly Liberal approach. Pension entitlements could be entirely ring-fenced from other elements of social security budget, in contrast to the status quo, where National Insurance contributions are linked to an ensemble of other benefits. This would bring extra transparency to the state's pension liabilities (and assets) and lead to a more informed political debate.

→ A funded scheme does not have to be presented as a tax, and may make it possible to raise significantly higher contributions than would be acceptable under a 'pay-as-you-go' system. It is clear that, for most people, National Insurance has come to be seen as 'just another tax'. It is not specifically associated with pensions and it is not trusted. In contrast, the Australian experience gives an encouraging insight into the public acceptance of a separate funded scheme. While initial contributions (in 1992) were set at 3% of earnings, it has subsequently been possible for the Government to raise this to 9% by 2002/3 with no serious opposition.

→ A funded scheme may improve the savings rate. The Association of British Insurers (ABI) has famously estimated that Britain has a savings deficit of £27 billion. According to the most recent ABI survey, 36% (10 million) of the working population are not saving enough and 80% of those (8 million) are not saving at all. Unsurprisingly, the savings gap is particularly marked amongst the young. A consistent finding of surveys is that those under 30 think very little about retirement, and in many cases saving for retirement

289

is postponed until 35 or even 40. The current Brownian settlement, which combines an unfunded state pay-as-you-go scheme with voluntary private savings and means-testing, does little to address this problem.

The failure of a voluntary system to produce adequate savings can be explained either as a market failure (people have imperfect information about their future spending needs and the savings required to meet them, and therefore fail to make enough provision) or as a result of moral hazard (people assume that the state will always provide if their income falls below subsistence, so they do not need to make their own provision), or both. Either way, the fact is that voluntary savings schemes do not work well, and certainly not well enough to be the cornerstone of a savings system.

The most recent (in fact, a fully live) example of the failure of voluntary schemes is the Government's Stakeholder Pension, introduced in April 2001 (although, prior to Stakeholder, PEPS, ISAs and personal pensions have all been, to greater or lesser degree, failures). Stakeholder is a funded pension aimed at those on modest incomes between £9,500 and £20,000 per annum. It is compulsory to the extent that all employers who have five or more employees, and who do not offer an occupational pension or a personal pension to which they make contributions of at least 3% of their employees' earnings, will have to offer their employees access to a Stakeholder Pension. But it is non-compulsory in the sense that no one is forced to take it up. And, sure enough, by the end of 2002, almost two years after launch, over 90% of the 1.25 million Stakeholder schemes set up were empty shells.

There is clearly scope for debate about how much the introduction of a compulsory funded scheme will increase overall national savings, as the increase in compulsory savings may merely displace voluntary savings. However, evidence exists that funded pension schemes can increase national savings, notably when groups that traditionally save only low amounts are required to participate.

→ A compulsory funded scheme will be more cost-effective than voluntary schemes. Because voluntary savings schemes do not generally work without some form of bribery, the state has spent substantial amounts of taxpayers' money in subsidies to encourage take-up. It has been estimated that the total cost to the Exchequer of tax relief for pensions (including occupational and personal pensions) averages around 1.5% of gross domestic product (GDP). In 1999/2000 it cost around £12 billion, and estimates for 2002/3 are around £14 billion.[16]

In addition to tax relief, there is the cost of advice. For example, the Government has allowed for Stakeholder providers to charge for advice at up to 1% per annum of the Stakeholder funds under management. Frank Field has calculated that such a charge over a working life of 40 years would amount to about 20% of the fund's value.[17]

→ Simplicity. This is not a negligible issue. Given the complexity of decisions involved in making financial provision, any Government scheme needs to be straightforward and understandable if it is to gain popular acceptance. Such was the case with Beveridge. Sadly, the Brownian settlement is so complex that even financial advisers have trouble explaining it.

Objections to a universal funded scheme
Compulsion

The most common objection to a funded pension scheme is that it extends compulsion. This is muddle-headed. All taxes are compulsory levies. Existing state pension schemes (the basic pension,

SERPS and now the State Second Pension) are also compulsory levies, with the distinction that they are supposed to operate on the contributory principle, such that today's contribution translates into tomorrow's entitlement. However, as we have seen above, there is no protection for this entitlement and those who contributed in the 1950s and 60s and are now in retirement have suffered a major default on the original pension promise. The bottom line is that everybody will have to pay for their pension and if they do not do so today they (or others) will be forced to pay in some way later.

Any compulsory funded pension scheme introduced today (and certainly that proposed here) would in the main part be replacing the existing compulsory pay-as-you-go arrangements with a compulsory funded scheme. Arguably, the funded scheme should also be extended to replace some existing voluntary schemes (notably Stakeholder), but for the very good reason that the latter do not work.

Transitional arrangements

The second objection to a funded scheme is the very practical one of where you start. Imagine you were mayor of a small village of a thousand souls and were responsible for introducing a pension scheme. If all the villagers were 25 years old, it would be very straightforward to introduce a communal scheme where everyone saved at the same rate for their mutual retirement. However, if there was a normal age distribution and, furthermore, the older members had already been contributing on a pay-as-you-go basis, it would be much more difficult to determine an equitable place to start.

In the transition from a pay-as-you-go to a fully or (in this case) partially funded system, pension liabilities that are implicit in the old scheme are made explicit. The current workers' contributions can no longer be used for the payment of current pensions, as they must be accumulated to build retirement capital. At the same time, previous contributions to the pay-as-you-go scheme have to be honoured. Thus, the implicit debt is crystallised and the Government has to come up with a financing mechanism to repay it. Such a crystallisation of Britain's existing pension obligations would be an entirely healthy development (we are effectively carrying a debt burden from the first generation of pay-as-you-go pensioners who received a pension without having paid contributions).

The most equitable way of dealing with the transitional debt burden is to spread it as thinly and as evenly as possible. Ironically, one precondition for this is already in place in the form of the downsizing of the existing pay-as-you-go system. The Government's commitments to the present generation have already been substantially reduced without any political backlash. This will make the transition much less expensive than it might have been (and, arguably, has created room for a second pillar).

The most gradual transition to a funded system (and that proposed here) would be to allow only new entrants to the labour force to join the funded system. The cash-flow requirements for the Government would then consist initially only of covering the gap caused by the diversion of the new entrants' contributions. Deficits would increase gradually as more and more workers retired from the old system.

The burden of transition would be further lightened by retaining the pay-as-you-go system as a first pillar of pension provision, so that the shift to a funded pillar would be only partial.

Distrust of financial markets
Given the funding crisis which has embroiled many of Britain's occupational pension schemes, any proposal for a new compulsory funded pension is likely to encounter strong resistance from

293

those who have an ingrained distrust of financial markets (this may be a reason, incidentally, why 'old Europe' will be much slower to adopt this model than Anglo-Saxon, Asian or Eastern European governments).

The market turbulence of 2000/2 did considerable damage to occupational pension schemes, but it was not the primary cause of their distress. Their fundamental problem has been the mismatch between liabilities, which increased as interest rates fell, and assets, which were invested disproportionately in equities. Fund managers and trustees were clearly at fault for the extent of the overinvestment in a single asset class, a peculiarly British phenomenon that had no parallel, even in the USA. It would clearly be appropriate for any compulsory funded scheme to be bound by specific limits in relation to different asset classes – notably equities, fixed income and real estate – as well as to different international and currency exposures. Such limits are standard for existing schemes of this kind overseas.

Of course, over any reasonable period of time, financial markets pay you to invest in them via the risk premium. So the normal expectation for a funded pension is that over a lifetime it builds up substantial real returns (thereby offering another significant benefit over a pay-as-you-go scheme). In addition, a moderate amount of diversification will provide the beneficiaries with exposure to markets with substantially higher growth and productivity rates than the demographically-challenged UK.

The second pillar

The primary purpose of this chapter is to set out the case in principle for introducing a universal funded pension scheme as a second pillar of Britain's pension provision. Set out below is a brief outline of how such a scheme might work.

Structure

Britain should move to a three-pillar system of pension provision, with two pillars under the supervision of the state, comprising the existing pay-as-you-go system and the new compulsory funded pension. The third pillar would be based entirely on voluntary savings. Vis-à-vis existing arrangements, the second pillar would be primarily be replacing the State Second Pension/SERPS, Stakeholder Pension and the Pension Credit.

Benefit

The first two pillars should be coordinated in such a way that the combination of the basic benefit and the funded component are targeted to produce an aggregate benefit equivalent to, or slightly above, today's minimum income guarantee (currently circa £102 per week, but forecast to rise to £160.71 per week by 2040 in 2000 prices).[18]

Administration

Arguments about how a universal funded pension should be administered (public vs private sector) are actually quite balanced. Natural Liberal instincts favour a private sector solution, with multiple providers competing to look after people's savings. This is indeed the case under the Australian model, where administration of the compulsory funded scheme follows as much of a 'market-orientated' approach as possible. Employees are given a choice of schemes from a variety of providers, including both defined benefit and defined contribution. This introduces the maximum amount of competition into the system, and, more importantly, introduces the maximum amount of transparency. People are able to see their savings accumulate in their own pension accounts and thereby develop a sense of ownership. Such a system may also provide encouragement for people to save additional amounts that would go only into their own pension accounts. Finally, it would allow contributions to be clearly distinguished from taxes, making it much easier to achieve buy-in.

However, this private sector solution could result in highly varied outcomes when beneficiaries come to claim their pensions. In a compulsory system, this is a problem. It cannot surely be 'fair' that two people making identical *compulsory* pension contributions end up with substantially different pension incomes depending on the competence of their pension administrator/advisers. It could, of course, be argued that different outcomes are already a reality of life for schools, hospitals and other public services where people are equally being forced to make compulsory contributions. However, in the case of pensions, the different outcomes will be stark and incontestable, and it is easy to imagine them becoming a source of political controversy.

There is an additional drawback to freedom of choice in pension products, which is one of market failure. While all savers may have access to the same standard information about the products available, there would be a clear asymmetry of understanding. Few, except a small and privileged minority, have any real grasp of financial markets and savings products, and it is unrealistic to expect the majority to acquire this knowledge either quickly or easily. Over time, perhaps, a basic level of financial literacy should be taught at school as part of citizenship training. But as things currently stand, it is unfair to expect everyone to be able to make informed choices between different savings products.

An intriguing solution to this difficult problem of administration is to provide a twin-track approach. People could be offered a choice between a publicly administered scheme, where the state acts as provider and the outcome is guaranteed, and a privately administered scheme where they can choose between multiple providers, in the knowledge that there could be a more varied outcome. The public scheme would be defined benefit; private schemes could be defined contribution or defined benefit.

For the public scheme, it would obviously still be extremely important to maximise the sense of individual ownership for contributors. This can be achieved in a number of ways. Governance of the state scheme should be carried out through an independent body, accountable to but separate from the state, in such a way as to give beneficiaries the closest equivalent to property rights and to protect them from the depredations of the Government. The best analogy is with the Bank of England. Governance should be exercised through a board of trustees, part-elected and part-appointed, with powers to include the administration of the scheme, the appointment and dismissal of fund managers, and the setting of investment strategy. Parliament would have statutory powers to set investment restrictions and contribution rates. The trustees would be accountable to Parliament for the investment performance and administration.

In such a way, individual pension contributions would be quite distinct ('hypothecated') from other National Insurance contributions (in contrast to the status quo). To ensure maximum transparency, contributors would be sent an annual report detailing the performance of the scheme and the status of entitlements. Contributions could be varied by Act of Parliament, if the state scheme moved substantially into surplus or deficit vis-à-vis targeted benefits.

Competition could be introduced into the management of the state scheme through appointment of external fund managers, who would be expected to compete for mandates in the normal way but manage the assets within strict investment guidelines laid down in the scheme's statutes (and subject to parliamentary approval). These guidelines would, amongst other things, ensure the necessary diversification, as discussed above (see 'Distrust of financial markets').

For private schemes, people would have the choice between multiple providers, although the obvious starting point for administration would be the employer. In the context of the earlier discussion about 'fairness of outcome', schemes need to be carefully regulated and it would make sense both to apply the same investment restrictions as apply to the state scheme, and to limit the choice of investment managers to a state- (or FSA-?) approved list.

Individual savers should be given the opportunity to top up their 'second pillar pension' with voluntary savings of their own, and hopefully the existence of the second pillar will draw many who had not previously got into the habit of saving money.

In other respects, the same contributory arrangements could apply to the funded second pillar as to the 'pay-as-you-go' first pillar. Contributions would be set as a percentage of earnings above National Insurance (NI) lower earnings limit and below the upper earnings limit.

Whether or not contributions are collected from employers or employees seems to be largely a question of political presentation. The Australian system takes contributions from employers. Frank Field proposes more courageously in his Universal Protected Pension (UPP)[19] to take them from employees. Clearly, it is easier to pluck the goose if it does not have a direct vote, but in the long run most people understand that a charge on employers is a charge on employees.

Adequate benefit for all

The central objective of any pension reform must be to ensure adequate benefit for all. The definition of 'adequate' can be the basis for a chapter in its own right, but the most realistic starting point is the current minimum income guarantee (circa £102 per week), which is designed to be just above the poverty threshold (70% of median earnings). This compares with the basic state pension of £67.50 per week, so implies a very substantial uplift through the second pillar. Restoration of the basic state pension to the level of income support would also be very much in line with the spirit of Beveridge (from 1948 to 1967, the basic state pension was in line with, or slightly above, the level of income support; thereafter, it has fallen substantially below).

Such a scheme would be less generous than the universal protected pension proposed by Frank Field, which seeks to provide a guaranteed pension equivalent to 28.2% of average full-time earnings.[20] This was based on the Government Actuary's estimate of the level of retirement pension necessary to free people completely from means-tested benefits, but it is substantially (about 25%) above the minimum income guarantee.[21] Field's is a highly ambitious and generous target, and its excessive generosity may account for its failure to gain much political traction.

Clearly, if the state scheme is to be defined as a benefit, contributions will have to be varied from time to time in order to 'manage' the targeted outcome. It would make sense for the contributory rates in private schemes to move in line with those in the state scheme. The state scheme would thereby become, in one sense, a competitive benchmark for the private sector.

When combined with a rise in the pension age to 67 and a review of private sector subsidies, it is possible that the new second pillar could be introduced with little or no change to existing National Insurance contributions.

The third pillar – private savings

Private, voluntary pensions should be seen as the third pillar of pension provision; and following the introduction of a second pillar designed to underwrite adequate pension provision for all, there is a strong case that the current system of subsidies and tax incentives for voluntary savings could be reviewed.

Tax incentives for savings are extremely expensive. The net cost to the Exchequer in 2002, after deducting tax received from pensions in payment, was around £14 billion.[22] The number has fluctuated around 1.5% of GDP since the mid-1980s. Indeed, according to work by the IPPR, the Government spent £2.5 billion more in 1999/2000 on tax relief for pensions than on means-tested benefits for the elderly.[23] Some of these tax incentives are entirely justified. In particular, there is a strong argument that taxpayers should either obtain relief when they put money with their pension scheme, or when it is paid out – otherwise they will be taxed twice. But it is not clear that this relief should be against the top marginal rate of tax. Nor is it clear that people should obtain relief both when the money goes in and when it comes out. This is the effect of the tax-free lump sum, which gives people the ability to take 25% of their pension pot tax-free. The lump sum payment is regressive, with the subsidy almost twice as large for someone on the 40% marginal rate than for someone on the basic rate. At the very least, the tax-free lump sum needs to be reviewed, and could be a source of funding for reform discussed elsewhere in this chapter.

The regressive nature of tax incentives for savings is actually quite stark. Over half the money spent on tax relief for private pensions goes to the top income decile of taxpayers and a quarter to the top 2.5% of taxpayers.[24] The main reason these tax incentives are so regressive is that tax relief is available against the top marginal rate of tax, a huge boon for the happy 10% who earn above £34,500. Not only are these 10% likely to be the most financially literate and therefore most willing to save; the most wealthy of them take full advantage of the state subsidy by putting large amounts into their pension fund, in order to maximise the benefit of 40% 'grossing up' from the Government.

There are other inefficient savings subsidies. Following changes made to the treatment of ISAS in 2004, income tax advantages will largely disappear for basic rate taxpayers. The only tax benefit remaining will be exemption from capital gains tax – something that will only benefit the 100,000 or so people who each year become liable to capital gains tax! Like PEPS before them, ISAs, which were originally intended to encourage earnings by lower-income households, have become nothing more than a tax perk for the upper middle classes and City professionals.

Tax incentives of this kind seem to have grown in popularity with politicians the more state provision is seen to fail. A redesign of the existing state architecture, and in particular the creation of a second pillar, assuring adequate pension benefits for all, provides the opportunity to review the web of private sector subsidies.

Notes
1. Sir William Beveridge, *Social Insurance and Allied Services*, 1942, para. 14.
2. Beveridge's principle of 'universalism' only extended to those in work and so crucially neglected the needs of both unpaid carers and married women. There is a strong case that the definition of universalism should be revisited in the context of today's pensioner poverty, but any proper analysis of this issue is beyond the scope of this chapter.
3. Beveridge, op cit.
4. Ibid., para. 307.
5. It is likely that Beveridge's mistake related more to planning assumptions than to his neglect of the problem of intergenerational transfers. Indeed, Beveridge recognised the problem of inter-generational transfers in so far as it affected the introduction of National Insurance. He originally proposed that initial benefits were to be phased in over twenty years, so that people were only entitled to benefits in proportion to their contributions. His proposal was

rejected by the Attlee Government, which thereby created a hidden intergenerational liability.

6. *Abstract of Statistics for Benefits, Contributions and Indices of Prices and Earnings*, ONS, 2002.

7. Victoria Mayhew, *Pensions 2000: Public Attitudes to Pensions and Planning for Retirement*, DSS, 2001.

8. ONS/House of Commons Library/IFS.

9. *Long-term Public Finance Report: An Analysis of Fiscal Sustainability*, HM Treasury, November 2002.

10. Ibid.

11. Ibid.

12. *Quinquennial Review*, Government Actuary's Department, January 2000.

13. *Long-term Public Finance Report*, op cit.

14. *Economic Outlook No. 72*, OECD, December 2002.

15. See Michael Sherraden, *Assets and the Poor: A New American Welfare Policy*, George Warren Brown School of Social Work, Washington University, 1991.

16. *Equal Shares? Building a Progressive and Coherent Asset-Based Welfare Policy*, IPPR, 2003.

17. Frank Field et al., *Universal Protected Pension: Modernising Pensions for the Millennium*, House of Commons, 2001.

18. *Universal Protected Pension*, Pensions Reform Group, 2001.

19. Ibid.

20. Ibid.

21. According to the Government Actuary, Field's UPP would produce a pension in 2040 worth £210.20 per week in 2000 prices, compared with a projected minimum income guarantee in 2040 of £160.70.

22. Inland Revenue, 2002.

23. *Equal Shares?*, IPPR, 2003.

24. P. Agulvik and J. Le Grand, 'Tax Relief and Partnership Pensions', *Fiscal Studies*, Vol. 19, No. 4, pp. 403–28, November 1998.

Lightning Source UK Ltd.
Milton Keynes UK
UKOW05f0734200814

237193UK00002B/71/P